THACKERAY: THE MAJOR NOVELS

Thackeray
THE MAJOR NOVELS

JULIET McMASTER

UNIVERSITY OF TORONTO PRESS

© University of Toronto Press 1971
Printed in Great Britain
ISBN 0-8020-5240-1
Microfiche ISBN 0-8020-0017-7
LC 76-151380

UK and Commonwealth except Canada
Manchester University Press
316-324 Oxford Road
Manchester, M13 9NR, England
ISBN 0-7190-0472-1

To Rowland

Preface

THACKERAY IS A DIFFICULT WRITER TO DEAL WITH, AS CRITICS have found. He is devious and sometimes evasive, apparently retreating from one position to another, and yet disconcertingly frank in his admission within the novels themselves that, in James's phrase, he is only 'making believe.' It is noticeable that much of the critical attention he has received has been hostile: it seems that even those who do not admire him would rather attack than dismiss him, for his combination of slipperiness and confidential geniality can both fascinate and exasperate. It is my own contention, however, that Thackeray is a consummate artist very much in control of what he is doing, whose major novels are works of thematic coherence and aesthetic integrity; and that he is also a highly sophisticated ironist, exploiting to the full the potential of the various personae he adopts, and introducing ambiguity deliberately, to sharpen our moral perception and to evoke the complexity of experience itself.

In constructing my study I have chosen to handle the general questions of technique, tone, social analysis, and moral and psychological vision in separate chapters, using one of the novels as the chief exemplar of each discussion. Thus, although the study of each aspect illumines every novel, I have connected my treatment of narrative technique more particularly to *Vanity Fair*, social commentary to *The Newcomes*, and so on, as seemed to me appropriate. The chapters are to this extent independent of each other, and their sequence is partly determined by the order of the novels' publication.

Though my intention has been to examine the novels for their own sake, I have also had it in mind to answer some of the recurrent critical charges against Thackeray. Most of them originated in his own lifetime, but they are still current today, in some form or another. It has been asserted that Thackeray is a careless artist; that he is morally obtuse or perverse, presenting insipid characters like Amelia for our veneration; that he has a weak mind, and is unable to address himself to the real social problems of his day; that he is unable to construct an integrated novel, producing instead random reminiscences and diffuse pictures of manners; and finally that he is not interested in human relations. Collected and stated baldly in that way the charges sound absurd, and no single critic that I know of has propounded them all; yet each has had its considerable defenders, among them figures of the stature of James, Leavis, and Edmund Wilson.

Against the contention that Thackeray was a dilettante, too careless as an artist to mind whether his reader believed in the imaginative reality of his creation or not, I suggest that he was as conscious and painstaking in his art in his way, and as successful, as Keats or Sterne or James were in theirs, and that his commentary, his infamous 'lyric leak,' has its positive uses in involving the reader and so subtly increasing the 'sentiment of reality' of the novel. I read *Pendennis* as a novel of ideas, an exploration of the individual's search for reality and the artist's quest for truth, and *The Newcomes* as a social anatomy, no 'loose baggy monster,' but a highly articulated work of art in which language and imagery are fully integrated with theme. A study of the 'good' characters, which includes an ironic reading of *Henry Esmond*, reveals the complex nature of Thackeray's moral vision; and finally, in an exploration that includes all the novels, I examine the active psychic life of his characters that underlies their more overt social concerns.

Parts of this study have already been published in *Literature and Psychology* and *Thackeray: A Collection of Critical Essays*, edited by Alexander Welsh, and in *Nineteenth-Century Fiction*. My thanks are due to the editors of the journals for their generous permission to reprint. For reproduction of the illustrations from Thackeray's novels I am indebted to the Bodleian Library, Oxford. I am also grateful to the University of Alberta for a grant that enabled me to do some of my research in England. To R.D. McMaster, who, first as my supervisor and then as my colleague and finally as my husband, has contributed more to the successive stages of my work than I can describe, I have tried to express my appreciation in the dedication. I would also like to acknowledge the friendly encouragement of my colleagues in the English Department at the University of Alberta, and the stimulating exchanges with my students during the give and take of teaching.

This book has been published with the help of grants from the Humanities Research Council, using funds provided by the Canada Council, and from the Publications Fund of the University of Toronto Press.

J.M.

Contents

Illustrations

ABBREVIATIONS

1
Narrative Technique:
Vanity Fair

TOO MANY TWENTIETH-CENTURY CRITICS OF THACKERAY HAVE started with a theory of how novels ought to work and then rejected his because they do not live up to it. I would rather go about it the other way, starting with what I find has a more positive existence – the undeniable life of his novels – and going on from there to a critical analysis of some of the means by which he creates it.

The 'life' of a novel cannot of course be physiologically demonstrated, as in a biological organism. I speak then only of an impression; but I believe it is a common one, experienced by most readers and quite without the application of sophisticated critical techniques. Anyone who has read *Vanity Fair*, I think, remembers it; its impact on him may be less immediate than that of *Jane Eyre* or *Great Expectations*, less subtle, perhaps, than that of *The Ambassadors*. But even years afterwards *Vanity Fair* is still packed away in his mind as part of his experience. The details of the action may be lost, but he remembers a world that he has inhabited, or that has somehow overlapped with his own. The concept of Vanity Fair itself, with all its social and religious reverberations, now takes his imagination back rather to Thackeray than to Bunyan or Ecclesiastes. And he remembers the people – Becky Sharp will come to mind as readily as Satan in any dispute on the specious attractions of evil; Amelia will recurrently figure in discussions of the appeal (or the reverse) of clinging women; Lord Steyne becomes for him the embodiment of Regency aristocracy, and Jos Sedley on his elephant the icon of the British empire. Accounts of the battle of Waterloo will have gathered the resonance of Thackeray's booming cannons, and certain London streets will echo for him with the footsteps of Sedleys, Osbornes, and Crawleys. Chesterton called Thackeray the novelist of memory, and it was Thackeray's achievement so to interweave his fiction with our lives that we draw on our memories of his novels almost as we draw on the material of our own past experience.

How is it done? To a large extent, I would suggest, by the presence of one character whom, if the reader has not been too much imbued with post-Jamesian criticism, he will perhaps have remembered and enjoyed as much as any of the others – Thackeray himself: or at least those facets of himself that he chooses to show us. And here we come, of course, as we were bound to, to the question of the authorial commentary. It has been plentifully dealt with by others, both attackers and defenders, and perhaps most extensively by Professor Geoffrey Tillotson.[1] What I want to emphasize is the direct relation between that life of the novels and the commentary, and the extent to which the one depends on the other. Thackeray's novels are great works of art for various reasons, but not the least of them is the author's presence: they live because of his commentary, not in spite of it. Sounding through those great organisms, *Vanity Fair*, *Pendennis*, and *The Newcomes*, like the heartbeat in the body, is the unifying tone of the narrator, a regular and reassuring reminder of the life and harmony of the whole. For the life of the novels comes not just from the vitality of the characters and action depicted in them, but from the tone and reactions of the man who tells the story; and more – from the reader's own personal responses, elicited, though not determined, by his.

From the first we are coaxed into an intimate relation with the narrator by his incomparable ease of style; Thackeray had a right to claim as he did that the author of *David Copperfield* had something to learn from the author of *Vanity Fair* in terms of simplicity of style and vocabulary.[2] It is

1 *Thackeray the Novelist* (Cambridge 1954)
2 ‘ Have you read Dickens? – O it is charming. Bravo Dickens. It has some of his very prettiest touches – those inimitable Dickens touches wh. make such a great man of him. And the reading of the book has done another author a great deal of good. In the first place it pleases the other Author to see that Dickens who has long left off alluding to his the o a's works has been copying the o a, and greatly simplifying his style and foregoing the use of fine words. By this the public will be the gainer and David Copperfield will be improved by taking a lesson from Vanity Fair.’ *The Letters and Private Papers of William Makepeace Thackeray* ed. Gordon N. Ray (London 1945) II 531. Subsequent references to Thackeray's letters, and inci-

partly by his familiar tone and colloquial rhythms that he is able to sustain a relation with his reader. Here is Mr Batchelor, for instance, turning from his story to the reader, to reminisce about the first Mrs Lovel, deceased:

> What Fred found in her to admire, I cannot tell: lucky for us all that tastes, men, women, vary. You will never see her alive in this history. That is her picture, painted by the late Mr. Gandish. She stands fingering that harp with which she has often driven me half mad with her 'Tara's Halls' and her 'Poor Marianne'. She used to bully Fred so, and be so rude to his guests, that in order to pacify her, he would meanly say, 'Do, my love, let us have a little music!' and thrumpty – thrumpty, off would go her gloves, and 'Tara's Halls' would begin. 'The harp that *once*,' indeed! the accursed catgut scarce knew any other music, and 'once' was a hundred times at least in *my* hearing. [LW 77][3]

Perhaps the main narrative has been suspended: by Batchelor's own admission Cecilia Lovel never appears in the story, and she is scarcely significant in the plot. There is too, some extraneous philosophizing. But the prose fairly crackles with the narrator's freshly remembered exasperation. His harangue, with its personal emphasis and idiomatic swing, comes across with an explosive immediacy.

Of course Mr Batchelor is a participating character as well as the narrator of *Lovel the Widower*, and it might be argued that his commentary is thus dramatically appropriate in a way that the less directly assigned commentary of *Vanity Fair* and *Pendennis* is not. However, there is essentially less difference between them than would appear. The commentary in the major novels is dramatic too, in that it belongs perceptibly to a personality and a mood, which are open to our judgment just as are Batchelor's splenetic outbursts and neurotic hesitations. *Lovel the Widower* is interesting because it represents a late stage in the evolution of this narrative voice. In *Vanity Fair* and *Pendennis* the narrator, though

dentally to Ray's excellent accompanying notes and commentary, will be given in the text, by volume number and page.

3 References throughout are to *The Oxford Thackeray* ed. George Saintsbury (London 1908) 17 vols

characterized by the inclusion of fragmentary details of his life as well as by his tone and his expressed values, remains anonymous. *Henry Esmond* shows a further stage in the evolution of the narrator, who now has a strictly limited point of view. Thackeray then returned to the kind of narrative in which the narrator is not the protagonist; for *The Newcomes* and *Philip* he hit upon what he felt to be the highly satisfactory scheme of using Pendennis as his persona, thinking in this way to shield himself from the automatic supposition of naive readers that he meant all he said.[4] The narration of *The Virginians*, partly anonymous and partly by George Warrington at a reflective rather than active stage of his career, is again halfway between the two methods of *Vanity Fair* and *Esmond*. In *Lovel the Widower* the story is Lovel's: he is the one with the title role, and the one who marries the heroine. But the point of view and emphatic tone are Batchelor's: he is only the narrator, and the one who *doesn't* marry the heroine. But by this time tone has definitely taken precedence over narrative and, as in certain characteristic James novels, we are in fact more interested in what does not happen to the watcher than in what does happen to the people he watches.[5] The *Roundabout Papers* complete the process by being, as it were, all tone and no narrative, and hence ceasing to be fiction. And 'Mr Roundabout,' as he inevitably becomes – Thackeray could not help creating personae even when he had full licence to be frankly personal – sounds very like Mr Batchelor, or Mr Pendennis, or Mr Warrington, in certain moods.

In Lubbock's classic distinction between 'drama' and 'panorama' in fiction[6] Thackeray is taken as the major example of the 'omniscient' author writing the 'panoramic' novel, and literary histories, using Lubbock's terms without his skill and insight, somewhat glibly follow this judgment, often taking this kind of novel to be, in some absolute

---

4 Even here, however, Thackeray had to explain to a reviewer that it was only Pen and not he who was responsible for 'the pragmatic assumption about [Laura's] goodness.' See Whitwell Elwin's review of *The Newcomes* in the *Quarterly Review* of September 1855, 360, and Letters III 469.

5 Geoffrey Tillotson points out the affinities between Mr Batchelor and certain James characters in *Thackeray the Novelist* 299–300.

6 *The Craft of Fiction* (London 1921) chapter 7 and *passim*

sense, inferior to the 'dramatic' novel of James and his followers. It is characteristic of Lubbock that he should prefer *Esmond* among Thackeray's novels, and under his influence critical emphasis this century has shifted away from *Vanity Fair*. *Esmond* is 'dramatic' because there we have all the characters set in motion before us and described and assessed only by one of themselves, with no author's voice intervening between us and the characters' own responses. Esmond himself editorializes and interprets, but his interpretations are strictly subject to his own personal limitations. But *Vanity Fair, Pendennis,* and the rest are to some extent dramatic in this sense too, because that authorial presence is not the artist himself, but a humanly fallible narrator, whose failures in assessment and personal idiosyncracies are as open to our judgment as are those of Pamela or Esmond or Strether, or any of the other limited consciousnesses; he is a narrator with whom, though he both invents and tells the story, we may choose to disagree. And hence the novels are dramatic in another sense as well: they are not only concerned with the staging of confrontations between the characters; they themselves constitute a confrontation in a different direction, between author and reader.

Of course there is nothing new about this in itself. A relation of some kind between teller and hearer must be as old as story-telling itself; it is only in the modern novel that it has been outlawed. Fielding valued the relation with his reader, and insists that the passages in which he directly addresses his reader are essential to his kind of writing. Conversation and often outright war with his reader was Sterne's *modus operandi*, and Jane Austen's assumption of a firm understanding in common with her readers is the basis of her irony. But that relation is nowhere so large a part of the total experience of the novel as in Thackeray's – except of course in *Tristram Shandy*, where, however, the writer is so outrageously eccentric that we rather stand back to watch his antics than participate in friendly discussion as Thackeray invites us to do. Fielding sounds a little too formidable to tangle with, and Jane Austen is inaccessible as a personality. But in Thackeray's novels we have the sense that we are being told the story by a fellow human being: he is informative, though not usually analytical, about the characters and the context in which they act, and sympathetic in his relation of its relevance to his and our own lives, if often questionable in his preferences and values. The paragraph that opens the chapter on the deaths of old Sedley and Osborne is one that an enthusiast for pure scenic presentation might prune away as extraneous matter; nevertheless, although here Thackeray turns his focus momentarily away from his immediate subject, it is as essential to the total experience of the novel as the account of the deaths themselves. It is a passage that deserves quoting at length:

There came a day when the round of decorous pleasures and solemn gaieties in which Mr. Jos Sedley's family indulged, was interrupted by an event which happens in most houses. As you ascend the staircase of your house from the drawing- towards the bed-room floors, you may have remarked a little arch in the wall right before you, which at once gives light to the stair which leads from the second story to the third (where the nursery and servants' chambers commonly are), and serves for another purpose of utility, of which the undertaker's men can give you a notion. They rest the coffins upon that arch, or pass them through it so as not to disturb in any unseemly manner the cold tenant slumbering within the black ark.

That second-floor arch in a London house, looking up and down the well of the staircase, and commanding the main thoroughfare by which the inhabitants are passing; by which cook lurks down before daylight to scour her pots and pans in the kitchen; by which young master stealthily ascends, having left his boots in the hall, and let himself in after dawn from a jolly night at the club; down which miss comes rustling in fresh ribbons and spreading muslins, brilliant and beautiful, and prepared for conquest and the ball; or Master Tommy slides, preferring the banisters for a mode of conveyance, and disdaining danger and the stair; down which the mother is fondly carried smiling in her strong husband's arms, as he steps steadily step by step, and followed by the monthly nurse, on the day when the medical man has pronounced that the charming patient may go downstairs; up which John lurks to bed, yawning with a sputtering tallow candle, and to gather up before sunrise the boots which are awaiting him in the passages: — that stair, up or down which babies are carried, old people are helped, guests are marshalled to the ball, the parson walks to the christening, the doctor to the sick-room, and the undertaker's men to the upper floor – what a memento of Life, Death, and Vanity it is – that arch and stair – if you choose to consider it, and sit on the landing, looking up and down the well! The doctor will come up to us too for the last time there, my friend in motley. The nurse will look in at the curtains, and you take no notice – and then she will fling open the windows for a little, and let in the air. Then they will pull down all the front blinds of the house and live in the back rooms – then they will send for the lawyer and other men in black, &c. – Your comedy and mine will have been played then, and we shall be removed, oh how far, from the trumpets, and the shouting, and the posture-making. If we are gentlefolks they will put hatch-ments over our late domicile, with gilt cherubim, and mottoes stating that there is 'Quiet in Heaven'. Your son will new furnish the house, or perhaps let it, and go into a more modern quarter; your name will be among the 'Members Deceased', in the lists of your clubs next year. However much you may be mourned, your widow will like to have her weeds neatly made – the cook will send or come up to ask about dinner – the survivors will soon bear to look at your picture over the mantle-piece, which will presently be deposed from the place of honour, to make way for the portrait of the son who reigns. [768–9]

Beginning with the death of Sedley, Thackeray goes on to write an essay, vividly enlivened by the precise imagery relating to his symbol of the stair-arch, on the incongruous presence of death through the whole span of life in Vanity Fair. It is characteristic of Thackeray's philosophizing that his abstract concept should be so promptly embodied, that he should shift immediately from the mystery of Death to the detail of domestic architecture that is its familiar memento. He had a right to scoff at the inflated abstracts that Bulwer Lytton introduced in some of his grandilo-quent purple passages, having himself so sure a touch, not only in avoiding the portentuous tone in preference for the genially ironic, but in evoking the remote through the familiar, and making the word flesh. And so also with his story; as he reminds us of the practical accommodation for the coffin on the stairway among all the scenes of life enacted there, presently it is not just Sedley, a character in the story, who is dying, but 'we'; and then, more specifically, the reader himself is asked to envisage his own body lying inert as the nurse takes professional note of his demise, and to picture his name in the list of 'Members Deceased' at his club. The social details, like the domestic architecture, have perhaps changed in the last century or so, but a modern reader, if he takes the time to read perceptively, can still be touched with a particular chill. Thackeray's 'lyric leak,' to use Edmund Wilson's delightful phrase, the direct personal cry from writer to reader, has in fact some of the power of the lyric, for all its humorous tone. And it has its uses for the novel, too: for the reader, having been made to contemplate his own death, returns to the contemplation of Sedley's and Osborne's with a new sympathy. The passage is woven into the fabric alike of the story and of the reader's experience.

The authorial presence is familiar and congenial enough to inspire initial trust and commitment, as the roles he adopts provoke reassessment and reaction. And it is that interchange that is Thackeray's object in his novels. According to an anecdote told by one of his *Punch* colleagues, it was one of Thackeray's jokes to declare that he was unable to think of a rhyme for the second line of a little poem beginning 'The mouse lay cosy in her hole and nothing could be snugger,' whereupon, to Thackeray's huge enjoyment, someone would inevitably suggest the obvious word.[7] For all Thackeray's own explicit objections to Sterne for just this kind of sly implication of the reader in his bawdry, the joke would be as characteristic of the one novelist as the other: it fulfils their major objective of audience participation. In his fiction, of course, Thackeray was to make manifold use of this participation. His novels are certainly about Amelia, Becky, Arthur Pendennis, Clive Newcome, and the rest; but they are also *about*, and in no superficial way, our response to these characters and to the world they live in. His authorial presence is his strategy to elicit this response. And the moral experience of the novel is largely a matter of the

7 See Arthur A. Adrian *Mark Lemon, First Editor of Punch* (London 1966)

reader's decision as to where he wants to place himself among the various attitudes dramatized for him in the author's commentary.

A standard objection to what has come to be known as 'authorial intrusion' is that it consists of *telling*, whereas it is the author's business to *show*, and the reader's to make up his own mind.[8] To refute this charge one need only repeat that the commentator in Thackeray's novels is no ultimate authority. The commentary does not constitute the 'moral' of *Vanity Fair* or of any of the other novels, though it certainly is part of the moral experience of reading them. The reader has to be prepared to make his own independent judgments just as much in the passages of commentary as in the passages of direct scenic presentation, and frequently more so, because of the deceptive plausibility of the commentator's arguments.

For example, we might consider a rather puzzling passage of evaluation and straight moral statement at the beginning of *Vanity Fair*. Amelia reproaches Becky for her 'wicked, revengeful thoughts,' as they both leave Miss Pinkerton's academy.

'Revenge may be wicked, but it's natural,' answered Miss Rebecca. 'I'm no angel.' And, to say the truth, she certainly was not.

For it may be remarked in the course of this little conversation (which took place as the coach rolled along lazily by the riverside) that though Miss Rebecca Sharp has twice had occasion to thank Heaven, it has been, in the first place, for ridding her of some person whom she hated, and secondly, for enabling her to bring her enemies to some sort of perplexity or confusion; neither of which are very amiable motives for religious gratitude, or such as would be put forward by persons of a kind and placable disposition. Miss Rebecca was not, then, in the least kind or placable. All the world used her ill, said this young misanthropist, and we may be pretty certain that

8 See Wayne C. Booth *The Rhetoric of Fiction* (Chicago 1961) chapter 1 and throughout, for a comprehensive handling of this whole debate, and Gordon Ray's article, '*Vanity Fair*: One Version of the Novelist's Responsibility' *Essays by Divers Hands* xxv (1950) 87–99, for a more specific reference to Thackeray.

persons whom all the world treats ill, deserve entirely the treatment they get. [15]

Now that does not sound like irony, at least of the simple kind that means the opposite of what it says. But can we take it at its face value, as direct and reliable assessment? To be sure, Becky *is* no angel, and of course there is a certain justice in her receiving no more love from others than she devotes to them. But on the other hand, that automatic assumption of the narrator, that misfortune must be deserved, certainly does not tally with his tender lamentation over Amelia elsewhere in the novel. It has the severity rather of the Calvinistic doctrine of the reprobate who, being preordained to be cast out, is thus justly inflicted in this world and damned in the next. And here is the clue to Thackeray's irony – a complex irony that is frequently true to some extent in both senses. While he wants us to make no mistake about Becky's unscrupulous self-seeking, he uses his narrator to expose the pharisaical confidence of the puritan respectable classes in the just distribution of their own comforts and the miseries of others. Here as elsewhere he assumes the role of spokesman for those who protect their conscience by calling the poor 'undeserving' and by citing Malthusian laws about the economic necessity of starvation. The role is assumed unobtrusively, but the reader must recognize it as part of the constant moral testing he is undergoing while reading the novel.

Again, it is clear from the facts that Becky's has been a life of hardships by the side of which Amelia's agonies over her unworthy fiancé are enormously inflated: yet there is a deliberate though humorous callousness about the narration of it that suggests Becky is to be blamed rather than pitied.

Her mother being dead, her father, finding himself not likely to recover, after his third attack of *delirium tremens*, wrote a manly and pathetic letter to Miss Pinkerton, recommending the orphan child to her protection, and so descended to the grave, after two bailiffs had quarrelled over his corpse. [16]

The early numbers of *Vanity Fair* are dominated by this voice of respect ability – not the Gaunt House or Mayfair version of respectability, but the Russell Square version, which is a more humdrum and domestic affair – though, like Mr Sedley, not without its moments of facetiousness. The respectable folk of Russell Square like their world morally ordered, their incomes secure if not vast, and their women modest, helpless, and pre-ferably lachrymose: hence we have the dominant preference for Amelia, who is nominated here as heroine [15], and the somewhat scandalized reaction to Becky. Later, as we follow Becky's progress up among the baronets, generals, and lords, the dominant tone changes to express a more patrician admiration for a woman of resourcefulness and wit, and in the Waterloo number, when she is expertly looking after her own interest, it is she who is awarded the title of heroine: 'If this is a novel without a hero, at least let us lay claim to a heroine. No man in the British army which has marched away, not the great duke himself, could be more cool or collected in the presence of doubts and difficulties, than the indomitable little aide de camp's wife' [369].

Neither attitude is fully Thackeray's own, of course, though he may lean more to the first than the second. The passages of commentary are not directives on what to think. Each is at best only one way of looking at the matter; and the next may be a different way, or emphatically the wrong one. 'What Thackeray is saying' about the characters is to be found in the facts of the narrative, and only fragmentarily and often mis-leadingly in the commentary. The reaction of those readers of Thackeray who wish that he would stop *talking* and get on with his subject is thus misguided, for the talk, with the attitudes expressed in it, is itself part of the subject.

Tristram Shandy, when for the space of several chapters he has left Uncle Toby in mid-sentence, with his pipe poised for the emphasis of the point he is about to make, enlarges on his 'digressive skill' whereby he 'manages to order affairs so, that my main business does not stand still in my absence':

I was just going, for example, to have given you the great outlines of my Uncle *Toby's* most whimsical character; – when my aunt

Dinah and the coachman came a-cross us, and led us a vagary some
millions of miles into the very heart of the planetary system: Not-
withstanding all this you perceive that the drawing of my uncle
Toby's character went on gently all the time; – not the great contours
of it, – that was impossible, – but some familiar strokes and faint
designations of it, were here and there touch'd in, as we went along, so
that you are much better acquainted with my uncle *Toby* now than
you was before.

By this contrivance the machinery of my work is of a species by
itself; two contrary motions are introduced into it, and reconciled,
which were thought to be at variance with each other. In a word, my
work is digressive, and it is progressive too, – and at the same time.
[I, xxii]

Thackeray's novels are also digressive and progressive too – and at the
same time. For just as in *Tristram Shandy* we are gathering dropped
hints and faint murmurings about Uncle Toby's character as Tristram
proceeds on his erratic way, and partly by inference from the kind of man
his nephew is, so we are filling in details here and there on the map of
Vanity Fair as it is peripherally referred to by this native inhabitant.

In generalizing about the nature of the authorial presence in Thackeray's
novels, one inevitably becomes involved in a series of qualifications; for it
is a lambent light, playing on the fictional world sometimes brilliantly,
but sometimes like an ultraviolet ray, invisible but still effective. None of
the various names we use for this presence – Thackeray, the narrator, the
persona, the implied author, the omniscient author – fully defines its
nature, though they have their local applications. There are the various
roles that the author chooses to play within the world of his characters – so
at one point we hear how he actually met Dobbin and Amelia in Pumpernickel. And there are the roles he adopts as historian and commentator,
with the attitudes, ranging from worldly wise to sentimental, that go with
them: one of these roles is that of the writer amused at the fictional
extravagances of his colleagues, and delighting in showing them up to his
reader by passages of burlesque and portentous talk about conquering
heroes. Somewhere there is Thackeray the man (with his 'broken nose

and myopic spectacles,' as Ford Madox Ford described him[9]), who talks to the reader with a quite human set of preferences about his characters, almost as though they were autonomous beings, and who occasionally, as at the end of *The Newcomes*, gives us details about his own family and activities, and the conception of his story. And comprehending them all is Thackeray the artist, who is, one suspects, rather wiser than Thackeray the man, though the great wisdom of the man is that, like Socrates, he knows his limitation. That range of interlocked roles extends continuously from the fiction to the history, from the imagined world to the actual world. Thackeray may infringe the rules of consistency, but in the process he can connect the novel's world with his reader's, and involve us personally in the lives of his characters.

In this context it is useful to examine the prologue to *Vanity Fair*, 'Before the Curtain.' Critics have traditionally denounced Thackeray's puppet metaphor as a derogation of the artist's duty to create life and to convince us of the imaginative reality of the world he presents. Ford Madox Ford, for instance, held up his hands in horror at Thackeray's propensity, reflected here, to expose his illusion.[10] Nevertheless, the prologue, far from being a piece of artistic irresponsibility, seems to me to be a study, as carefully wrought as one of Keats' odes, of the nature of the artist's relation to his artifice, and of both to the perceiver, the man to whom the artist's vision is to be communicated.

'Before the Curtain' was written when the novel was virtually complete, appearing with the last number of the serial publication and then prefixed to the novel when it appeared as a volume. Thus, although it stands as an advance program to the book, it was written more as a review, or at least with the knowledge of achievement as well as intention.[11] It is in its way a kind of epitome of the whole novel: a concentrated statement of the content as well as the technique, proceeding not by descriptive analysis but, like a poem, by a series of images. The passage is familiar

9 *The English Novel from the Earliest Days to the Death of Joseph Conrad* (Philadelphia 1929) 144

10 Ibid. 15

11 See Joan Stevens, 'A Note on Thackeray's "Manager of the Performance"' *Nineteenth-Century Fiction* XXII (1968) 391

enough, but since I want to consider it in some detail, I quote it at length:

As the Manager of the Performance sits before the curtain on the boards, and looks into the Fair, a feeling of profound melancholy comes over him in his survey of the bustling place. There is a great quantity of eating and drinking, making love and jilting, laughing and the contrary, smoking, cheating, fighting, dancing, and fiddling: there are bullies pushing about, bucks ogling the women, knaves picking pockets, policemen on the look-out, quacks (*other* quacks, plague take them!) bawling in front of their booths, and yokels looking up at the tinselled dancers and poor old rouged tumblers, while the light-fingered folk are operating upon their pockets behind. Yes, this is VANITY FAIR; not a moral place certainly; nor a merry one, though very noisy. Look at the faces of the actors and buffoons when they come off from their business; and Tom Fool washing the paint off his cheeks before he sits down to dinner with his wife and the little Jack Puddings behind the canvas. The curtain will be up presently, and he will be turning over head and heels, and crying, 'How are you?'

A man with a reflective turn of mind, walking through an exhibition of this sort, will not be oppressed, I take it, by his own or other people's hilarity. An episode of humour or kindness touches and amuses him here and there; – a pretty child looking at a gingerbread stall; a pretty girl blushing whilst her lover talks to her and chooses her fairing; – poor Tom Fool, yonder behind the wagon, mumbling his bone with the honest family which lives by his tumbling; – but the general impression is one more melancholy than mirthful. When you come home, you sit down, in a sober, contemplative, not uncharitable frame of mind, and apply yourself to your books or your business.

I have no other moral than this to tag to the present story of *Vanity Fair*. Some people consider Fairs immoral altogether, and eschew such, with their servants and families: very likely they are right. But persons who think otherwise, and are of a lazy, or a benevolent, or a sarcastic mood, may perhaps like to step in for half an hour, and look at the performances. There are scenes of all sorts; some dreadful combats, some grand and lofty horse-riding, some

'Come, children, let us shut up the box and the puppets, for
our play is played out': *Vanity Fair* 878

scenes of high life, and some of very middling indeed; some love-
making for the sentimental, and some light comic business; the whole
accompanied by appropriate scenery, and brilliantly illuminated
with the Author's own candles.

What more has the Manager of the Performance to say? — To
acknowledge the kindness with which it has been received in all the
principal towns of England through which the Show has passed, and
where it has been most favourably noticed by the respected conduc-
tors of the Public Press, and by the Nobility and Gentry. He is proud
to think that his Puppets have given satisfaction to the very best
company in this empire. The famous little Becky Puppet has been
pronounced to be uncommonly flexible in the joints, and lively on the
wire: the Amelia Doll, though it has had a smaller circle of admirers,
has yet been carved and dressed with the greatest care by the artist:
the Dobbin Figure, though apparently clumsy, yet dances in a very
amusing and natural manner: the Little Boys' Dance has been liked
by some; and please to remark the richly-dressed figure of the

Wicked Nobleman, on which no expense has been spared, and which Old Nick will fetch away at the end of this singular performance.

And with this, and a profound bow to his patrons, the Manager retires, and the curtain rises. [1–2]

That puppet metaphor is one that he uses again at the end of the novel: 'Come, children, let us shut up the box and the puppets, for our play is played out' [878]; and the accompanying illustration shows the lid of the box closing on Dobbin's family group, who still remain upright, while Rawdon and others are jumbled inside; Becky, crushed in the arms of a puppet-fiend, and Lord Steyne have fallen outside, as figures too dangerous, perhaps, for children's play, or again too vital to remain within the pale of respectability. The puppets also appear in the title page illustration to the first edition.[12]

But this is not the only image for the relation between the author and his fictional creations. He is also the 'Manager of the Performance,' who may direct the actors on the stage, but who cannot control them in their own lives. This again is a metaphor which is used in the course of the novel, in an equally famous passage:

As we bring our characters forward, I will ask leave, as a man and a brother, not only to introduce them, but occasionally to step down from the platform, and talk about them: if they are good and kindly, to love them and shake them by the hand; if they are silly, to laugh at them confidentially in the reader's sleeve: if they are wicked and heartless, to abuse them in the strongest terms which politeness admits of. [96]

The characters are no longer puppets, to be galvanized by the twitch of a

12 There is another, though debatable, appearance of a puppet in the initial illustration for chapter 61, the opening of number 18 for June 1848. If this is indeed a puppet – and it certainly looks like a little figure of the dead soldier George Osborne, which would be appropriate enough for the material of the chapter – it would suggest that Thackeray had got his idea in time for the penultimate as well as the final numbers, in spite of Eyre Crowe's assertion.

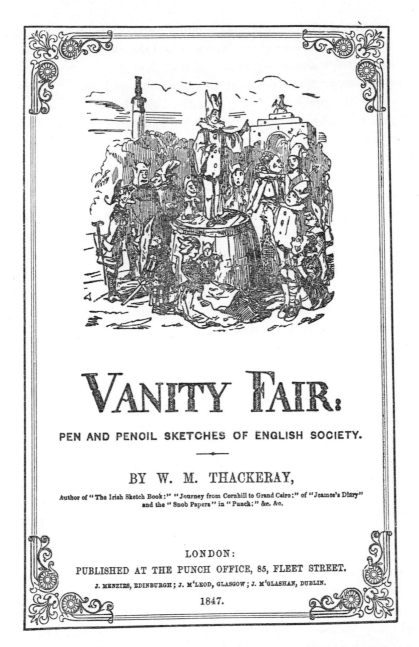

VANITY FAIR:

PEN AND PENOIL SKETCHES OF ENGLISH SOCIETY.

BY W. M. THACKERAY,

Author of "The Irish Sketch Book;" "Journey from Cornhill to Grand Cairo;" of "Jeames's Diary" and the "Snob Papers" in "Punch;" &c. &c.

LONDON:
PUBLISHED AT THE PUNCH OFFICE, 85, FLEET STREET.
J. MENZIES, EDINBURGH; J. M'LEOD, GLASGOW; J. M'GLASHAN, DUBLIN.

1847.

'The moralist ... holding forth on the cover': cover design for *Vanity Fair* string or eliminated at the whim of the puppeteer; they are human beings, of the same size and species as the Manager and the audience, and qualified to shake hands with the one or the other.

The Manager himself sits in an ambiguous position – 'before the curtain on the boards' – looking into the Fair. Behind him is the little universe where he commands, before him is the life of the Fair, the very life which he intends to present, perhaps, in his performance to us. And now, by a strange metamorphosis, he sees himself as just one more of the turbulent throng of 'quacks (*other* quacks, plague take them!) bawling in front of their booths.' This inclusion of himself in his own satirical vision is characteristic too, and it not only operates in the novel as that plausible voice of respectability in which he speaks, but is also apparent in the cover design to the monthly parts, of the fool addressing other fools from a barrel, and in his explanation, 'the moralist, who is holding forth on the cover (an accurate portrait of your humble servant), professes to wear neither gown nor bands, but only the very same long-eared livery in which his congregation is arrayed' [95].

That long-eared livery is also the costume of Tom Fool, the classic figure of the clown who must mask his melancholy, his world-weariness, and his domestic cares behind a smiling face for the world's entertainment. There is another picture of this figure, clothed in motley, with the fool's bauble, at the foot of chapter 9: and the worried face that he reveals as he lowers his comic mask is Thackeray's own. That too is part of Thackeray's achievement in 'Before the Curtain,' and in *Vanity Fair* as well – to see his own identity with the meanest figure of his creation, 'poor Tom Fool, yonder behind the wagon, mumbling his bone.' Chesterton, who has an unerring instinct in singling out what is great in Thackeray, so describes his place among Victorian moralists: 'The one supreme and even sacred quality in Thackeray's work is that he felt the weakness of all flesh. Wherever he sneers it is at his own potential self ... He stood for the remains of Christian humility, as Dickens stood for the remains of Christian charity. Dickens, or Douglas Jerrold, or many others might have planned a Book of Snobs; it was Thackeray, and Thackeray alone, who wrote the great subtitle, "By One of Themselves."'[13] This

13 Introduction to *The Book of Snobs* (London 1911) ix

'Under the mask satirical there walks about a sentimental gentleman who means not unkindly to any mortal person': Letters II 539. Thackeray's self-portrait, *Vanity Fair* 104

humility, as well as the godlike confidence of the puppeteer, is embodied in *Vanity Fair* as in its prologue.

Accompanying this set of metaphors for the author's relation to his characters, there is a corresponding set of views of humanity. One is the view of man as a puppet, operating under some outer necessity, divinely proposed and disposed of, and finally insignificant in the total span of disappointed aspiration (though Thackeray's playful handling of his image suggests something less despairing than Hardy's vision of man as the plaything of the President of the Immortals). Another is the satirical vision of the Fair, with its dominant population of quacks and pickpockets. And then there is the compassionate view of man as a figure of pathos, like Tom, who is the prey rather than the predator, and yet perhaps the more Fool for being so.

It is Thackeray's version of Langland's Field full of Folk. And in the novel he expands it: we may indeed see his characters, even the determined and active Becky, as acting under the compulsion of the world they live in. At the same time, we can see her, like the quacks and pickpockets, as one of the elements that make it what it is. Poor Tom Fool, with his domestic concerns, stands for Amelia's and Dobbin's part of the story: equally, though perhaps not so reprehensibly, belonging to the Fair – just as in Bunyan's Vanity Fair 'wives, husbands, children' are on sale as well as 'trades, places, honours, preferments, titles,' which are Becky's concerns.

But there is another figure of concern in the prologue, and that is the 'man with a reflective turn of mind' who walks through the exhibition – the reader. He is partly just another inhabitant of the Fair, but since he buys rather than sells he is to be enticed and amused with advertisements of 'some dreadful combats, some grand and lofty horse-riding,' and so on. Partly too he is invited to be merely a detached spectator of the Fair, as though he were not part of it; though his books and his business, which may seem more solid and sensible to him, are perhaps only his own version of 'cheating, fighting, dancing and fiddling.' There may be some who 'consider Fairs immoral altogether, and eschew such,' – but they cannot well avoid this one, though they may choose to shut their eyes to it; for even Christian and Faithful had to pass through Vanity Fair.

In the prologue, as in the novel, we notice Thackeray's tendency to slide away from the substance of the vision to the evaluation of it, and a consideration of its effect on the viewer. 'Yes, this is VANITY FAIR; not a moral place, certainly; nor a merry one, though very noisy.' The focus changes from the jumble of life presented to the spectator's response: 'the general impression is one more melancholy than mirthful. When you come home, you sit down, in a sober, contemplative, not uncharitable frame of mind, and apply yourself to your books or your business.'

And this is what he chooses as his moral, so far as he has one. It is no extravagant program of reform that he has undertaken; only that his reader should look, and know; respond, and gain in sympathy from his response; and then that he should proceed with his own business of living in a 'not uncharitable frame of mind.' It is the best that a preacher in and of Vanity Fair can hope to achieve.

To see how this appeal for the reader's response operates in the novel we might turn to a passage in which Thackeray recurs to his image of the Fair. It is in the chapter where he shows how Miss Crawley, universally pampered and flattered for the size of her bank balance, has her private hours of sickness and hysterical fear of death:

> Without preaching, the truth may surely be borne in mind, that the bustle, and triumph, and laughter, and gaiety which Vanity Fair exhibits in public, do not always pursue the performer into private life, and that the most dreary depression of spirits and dismal repentances sometimes overcome him. Recollection of the best ordained banquets will scarcely cheer sick epicures. Reminiscences of the most becoming dresses and brilliant ball-triumphs will go very little way to console faded beauties ... and the success or the pleasure of yesterday become of very small account when a certain (albeit uncertain) morrow is in view, about which all of us must some day or other be speculating. O brother wearers of motley! Are there not moments when one grows sick of grinning and tumbling, and the jingling of cap and bells? This, dear friends and companions, is my amiable object – to walk with you through the Fair, to examine the shops and the shows there; and that we should all come home after the flare, and the noise, and the gaiety, and be perfectly miserable in private.
> [227–8]

As preacher he asks us to judge the worldly old hypocrite for what she is; but as himself, an inhabitant of the same world, and speaking to other inhabitants with the same awareness of the incongruous proximity of death in Vanity Fair, he creates understanding and sympathy. The play of irony about his 'amiable object' to make us go home to 'be perfectly miserable in private' is a further appeal, since it unites reader and writer in a kind of self-mockery.

It is a marvellous piece of work, that prologue – a kind of distilled essence of the novel, without being in any crude way an explanation or an apology or a synopsis. It not only gives a preview of the content of the novel – establishing the symbolic setting of the Fair, promising for those who will appreciate the touch of burlesque the 'grand and lofty horse-riding' as well as love-making and comic business, and introducing in their puppet shape the figures who are so fully to expand in the course of the novel; but it gives also a foretaste of the method, offering a series of metaphors for that varying presence of the artist in his work, and preparing us for the tone and changing moods of the narrative and for the part that we, as spectators and evaluators, are to play ourselves.

So I do not defend Thackeray from the charge of exposing his own illusion. He certainly does assert his liberty to juggle with his characters, not just in calling them puppets (which, by the way, is a matter of almost literal truth – the writer *is* the omnipotent being who proposes and disposes of his characters; Thackeray differs from other authors only in admitting it), but in various other ways in all his novels. For instance, in *The Virginians* he reassures us about the fate of Harry Warrington when he is knocked unconscious by telling us that he has no intention of squandering his hero so early in the novel [212], and in *The Newcomes* confesses that it was a matter of expediency that he eliminated Lady Kew when he did [1009]; and he speaks of Philip Firmin as being 'so rude and overbearing that I really have a mind to depose him from his place of hero – only, you see, we are committed. His name is on the title page overhead, and we can't take it down and put up another' [144]. But this is only one end of the scale; and his characters in his own mind and as he embodies them in words certainly do not lack imaginative life. This capricious being also spoke of his creations as though they were so real as to act beyond his control: he was not responsible for the marriage of Esmond and Rachel, he told a friend, for they 'married themselves'; he complained that he was losing sleep, during the course of writing *The Newcomes*, because Colonel Newcome was so perversely 'making a fool of himself.' 'The characters once created *lead me*, and I follow where they direct,' he admitted [Letters III 438n]. Gulliver is no longer among the Lilliputians: it even seems as though the puppets had power to manipulate the puppeteer.

   Now, the one attitude may not compensate for the other. James thinks the author's admission within the novel that he and the reader are only 'making believe' is 'a terrible crime' – though at the time he was speaking of Trollope and not Thackeray.[14] And almost as influential a critic, Ortega y Gasset, would simply deny Thackeray's books the title of novels:

> The author must begin by luring us into the closed precinct that is his novel and then keep us there cut off from any possible retreat to the real space we left behind ... [He] must build around us a wall without chinks or loopholes through which we might catch, from within the novel, a glimpse of the outside world ... In my judgment, no writer can be called a novelist unless he possesses the gift of forgetting, and thereby making us forget, the reality beyond the walls of his novel. Let him be as realistic as can be; that is to say, let the microcosm of his novel consist of unquestionably true-to-life elements – he will have lost out if he cannot keep us from remembering that there exists an extramural world.[15]

Thackeray, I think, would be almost as incredulous of Ortega's theory as Ortega would be shocked at Thackeray's practice. It was part of both his moral and artistic purpose to force the reader, during the act of reading, to make comparisons from one world to the other, to bring to bear his knowledge of one on the evaluation of the other; in fact, to break down, or at least as far as possible to overlook, that barrier between illusion and reality. That is why he lets his characters wander from one novel to the next, delights in introducing historical figures and happenings into them, so that they seem to be 'hanging on to the skirts of history' [VF 211], appears himself in them as friend to the characters, talks to the reader as though he is likely to know or at least to meet Becky and the rest, and invites him to make comparisons from the character to himself, and himself to his friends.

The kind of novel Ortega describes bears a different relation to the reader's experience. James, for instance, dramatizing the unfolding consciousness of a single character, invites us to live *through* Strether,

14 See 'The Art of Fiction'
15 *The Dehumanization of Art and Notes on the Novel* trans. Helene Weyl (Princeton 1948) 91–2

feeling and understanding as he does (even if we are simultaneously aware, sometimes, of his mistakes and limitations); so that our own identities and our own concerns are, for the duration of the novel, in some sort suspended. But Thackeray does not try for this kind of intensity. He persuades us to live not *through* his characters but, in our own identities, *with* them, and makes us feel that our lives unfold together.

He achieves this partly through his use of serial publication. It seems as though he had a concept of the serially published novel as almost a genre in itself: certainly *Esmond*, written for publication as a whole, is a work different in kind from his other novels; with its limited point of view and sustained emotional intensity, it is more like the kind of novel Ortega describes. The difference is not just a matter of the composition of the shorter monthly units, which must be structurally sound on their own as well as being integral parts of the whole. The publication over many months has some effect on the mood and action of the novel, as well as on its structure. As the time of writing and of reading is extended, so the time of the action is protracted. These novels are not concerned with any single conflict of wills, any decisive break-through of experience, as, say, Jane Austen's or George Eliot's are. His characters get older, they act themselves out; they gain in wisdom in one direction, perhaps, while their receptivity in another fades. Meanwhile, the narrator gets older, and reminds us that we are getting older too. That continuous fabric of existence goes on, over months or years, with its dramas and disappointments but without resolution, for the novel's characters as for its readers. Intensity cannot be sustained for months on end: so the gaps are filled in with editorializing, and we are asked to think about ourselves in relation to the characters. Think about thirty years ago when you were wildly and imprudently in love, like Pendennis with the Fotheringay. Think about next year, when you may die like poor broken Sedley or arrogant old Osborne.

And those yellow-covered parts by which the author maintained his contact with his public, getting their reactions and reacting to them during the course of composition, were also the common meeting ground, month by month, for hundreds of readers who, since they were reading the same number at the same time, would have a topic of conversation as immediate as the latest railway disaster. Have you read this month's number of *Pendennis* yet? Do you think that artful Amory minx will really catch Pen? In my opinion, he's a self-satisfied young jackanapes who deserves all he gets. And so on. In literature today we have no equivalent, though radio and television have attempted the same effect. The serial soap opera, for instance, which prompts so many listeners to write letters pleading that a marriage should come about or that an impending death be averted, taps the same source of interest; Thackeray too builds up complicated family trees that overlap the divisions between the novels, so that his readers, keeping track of the Esmonds, Warringtons, Crawleys, and Newcomes, build up a sort of in-group scholarship as they do within their own families. The nearest approach today to the kind of gossipy interest that Thackeray managed to create with his fiction is in the popular magazines about public celebrities. One can imagine that in some sense Becky and Amelia were the Elizabeth Taylor and Jackie Kennedy of their age; there would be the same piquante immediacy about the marital adventures of the one and the widowhood and remarriage of the other. Their private lives would be as avidly discussed, their progress as eagerly followed.

Of course serial publication always provokes speculation among readers about what is going to happen, and argument about which character is most congenial; but among the great Victorian novelists Thackeray, I think, is the one who most fully exploited that analogy of serial publication with the news media, making it a means of blurring the distinction between art and life, and so of giving his fictional creations a lifelike existence. For all the teeming life in a Dickens novel and for all the vitality of its characters one does not feel that they are apt to step out of the confines of their volume, as we feel of Jos or Major Pendennis. Dickens used serial publication more for the accumulation of suspense than to provoke discussion among his readers about the morals and attractions of his characters. They do not tempt one to argue to and fro about them, as we argue about whether Becky could really have been a good woman if she had had five thousand a year, or whether Colonel Newcome behaved like an old trump or an old fool in his last exploit. That kind of argument presupposes an existence of the characters outside the novel, and it is Thackeray's achievement to make us think of his characters as we think of public figures or our own acquaintance.

Another writer who achieves this kind of life for his characters (and it is a particular *kind* of life I am speaking of, and not a question of degree) is Sterne in *Tristram Shandy*, where serial publication and the close communication between writer and reader again have something to do with it. Sterne, too, managed to get his readers feverishly speculating about Uncle Toby's amours and the exact location and effects of his wound in the groin. And the most solemn of modern critics still talk unembarrassedly about 'my Father' and 'my Uncle Toby.' The writer of *Tristram Shandy*, too, is both within his story, with a limited consciousness, and outside it, with access to information that would hardly have been available to Tristram; and there are times when the fictional Tristram and the historical Sterne are as indistinguishable as Pendennis and Thackeray. I believe it is that dual role which, while in some sort exposing the illusion, creates a new one. In his relation with his readers the author must in honesty at some time speak in his own person, and so admit to the perpetration of a fiction; but since he stands also in a human relation to the characters within his novel, he manages to make us believe, momentarily, that we all inhabit the same world. At least this is the effect of looking back to a Thackeray novel we may have read years ago: we remember Becky as we remember some vivid figure from our own experience. There are still people who make a practice of reading *Vanity Fair* every year, as they might regularly holiday at the same resort, to meet the people they know.[16] In Thackeray's novels the firm location of 'illusion here, reality there' is shifted and adjusted, so that we can readily relate to either plane. And Vanity Fair becomes co-extensive with our own world.

Certainly Thackeray's contemporaries testified to suspending their disbelief in this way. Whitwell Elwin, one of his best reviewers, spoke admiringly of Thackeray's ability 'to interweave his fictions into the daily existence of his readers, and bring his mimic characters into competition with the living world, till forgetting they were shadows, we have

16 For example, see Joan Evans's letter to the *Times Literary Supplement* 5 December 1953: "I have been reading *Vanity Fair* once a year now for more years than I care to reckon' 1011.

followed their fortunes, and discussed their destinies and conduct as though they had been breathing flesh and blood.' Thackeray, he says, has the gift of waking our sympathy, and seizing upon our credulity, 'so that we believe in his people, speculate gravely upon their faults or their excellences, and talk about them as if we had breakfasted with them this morning.'[17] And *The Times* reviewer fastened on the same quality:

> Of course we all know the Newcomes. We may not visit at Park-lane or Bryanston or Fitzroy squares. We may have been too late a summer or two since to meet them at Baden. We should not bow nor perhaps recognize them individually if we did meet. But they are people with whose habits and motives we are familiar – about whom we have talked pleasantly for months – who have been more, perhaps, to each of us than many families of his or her acquaintance. If we question our respective impressions, we may even find that to many intents we have looked upon these 'Newcomes' as real personages, as helping to people our world, to attract or repel us, and to point or adorn our moral speculations.[18]

Yet Thackeray had never tried to make people believe in his fictions in any literal sense – as, say, Defoe might have hoped to make a few readers believe in the existence of a historical Moll Flanders. Paradoxically, his very exposure of his story as fiction made his readers the more ready to think of it almost as fact, for they had been invited to participate with the author in the whole process of creation. Those reviews were written on the heels of a novel that had ended with an image of its characters fading away into fable-land:

> As I write the last line with a rather sad heart, Pendennis and Laura, and Ethel and Clive fade away into fable-land. I hardly know whether they are not true: whether they do not live near us somewhere. They were alive, and I heard their voices; but five minutes since was touched by their grief. And have we parted with them here on a sudden, and without so much as a shake of the hand? [1007]

17 *Quarterly Review* XCVII (1855) 377–8
18 29 August 1855

So the illusion that has been laboriously constructed through two years and a thousand pages dissolves in an instant. Nevertheless, it is a great moment, touched with the pathos of the fading vision. In its use of the suddenly diminishing perspective, the passage has something in common with the ending of *The Eve of St. Agnes*, a poem which up to the last stanza maintains an atmosphere of almost tactual immediacy:

> And they are gone: aye, ages long ago
> These lovers fled away into the storm.

Illusion and reality are momentarily illuminated in the same instant; and if this is done successfully, the one can enhance rather than dispel the other.

'Fled is that music: – do I wake or sleep?' That is the ending of another of Keats' poems concerned with the nature of the artistic illusion. And Thackeray, like Keats, was constantly concerned with the same question: 'And have we parted with them here on a sudden, and without so much as a shake of the hand?' What Thackeray and Keats were trying to communicate was the totality of their vision, and this involved the acknowledgement of its visionary nature. However, if a novelist can make his creatures as real for us as they are for him, it is no mean achievement; and we too are left with a dreamlike wondering: 'I hardly know whether they are not true.'

In one of his initial illustrations for *The Newcomes*, Doyle has aptly depicted Thackeray's almost physical relation with the imagined world he creates. It shows the crowd attending Rosey Newcome's '*omnium gatherum*' at the splendid new mansion in Tyburnia. Clearly distinguishable are Honeyman and Binnie, Colonel Newcome, the Sherrick ladies, Rosey and her mother, and the artists J.J. Ridley and McCollop, all figures with whom we have become familiar in the course of the novel, and representing between them the great institutions of the Victorian world – the church, the law, the empire, the family, commerce, and the arts [820]. Right in the centre is a figure identifiable as Pendennis by the presence of Laura with the laurel wreath by his side: the features, however, are not Pen's, but unmistakably Thackeray's. The drawing is no

Thackeray at Rosey Newcome's '*omnium gatherum*': *The Newcomes* 828

doubt a little joke of Doyle's, but it is nevertheless an appropriate representation of Thackeray's intention to involve us personally in his world, as he involves himself. The reader may, if he chooses, see himself in one of the various unidentified figures in the gathering.

Another means by which Thackeray cements the relationship between himself and the reader, which to so large an extent sustains his created illusion, is his use of burlesque. It is characteristic of the novelist who depends on irony and an intimate communication with his readers, like Fielding, Sterne, Jane Austen, and Thackeray, that parody is an initial creative impulse. Witness *Shamela, Joseph Andrews, Love and Freindship, Northanger Abbey*, and *Tristram Shandy* itself. In many ways, Thackeray's *Punch* parodies of his contemporaries, *Novels by Eminent Hands*, were as much preparation for his style and tone in *Vanity Fair* as *The Book of Snobs* was for its content. For in making fun of the inflated rhetoric of

Bulwer Lytton and the ultra-high society and heroic posturing of Disraeli, he was defining for himself his own principles of simple and direct language, and characters by and large 'very middling indeed.'

There are still some passages of direct parody in his novels,[19] addressed to readers familiar with the Newgate novel, the silver fork novel, and the historical romance of the kind G.P.R. James wrote. The most obvious of these was the passage (which Thackeray subsequently excised) at the beginning of the Vauxhall chapter of *Vanity Fair*, in which the author undertakes to write his story first in the Newgate style, with the characters as criminals talking Thackeray's version of the flash language familiar in Ainsworth's novels ('I'll gully the dag and bimbole the clicky in a snuffkin'!); and then in the 'genteel rose-water style,' in which the protagonists become the Marquis of Osborne, Lady Amelia, and Lord Joseph, and speak a jargon of English, French, and German [882–3]. And one chapter of *The Newcomes* begins with the two cavaliers on a November afternoon that were the trademark of G.P.R. James [669].

But for the most part Thackeray gave up direct parody in his novels for a light texture of burlesque supported by a sophisticated pattern of allusion, and frequent remarks on how 'I disdain, for the most part, the tricks and surprises of the novelist's art' [N 901], and on his determination to write about men and women, not heroes and heroines, about the everyday occurrences of ordinary life, not the wild coincidences and providential resolutions of romance, and so on. His principle of realism, of course, prompted him in his reaction from romance, just as it has prompted similar remarks in most novelists who, as a matter of tradition, deny heroic status to their protagonists. He followed up his brief parodies in *Vanity Fair* with the disclaimer:

> Thus you see, ladies, how this story *might* have been written, if the author had but a mind; for, to tell the truth, he is just as familiar with Newgate as with the palaces of our revered aristocracy, and has seen the outside of both. But as I don't understand the language or manners of the Rookery, nor that polyglot conversation which,

19 See John Loofbourow *Thackeray and the Form of Fiction* (Princeton 1964) 14–50, for a detailed handling of the texture of parody in *Vanity Fair*

according to the fashionable novelists, is spoken by the leaders of *ton*; we must, if you please, preserve our middle course modestly, amidst these scenes and personages with which we are most familiar. [884]

But Thackeray makes thematic use of his reaction. *Vanity Fair* deserves its subtitle of 'A Novel without a Hero,' because the specifically unheroic nature of man – and of woman too, for all the ironic claims for that title alternately for Amelia and Becky – is his subject.[20] Literary, as well as social, pretension is to be Thackeray's satirical butt.[21] It is to be the reader's business in *Vanity Fair*, as it is Catherine Morland's in *Northanger Abbey*, to distinguish between the true and the false, both in life and in literature. And just as she has to learn to see through the wiles of the Thorpes, so we have to see, by a process of contrast between the real and the romantic, through the wiles of far more complex beings like Becky, and Amelia too (for Amelia's poses are so much the more deceptive because they are unconsciously assumed). The analogy suggests again how integral a part of the novel Thackeray makes his reader's response. Jane Austen builds in a character to learn her lesson about truth and artifice, and Catherine in a sense is the reader on-stage. Thackeray, with the same theme, allows the reader to retain his own location and his own identity, but makes him experience the novel's delusions and enlightenments for himself. That is partly why the progress of his plot does not depend on any crucial development of a character's consciousness: it is the reader who must do the developing. Tristram's demand that his reader should replace the asterisks with the requisite salacities and fill in the description of the Widow Wadman for himself begins to look like a relatively moderate requirement!

Thackeray's background of recurrent ironic allusion to heroes and heroines enables us to see through the characters as they strike various romantic attitudes. *We* know that the inhabitants of Vanity Fair are not

---

20 See A.E. Dyson '*Vanity Fair:* An Irony Against Heroes' *Critical Quarterly* VI (1964) 11–31

21 Harriet Blodgett has touched on this in a perceptive article 'Necessary Presence: the Rhetoric of the Narrator in *Vanity Fair*,' *Nineteenth-Century Fiction* XXII (1967) 216

heroic, but they recurrently see themselves in that light, and the incongruity makes for a good deal of the life and humour of the novel. 'It's not myself I care about,' George tells Amelia with noble simplicity: 'it's you' [301]; though he has just been fulminating to Dobbin, with some emphasis on the first person singular, 'How the deuce am I to keep up my position in the world on such a pitiful pittance?' [295]. 'You were pure – Oh yes, you were pure, my saint in heaven!' exclaims Amelia [846], casting her eyes up at the portrait of the husband who had tried to break his engagement with her, neglected her after a few days of marriage, and propositioned another woman within weeks. 'A defeat!' exclaims Jos contemptuously from his bed on the morning of Waterloo, 'D—— it, sir, it's impossible. Don't try and frighten *me*' [371]. It is even a relief to turn from these feats of deliberate self-delusion to Becky's professional gusto in her acting, as she plays the injured wife for Jos's benefit: 'I have had so many griefs and wrongs, Joseph Sedley, I have been made to suffer so cruelly, that I am almost made mad sometimes' [833]. So one of Thackeray's means of making his characters lifelike is to show them striking poses that are fiction-like.

That emphasis on the incongruity between romance and reality, or between the pose and the truth, is both subject and technique in *Vanity Fair*. Frequently the reader is ironically invited to see the sordid facts of the lustful and rapacious world through the rose-coloured spectacles of the novel of sentiment. In the number following the scene of old Sir Pitt's proposal to Becky the writer congratulates himself that 'every reader of a sentimental turn (and we desire no other) must have been pleased with the tableau with which the last act of our little drama concluded; for what can be prettier than an image of Love on his knees before Beauty?' [179]. We are meant to enjoy the contrast between this image and the one we had been left with: the leering old satyr before the scheming adventuress. But at the same time we must appreciate the extent of its justice: now if ever is the moment of sentiment in the lives of these two worldly sinners. The scene is indeed an emotional crisis in Becky's life – she 'wept some of the most genuine tears that ever fell from her eyes' [178]. And Sir Pitt's avowal, 'You shall do what you like; spend what you like; and 'av it all your own way. I'll make you a zettlement. I'll do everything reglar' is no

'The old man fell down on his knees and leered at her like a satyr.' Sir Pitt Crawley proposes to Becky: *Vanity Fair* 178

doubt as sincere a profession of love as he has made in his life.

Thackeray has a knack of reminding us of a character's humanity by his implied contrast with a heroic stereotype. He shows people with little fragments of heroism in them, even if only in the form of a desire to be heroic. So all the male characters partially embody some aspect of heroism, but never achieve the full status: Dobbin, whose moral strength might qualify him for hero, has a lisp and big feet; Rawdon, who has the appropriate courage and class, is a roué; George, who has the looks and the bearing, is a self-satisfied cad. Take Dobbin's mind, and Rawdon's heart, and George's body, and you might patch up a heroic mould. Take Dobbin's clumsiness and embarrassment, and George's conceit, and Rawdon's brains, and add a large measure of cowardice, and you have Jos, the negative embodiment of a hero, although, perhaps even more than

George, 'Waterloo Sedley' has a heroic concept of himself. It is clear how intrinsic a part literary satire is of Thackeray's more comprehensive social satire, for man's false pretension to heroic status is equally Thackeray's subject with man's struggle for social status. His characters often seem to have an extra dimension of life because of that implied contrast. For example, after the dramatic scene in which Rawdon bursts in on Becky and Steyne, there is a situation that readily lends itself to the full melodramatic treatment, where the hack novelist would pull out all the stops. Rawdon is a soldier and a man of honour, and his honour has been stained by an unscrupulous blackguard. And indeed he does act in the manner prescribed: he seeks out a comrade to stand as his second, and challenges Steyne to a duel. But his second is the bloated, unshaven old Captain McMurdo, and the 'affair,' though handled with the conventional ritual, ends with a whimper, not a bang.[22] The scene in which Pitt hears the news of Becky's betrayal is comparable:

> 'Your marriage was your own doing, not mine.'
> 'That's over now,' said Rawdon. – 'That's over now.' And the words were wrenched from him with a groan, which made his brother start.
> 'Good God! is she dead?' Sir Pitt said, with a voice of genuine alarm and commiseration.
> 'I wish *I* was,' Rawdon replied. 'If it wasn't for little Rawdon I'd have cut my throat this morning – and that damned villain's too.'
> [680–3]

Fiction's conventional answer to Pitt's perfect cue, 'Good God! is she dead?' is, of course, 'Would that she were!' and readers trained on the novels of Bulwer Lytton and his like would automatically expect something like it. Rawdon's morose and ungrammatical 'I wish *I* was' reminds the reader all over again of his humanity. The same device is in operation

22 John A. Lester, jr, in 'Thackeray's Narrative Technique' *PMLA* LXIX (1954), 392–409, points out how few of the duels threatened in Thackeray's novels actually take place. Lester attributes this to a constitutional reluctance on Thackeray's part to embark on a dramatic scene; I would suggest it is rather a further insistence on the unheroic nature of man.

in the characterization of Lady Lyndon in *Barry Lyndon*: she is actually kept in durance vile by an unmitigated villain, but because she sees herself as a heroine of romance, and is overweight to boot, she is the more believable. It is one of the positive sides of Thackeray's determination not to write romance.

Another of his strengths that partly stems from this determination is his power of understatement. The Waterloo number of *Vanity Fair* begins apologetically, 'We do not claim to rank among the military novelists' [361], and indeed he stays for the most part with the wives, where Lever or G.P.R. James would have been busy describing the muscular feats of the combatants. But the tension mounts the higher for this, for the enforced passivity of the civilians left behind (always excepting Becky, who skilfully conducts her own campaign) makes them more interesting objects of study, and the remote booming of the guns is the more ominous because they cannot see its effects. The battle itself is touched on briefly but brilliantly, for the number ends with the most memorable and effective passage in all Thackeray's writing:

> No more firing was heard at Brussels – the pursuit rolled miles away. Darkness came down on the field and city: and Amelia was praying for George, who was lying on his face, dead, with a bullet through his heart. [406]

A piece of information to which other novelists might have devoted chapters of ranting and posturing is relegated to a subordinate clause; herein lies its power. Through his reaction to the inflated narratives of lome of his contemporaries Thackeray had grasped the intensity of the low pitch. He is not characteristically the dramatist of the big scenes of sife, though he can write them magnificently if he wants to – witness Rawdon's discovery of Becky, or Esmond's reunion with Rachel at Winchester. But he can convey with intensity the long-drawn-out emotions and the changing relations that are the dominant shading of existence. That low note sounds with a haunting dominance through his novels: through Dobbin's fifteen years of fruitless devotion, through Esmond's somewhat bitter solemnity, through the sense of bartered aspirations in *The Newcomes*, and of pointless sacrifice in *The Virginians*, and through

C

Philip's long frustration in finding there is really nothing for a strong and able man to do in the china-shop of respectable society.

So here too Thackeray can make a virtue of what can theoretically be called a defect. Even Fielding was aware of the danger of burlesque, and introduced it only circumspectly into the diction of *Joseph Andrews*, being careful, for the sake of realism, to keep it out of character and action. But Thackeray's constant reminders that he is not writing a novel like Bulwer Lytton's, and occasional sallies into burlesque as if he were, themselves draw attention to the fact that we are reading fiction. It suits his purpose, however, because on the one hand by this means he invites complicity with his reader through talking about what, after all, the reader can be sure is really passing in his mind – that is, the problems of writing a novel; and on the other, he is expanding his themes of social pretension and emotional deceit, and the limited heroism of humanity.

The part of the novelist concerned to burlesque the excesses of his con-temporaries and to amuse his reader with topical literary jokes is of course only one of the writer's roles in Thackeray's novels. Those in which he speaks more as a man than a novelist can best be explored by a more detailed examination of the texture of certain passages.

In the preface to *Pendennis* Thackeray spoke of his novels as a 'sort of confidential talk between writer and reader,' and asks us to believe that he does 'tell the truth in the main.' In the main, yes, and, in the total move-ment of his novel, we can acknowledge the justice of this, but it does not mean that we can relax our guard and take everything he says at face value. For the same writer also exclaims devoutly, 'Oh, let us be thankful not only for faces, but for masks! ... Whilst I am talking, for instance, in this easy chatty way, what right have you, my good sir, to know what is really passing in my mind?' [v 577]. The challenge is one we have to meet, and one of the pleasures of *Vanity Fair* is that it is *strenuous* reading, if we are ready to listen to it and give our minds to what is going on. That relation with the narrator is not a passive one where he tells and we listen – it is a two-way affair, in which we must exert ourselves to detect and see through his various masks, in which we must often disagree vigorously with what we are told, and always think for ourselves.

For all Ford Madox Ford's strictures about Thackeray's intruding his broken nose and myopic spectacles into his novels, the author has been quite explicit in the pages of the novel itself about the fact that he plays roles. And it is hardly necessary to explain the often contradictory attitudes by postulating, as a recent critic has done, that the 'implied author' has two contrary neuroses;[23] Geoffrey Tillotson has made a far more complete examination of what he calls 'the content of the authorial "I".'[24] But Thackeray himself warns us not to take his first person too seriously: '"I" is here introduced to personify the world in general – the Mrs. Grundy of each respected reader's private circle' [453]. There is frequently a sense of him as a personal and even physical presence, with a set of friends at the club and a healthy appetite for good food and vintage wine. But that personal presence is as Protean as his artistic presence. Sometimes he chats about his own private experience – about the hangover, contracted from two glasses of rack punch at Vauxhall gardens, which he can still remember after twenty years [70], or how, fifty years ago (Thackeray was then thirty-six), when he was 'an interesting little boy' [526], he used to be ordered out with the ladies after dinner. In one place he speaks of 'my Julia' and his children [104], and in another of how he has loved in vain [216], and is a lonely and childless bachelor [65, 453]. To match this range of ages and domestic situations there is a comparable range of moral attitudes. We recognize the sentimental narrative voice that is concerned with the effusions of the girls at Miss Pinkerton's academy, and the heart-rending tone that laments, 'Our dear wounded Amelia, ah! where was she?' [420], as well as that voice of Vanity Fair that urges young ladies to be cautious, and 'never tell all you feel, or (a better way still) feel very little' [218], and that invents those worldly aphorisms scattered so delightfully through the novel: such as 'To part with money is a sacrifice beyond almost all men endowed with a sense of order' [559]. The narrator, in these moments, is no more than one of his own characters.

But that sense of a personal presence, and of a whole life of incident

23 Bernard J. Paris, 'The Psychic Structure of *Vanity Fair*' *Victorian Studies*
   x (1967) 389–410
24 *Thackeray the Novelist* 55–70

beyond but interlocking with the incident that is directly presented, is a means of communication with the characters, and of illumination of their actions. Our sense of the enormity of Becky's gesture of flinging Johnson's Dixonary back at Miss Pinkerton's academy is enhanced by the accompanying anecdote of the narrator's acquaintance:

> Miss Sedley was almost as flurried at the act of defiance as Miss Jemima had been; for, consider, it was but one minute that she had left school, and the impressions of six years are not got over in that space of time. Nay, with some persons those awes and terrors of youth last for ever and ever. I know, for instance, an old gentleman of sixty-eight, who said to me one morning at breakfast, with a very agitated countenance, 'I dreamed last night that I was flogged by Dr. Raine.' Fancy had carried him back five-and-fifty years in the course of that evening. Dr. Raine and his rod were just as awful to him in his heart, then, at sixty-eight, as they had been at thirteen. If the Doctor, with a large birch, had appeared bodily to him, even at the age of three score and eight, and had said in an awful voice, 'Boy, take down your pant —'? Well, well, Miss Sedley was exceedingly alarmed at this act of insubordination. [13–14]

Becky's action, of course, stands on its own, and needs no laboured underlining to make it memorable; Amelia's horror we can readily imagine for ourselves. So much will do for a fine scene. But Thackeray gives us more. That brief reference to the author's acquaintance provides a context that, for all its particularity of detail, is universal. It is an appeal to our common experience of childhood subjection – experience that remains vivid though generally overlaid by the concerns of adult life. The old man who lives his childhood fears again awakens and embodies our own subliminal memories, and against them Becky's act of rebellion stands out as a gesture of myth-making stature.

This interpolation of personal reminiscence is of course a delicate business. Thackeray has certainly over-stepped the bounds of tact for many modern readers, who find that his anecdotal habit rather distances the narrative than makes it more immediate. I would defend it on the grounds not that it is good in itself, but that Thackeray manages it consummately. He makes it work. For one thing he has so peculiar a power, with his precision of imagery and language, of evoking scenes and incidents tellingly; and for another, through his easily familiar tone and light touch, he can avoid the portentous threat of the bore who relentlessly insists, 'Let me tell you about myself,' and induce us to listen with a friendly interest. His reminiscence works as part of a strategy to elicit reminiscence from the reader too, and make him draw parallels between the narrative and his own life, and so to charge the fictional events with some of the power of remembered experience. Becky's hurling of the dictionary is staggering because we have been made to remember our own total subjection at school, and Jos's agonies of shame after the evening at Vauxhall are vivid because we have been genially invited to recall our own past indiscretions at places of public entertainment.

Because Thackeray speaks personally, the reader reacts personally, and is often provoked to take issue with the narrator on his judgments and allegiances among the characters. Such a reaction must be based on the supposition that somehow we know more of the characters and surrounding circumstances than he tells us — that is, that these are autonomous beings – people – whose faults and virtues may be speculated on, but not finally assessed. It is an unobtrusive process by which we are made to react in this way, for the comments to which we react are often diffused through the whole narrative, and take the form not only of passages of explicit evaluation but of brief interpolated phrases and adverbs, which may be from the narrator's personal viewpoint, or from that of some character in the action, or of some hypothetical reader. An early scene in *Vanity Fair* will illustrate this process. It occurs during Becky's campaign to capture Jos, while she is staying in the Sedley home and has Amelia's support:

How Miss Sharp lay awake, thinking, will he come or not to-morrow? need not be told here. To-morrow came, and, as sure as fate, Mr. Joseph Sedley made his appearance before luncheon. He had never been known before to confer such an honour on Russell Square. George Osborne was somehow there already (sadly 'putting out' Amelia, who was writing to her twelve dearest friends at Chiswick

Mall), and Rebecca was employed upon her yesterday's work. As Joe's buggy drove up, and while, after his usual thundering knock and pompous bustle at the door, the ex-collector of Boggley Wollah laboured upstairs to the drawing-room, knowing glances were telegraphed between Osborne and Miss Sedley, and the pair, smiling archly, looked at Rebecca, who actually blushed as she bent her fair ringlets over her netting. How her heart beat as Joseph appeared, – Joseph, puffing from the staircase in shining creaking boots, – Joseph, in a new waistcoat, red with heat and nervousness, and blushing behind his wadded neckcloth. It was a nervous moment for all; and as for Amelia, I think she was more frightened than even the people most concerned.

Sambo, who flung open the door and announced Mr. Joseph, followed grinning, in the collector's rear, and bearing two handsome nosegays of flowers, which the monster had actually had the gallantry to purchase in Covent Garden market that morning – they were not as big as the haystacks which ladies carry about with them nowadays, in cones of filigree paper; but the young women were delighted with the gift, as Joseph presented one to each, with an exceedingly solemn bow.

'Bravo, Jos,' cried Osborne.

'Thank you, dear Joseph,' said Amelia, quite ready to kiss her brother, if he were so minded. (And I think for a kiss from such a dear creature as Amelia, I would purchase all Mr. Lee's conservatories out of hand.)

'O heavenly, heavenly flowers!' exclaimed Miss Sharp, and smelt them delicately, and held them to her bosom, and cast up her eyes to the ceiling, in an ecstasy of admiration. Perhaps she just looked first into the bouquet, to see whether there was a *billet-doux* hidden among the flowers; but there was no letter. [43–4]

Now here, of course, there is a personal tone of voice perceptible throughout the narration, but it takes different forms in different places, and with various effects. Occasionally there is a reference to the actual historical background shared by William Makepeace Thackeray and the reader of his monthly instalment, who have in common an acquaintance with Mr Lee's conservatories, and perhaps the memory that Regency nosegays were delicate affairs, not to be confused with the ostentatious bouquets currently fashionable in 1847. Then there is the tone of the writer addressing a literarily sophisticated reader who will savour the touch burlesquing the sentimental novel: hence the description of the conquering hero, Joseph (thrice repeated), who, incongruously, appears as an obtuse and over-stuffed shirt, and of the angelically innocent and palpitating young *ingenue*, who is in fact a wily adventuress with a natural talent for intrigue, and already plenty of experience in it.

Besides this appealing invitation to intimacy there is the voice that seems to be telling us what to think but which is often a dramatic repre-sentation of somebody else's reaction; so we hear, apparently as mimicry of Amelia's own terminology and way of thinking, about her 'twelve dearest friends,' but must judge for ourselves whether each can justly claim that superlative place in her affections. When we read that Amelia was 'more frightened than even the people most concerned,' we realize that the 'even' was inserted by a sentimental consciousness, and it illu-minates both her tendency to excessive emotional reaction and the essen-tial passionlessness of the two principals in the love affair. Rebecca 'actually' blushed in her consciousness of being singled out as the object of Jos's romantic aspirations – this apparently from the point of view of some hypothetical reader who has already concluded she is a brazen hussy hardly to be induced to blush, or who is disgusted that she should be so consummate a hypocrite. Kettle, starting with the principle that anything but strictly neutral narration is an artistic blunder, declares (in a dis-cussion of an earlier but similar 'actually') 'The tone of that "actually" is the tone that puts almost everything in *Vanity Fair* at a distance.'[25] I can only disagree with him diametrically – that tone, whether scandalized or congratulatory, is what most involves us. It is only by knowing not only what the characters do but also how the world responds to them that we

25 Arnold Kettle *An Introduction to the English Novel* (London 1951) 158. The different 'actually' of which Kettle speaks ('Miss Sharp ... actually flung the book back into the garden') has the same tone as the 'actually' we are discussing.

can fully understand them as operative beings. And, through the biassed tone, momentarily we participate in or are induced to react from those built-in respectable assumptions. It comes through quite clearly, even in this brief passage, that Amelia is ingenuous, sentimental, and emotionally shallow, and that Becky is slily on the make, caring not at all for emotion save as a front to get on in the world, and is a talented actress who, at this stage in her career, is rather fatally inclined to overplay her part. But we arrive at these conclusions by a process not only of watching the action, but of responding to the various voices that praise or censure for the wrong reasons.

The novelist can speak as the final authority on the actions and the motives of the characters he creates, whereas the raconteur who is telling us an anecdote of people he knows, and that we may know too, will frequently, as a matter of honesty or in deference to our feelings, admit to a limitation in his knowledge. Now Thackeray often makes such an admission: '*I think* [Amelia] was more frightened than even the people most concerned,' he says, with an air of uncertainty. '*Perhaps* [Becky] just looked first into the bouquet, to see whether there was a *billet-doux* hidden among the flowers.' The narrator's professed ignorance, not just on minor matters like these, but also in matters of substance, is one more of Thackeray's devices for endowing his narrative with something like the quality of life. We cannot know *all* about his characters, as we cannot know all about a person. Much of his writing seems to assume, and so helps us to assume, the existence of his literary creations outside the limits of his volume. And besides this, his professed uncertainty is an invitation for the reader's participation. Our opinion counts too, and we are allowed to make up our own minds on Becky's piece of intriguing.

And again, there is the voice of the narrator that tells us of his own personal affections and convictions. Perhaps it is for this that Thackeray has been taken most to task. His cynical philosophizing was attacked through the nineteenth century, and twentieth-century readers have been disgusted by his sentimental drooling over such figures as Amelia. Dorothy Van Ghent is indignant at the 'unforgivable parenthesis' in which the narrator tells us how much he would like to kiss 'such a dear creature as Amelia,' and she calls his comments 'inane and distracting ... turning [our attention] on the momentarily flaccid mentality of the author.'[26] Arnold Kettle talks about the discrepancy between the vivid dramatization of Becky and the writer's comments on her: 'Thackeray, the Victorian gentleman, may tone down her rebellion by ambiguous adverbs and a scandalized titter, but the energy he has put into her is far more profound than his morals or his philosophy and she sweeps him along.'[27] This suggests that the commentary is all that Thackeray can be given credit for, and that Becky somehow managed to create herself. And this is just my point – that, by inducing us to react, the commentary (which indeed *is* often inane, or smug, or gushing, as it is also often worldly and cynical) endows the characters with a kind of life, and makes us feel that they are autonomous beings with an existence beyond their creator's mind.

We understand how Miss Bates in *Emma*, or Joseph in *Wuthering Heights*, are exasperating characters to the people who live with them, but for us they remain entertaining creations. Amelia, on the other hand, is exasperating directly and personally to the reader (as are Helen Pendennis, Colonel Newcome, or Philip Firmin in their different ways) because of just such remarks as that the narrator longs to kiss her. He provokes such reactions as that of the lady correspondent whom he quotes at one point: '"We don't care a fig for her," writes some unknown correspondent with a pretty little handwriting and a pink seal to her note. "She is *fade* and insipid"'; and he goes on to show that such adverse comments from one female on another are actually 'prodigiously complimentary,' because they must be prompted by jealousy for the insipid girl's success with men [131–2]. Amelia becomes here the issue on which the author bandies catty remarks with his readers. Whether Thackeray actually received such a letter or not does not really matter; we only know he *could* have, because Amelia has provoked similarly personal reactions in ourselves.

So the life and vigour of *Vanity Fair* (and to some extent of all

26 *The English Novel, Form and Function* (New York 1953) 139–40
27 *An Introduction to the English Novel* 164

Thackeray's novels) is a result of this reaction which the commentary, by various means, elicits from us. There is room for argument, and room for personal allegiance, and for personal animosity. That is why there has been so much critical debate on whether Amelia is or is not recommended to our sympathy, whether Becky is or is not capable of murdering Jos, whether Rachel Esmond is or is not a wicked women.[28] The issues are almost as extensively debated as the sanity of the governess in *The Turn of the Screw*, for Thackeray, 'the omniscient author,' is in his own way as ambiguous as James. We all feel we can put in our oar, and have our say, according to our convictions. In declaring, as it were, open season on his characters by discussing them with us himself, he has given them the stature and ambiguity of real people.

E.M. Forster's classic distinction between people in life and characters in fiction is that we can know all there is to know about a character, never about a person.[29] Thackeray deliberately blurs this distinction by leaving some major questions unanswered, as they must be in life about the private lives even of our closest friends. 'Was she guilty or not?' the narrator asks of Becky, à propos of her relation with Steyne. This again has offended Kettle, who accuses Thackeray of pusillanimity. But his reticence on the matter is certainly not because of a prudish reluctance to deal explicitly with adultery; and the question of Becky's guilt is in any case a far more complex one than whether or not she had gone to bed with Lord Steyne, or intended to.[30] After all, did she need to? She was pre-

28 As representative samples I cite the following: Mark Spilka has discussed Amelia in 'A Note on Thackeray's Amelia' *Nineteenth-Century Fiction* x (1955) 202–10; David Cecil's comments on Becky in *Early Victorian Novelists* (London 1934) started a debate that involved Russell Fraser, 'Pernicious Casuistry: A Study of Character in *Vanity Fair*' *Nineteenth-Century Fiction* xii (1957) 137–47, and John E. Tilford, jr, 'The Degradation of Becky Sharp' *South Atlantic Quarterly* lviii (1959) 603–8; and Tilford himself has shown the varied reactions to Rachel Esmond in 'The "Unsavoury Plot" of *Henry Esmond*' *Nineteenth-Century Fiction* vi (1951) 121–30, and 'The Love Theme of *Henry Esmond*' *PMLA* lxvii (1952) 684–701.
29 *Aspects of the Novel* (London 1927) chapter 3. Booth also notes this as a major difference at the beginning of *The Rhetoric of Fiction* 3.
30 G. Armour Craig, in a fine study, 'On the Style of *Vanity Fair*,' which

Becky and General Tufto, with Rawdon turning a blind
eye: *Vanity Fair* 349

sumably not physically attracted to him, and she had shown herself skilful
in the management of him. And what was her motivation? The money,
the jewels, and the prestige were what she was after, but to some extent
Rawdon benefited from these too – at least, this affair was different only in
degree and not in kind from all the others in which this domestic team
had worked together. Earlier in the novel, when George Osborne was
'carrying on a desperate flirtation with Mrs. Crawley ... losing money to

explores some of the implications of Thackeray's confidential relation with
the reader, has also considered the complexity of this question of Becky's
guilt. *Style in Prose Fiction* ed. Harold C. Martin (New York and London
1959) 87–113

the husband and flattering himself that the wife was dying in love for him,' we were told:

It is very likely that this worthy couple never absolutely conspired and agreed together in so many words: the one to cajole the young gentleman, whilst the other won his money at cards: but they understood each other perfectly well, and Rawdon let Osborne come and go with entire good humour. [354]

George, General Tufto, Jos, and young Lord Southdown are all lured in by Becky for Rawdon to fleece. In fact a pastoral metaphor is developed ironically in some detail: Becky is the 'innocent lamb,' Briggs the sheepdog, and Southdown the sheep to be shorn by the shepherd, Rawdon [473–5]. Is Becky entirely to blame if the shepherd draws the line at a different point, and decides that Steyne is not a sheep (though his fleece is of undeniable quality) but a wolf? Steyne himself appears to have thought that Rawdon was a complacent cuckold. Certainly, Becky had kept the money and the presents to herself; but she had indeed procured Rawdon the position of governor of Coventry Island, as the paper of the morning after the catastrophe testifies. 'I was only guilty of too much devotedness to Rawdon's service,' she defends herself. 'I have received Lord Steyne alone a hundred times before. I confess I had money of which Rawdon knew nothing. Don't you know how careless he is of it, and could I dare to confide it to him?' [694]. Like Pitt we find she makes a plausible case. However, considering the nature of that appointment, she might have procured a death sentence rather than a promotion for her husband. But then again, perhaps she knew nothing of the climate of Coventry Island and had intended to accompany him there. All this does not add up to innocence, obviously, but the proliferations of the question are such that we become aware of the impossibility of any final allotment of responsibility. If we are ready to consider them, we avoid the temptation to place ourselves among the Pharisees by concluding too glibly, 'Of course she is guilty, and so let's be done with it.' In that way, wretches hang that jurymen may dine.

On greater and lesser issues, we are invited to judge for ourselves. Did Becky murder Jos? The insurance company thought so, but then the insurance company had a vested interest in the matter. Was Amelia grieved or relieved to find out at last that her sainted husband had betrayed her [866]? Was it some kind of emotional masochism in Dobbin that made him so energetically promote the match between Amelia and George [238]? What was it old Osborne wanted to say before he died? Had he so conquered his long resentment as to want to ask for a reconciliation, or would he only have voiced anew his bitterness and rage [777]? And so on.

So, for all the novelist's reiterated claims to omniscience, there are key points at which he drops this claim and speaks only like the historian, who must be tentative in his conclusions about actual people in complex situations. Indeed, when he admits, as he does at one point, that the whole history is an elaboration of a dinner-time narration by one Tapeworm, and suggests that it could be, after all, only a proliferation of scandal, we begin to realize just how much in the way of assessment is left up to us.

That maxim, 'Judge not that ye be not judged,' which prompted Thackeray to include himself in his own satire, is in operation when Becky's whole career and character are under scrutiny. The ' Vagabond Chapter' on her activities after her downfall has a marvellous ironic tone that forces the reader to beware of glib moral judgments. On the one hand Thackeray develops that image of Becky as the 'siren, singing and smiling,' but with the 'monster's hideous tail ... writhing and twirling, diabolically hideous and slimy, flapping amongst bones, or curling round corpses' [812], and is concerned that we should know the full extent of the evils that have hitherto been only hinted of her. And on the other he sets his reader in 'the moral world, that has, perhaps, no particular objection to vice, but an insuperable repugnance to hearing vice called by its proper name' [812]. We hear enough of her doings in these days to know fairly precisely what kind of life she leads – for instance 'at that famous mansion kept by Madame de St. Amour, in the Rue Royale at Paris, where she began exercising her graces and fascinations upon the shabby dandies' [820] ; but yet, the author asks, ' has any the most squeamish immoralist in Vanity Fair a right to cry fie?' Becky is denounced by people who are no better than herself, and it is suggested that the reader may be one of them: 'The actions of very vain, heartless, pleasure-seeking people are very often improper (as are many of yours, my friend with the grave face and spotless reputation)' [813]. There are touches of pathos about Becky at this time, when she is getting her deserts: 'She was seized, not by remorse, but by a kind of despair, and absolutely neglected her person, and did not even care for her reputation.' In this outcast state, and moving, it sometimes seems, under some painful compulsion, she retraces the stages of her married life from Paris to Brussels. But the recurring assumption is that the reader is part of the respectable throng which casts her out and is then the more shocked that 'her taste for disrespectability grew more and more remarkable. She became a perfect Bohemian ere long, herding with people whom it would make your hair stand on end to meet' [822].

And so, intricately, the reader is lured into the world of Vanity Fair, and made to recognize it as his world, and to think of the characters, to whom he has been introduced by his friend the author, and about whose domestic lives he has heard some piquante gossip, as his acquaintances. Such a proceeding may be a sort of heresy to the reader or the critic trained in the Jamesian scheme, who may exclaim angrily about 'aesthetic distance,' and the 'closed precinct' that a novel ought to be. But Thackeray simply does not believe in aesthetic distance, at least in any strict application of the phrase. For him a close and personal relation with the reader, albeit a varied one, and a confidential intercourse with him about his novel and his characters, and the rights and wrongs of their actions in a fallen world that author, reader, and characters equally inhabit, and the concerns they have in common – all this is the life blood of the illusion he creates. *Vanity Fair* is a great novel not in spite of that authorial presence but because of it, for it is what gives the novel its peculiar immediacy of appeal as well as its universality of application. As Brownell put it, in a perceptive article which was written when Thackeray's reputation was beginning to decline under the influence of the aesthetic movement and the increasing authority of James, 'All this commenting and discursiveness, this arguing from Philip or Amelia to men and women in general, this moralizing over their traits and conduct, has the zest for us that similar criticism or gossip about real people, if any such were attainable, would possess. If it displeases any reader whose sense for "art" is keener than his interest in life, there is perhaps no more to be said.'[31] It is of course the creation of that zest that *is* Thackeray's art.

Qualification is necessary. Commentary, involving this rather dangerous process of breaking the illusion of reality, is not good in itself, but only when done well. Trollope, in his great admiration for Thackeray, tried and occasionally blundered: when he tells us that he himself dislikes shaking hands with Mr Slope, or that the reader need not be worried about Eleanor's fate, it strikes us, as it struck James, as a mistake.[32] And the long-drawn-out loquaciousness of Thomas Hughes at the beginning of *Tom Brown's Schooldays*, intended to be reminiscent of the opening to *The Newcomes*,[33] is merely tedious. Thackeray himself, of course, was not always successful: *The Virginians* breaks down under the weight of the commentary, which there becomes turgid and lacks the sparkle and bite of the earlier novels. But he *could* do it well; and at its best it is not only entertaining and thematically relevant, but it works as a sort of magic to build a bridge between us and the characters, from the actual world around us to the imaginary world of Vanity Fair. The novel lives up to the prologue's claim of being 'brilliantly illuminated with the Author's own candles.'

31 *Victorian Prose Masters* (New York 1901) 12
32 When in *Can You Forgive Her?* Trollope tried to raise the same kind of interest in the extent of his heroine's guilt as Thackeray had stimulated in Becky's, the young James reviewed the novel irritably: 'The question is, can we forgive Miss Vavasor? Of course we can, and forget her, too, for that matter. What does Mr. Trollope mean by this question? It is a good instance of the superficial character of his work that he has been asking it once a month for so long a time without being struck by its flagrant impertinence.' *Nation* (New York) 28 September 1865 i 409. Reprinted in *Trollope: The Critical Heritage* ed. Donald Smalley (London and New York 1969) 249–50.
33 So much is clear from his opening reference to Thackeray and Doyle.

2

Tone and Theme:
Pendennis

'WRITING NOVELS IS ... THINKING ABOUT ONE'S SELF,' THACKERAY wrote in a letter to his daughters [Letters III 645]. And in a discussion of his novels one must inevitably spend a good deal of time talking about Thackeray. That is why some of the best criticism, and notably Gordon Ray's,[1] has been biographical in its approach. Debates on his work have centred as often on the author as on the world he presents. Was he the great castigator of snobbery or, as Sadleir suggested, himself 'a snob who worked an ostentatious anti-snobbery to death'?[2] Was he a cynic who acquiesced in the pervasive evil of the world, or a sentimentalist who characteristically gushed over figures like Amelia, Helen Pendennis, and Colonel Newcome?[3] And the problem is complicated by the fact that he not only adopted different poses as author, but also built many of his own attitudes into his characters, who in turn become mouthpieces for his views and act out certain parts of his own experience. Thackeray is to be found not only in the narrator of *Vanity Fair*, but to varying extents in characters like Dobbin, Esmond, Clive Newcome, Philip, in Pen and Warrington in *Pendennis*, in George Warrington and General Lambert in *The Virginians*, and so on. We come to recognize the author as frag-

---

1 See particularly *The Buried Life* (London 1952), *Thackeray: The Uses of Adversity, 1811–1846* (London 1955), and *Thackeray: The Age of Wisdom, 1847–1863* (London 1958)

2 *Bulwer, a Panorama: Edward and Rosina, 1803–1836* (London 1931) 225. For an account of the varying biographical portraits of Thackeray, see Ray's introductory chapter in *Thackeray: The Uses of Adversity, 1811–1846* 1–9.

3 For a summary of the 'Cynic or Sentimentalist?' debate, see Walter Jerrold's article, *New World* May 1921, 481–90. More recently, Lambert Ennis called his book *Thackeray: The Sentimental Cynic* (Evanston Ill. 1950).

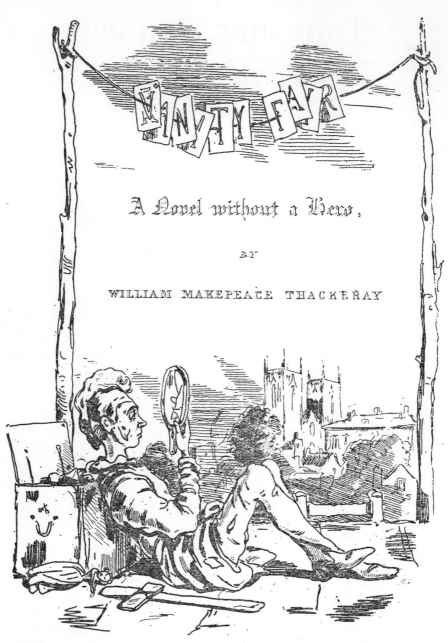

'That may-be cracked and warped looking glass in which I am always looking': Letters II 423. Title page to the first edition of *Vanity Fair*

mentarily incorporated in his novels, and we begin to distinguish certain characteristic tones. These tones have a definite bearing on the themes of the novels.

Thackeray's most typical alter egos are rich in ironic potential, for he characteristically chooses an attitude that contains a built-in contradiction, or at least a qualification of itself. His familiar pose of 'the moralist holding forth' is of course an example, in that he is simultaneously the satirist and the example of his own moral strictures. According to Swift, satire is the 'glass wherein beholders do generally discover everybody's face by their own,' but Thackeray's image is different: 'Good God,' he exclaimed, 'dont I see (in that may-be cracked and warped looking glass in which I am always looking) my own weaknesses wickednesses lusts follies shortcomings?' [Letters II 423–4]. It is an image he used for the title page of *Vanity Fair*. Another recurrent role is that of the determined bachelor and non-participant, who is relieved that the domestic woes of other men are not for him, and yet wistfully envious all the same; in other guises he is the old fogey, scornful of the romantic extravagances of other people's youth, but jealously proud of his own; or the urbane man of the world, concerned about money and comfort and proud of recognizing things as they are, and yet secretly ashamed of his worldliness, and attaching himself sentimentally to love and innocence in others. Even the Snob, the narrator of the *Book of Snobs* and a recurrent guise of the author in the novels, is determined to assert his own status only because he feels insecure about it within himself.

Titmarsh, Thackeray's favourite alter ego, is the typical outsider. He is always the observer rather than the participator, as are Mr Spec (the literary descendant of Mr Spectator), Dr Solomon Pacifico, and Edward Fitz-Boodle (whose adventures consist in *not* marrying various women).[4] But Titmarsh is not so content in his role as Mr Spectator – he is always looking into the world of action and thinking about participating, yet at the same time clinging desperately to his position beyond the pale when it seems that he will get drawn into the world which he observes. He dares not commit himself. He half-heartedly dallies with the notion that he is in

4 See Myron Taube, 'Thackeray and the Reminiscential Vision' *Nineteenth-Century Fiction* XVIII (1963) 247–59

love, but is evidently relieved, after the lady has accepted a more impetuous wooer, to be able to nurse a broken heart and retire to his position of
wistful detachment: 'Need I repeat that in the course of my blighted being,
I never loved a young gazelle to glad me with its dark blue eye, but when
it came to, &c., the usual disappointment was sure to ensue?' [x 290].
Titmarsh, through his relation to Lady Kicklebury, becomes Touchit in
the play *The Wolves and the Lamb*, and finally evolves into Mr Batchelor
in the adaptation of the play into the novel, *Lovel the Widower*. 'Who
shall be the hero of this tale?' he begins. 'Not I who write it. I am but the
Chorus of the Play' [57]; but the dramatic core of the story is not where it
is decided that Lovel will marry Bessy Prior, but where it is decided that
Batchelor will not. The situation arises when Bessy is being accosted by the
seedy libertine, Baker, and Batchelor overhears the scene from the garden.

> I was just *going* to run in, – and I didn't. I was just going to rush to
> Bessy's side to clasp her (I have no doubt) to my heart: to beard the
> whiskered champion who was before her, and perhaps say, 'Cheer
> thee – cheer thee, my persecuted maiden, my beauteous love – my
> Rebecca! Come on, Sir Brian de Bois Guilbert, thou dastard Templar!
> It is I, Sir Wilfred of Ivanhoe.' ... And I give you my honour, just as
> I was crying my war-cry, couching my lance, and rushing *à la
> recousse* upon Sir Baker, a sudden thought made me drop my (figura-
> tive) point: a sudden idea made me rein in my galloping (metaphori-
> cal) steed, and spare Baker for that time. [151–2]

His native hue of resolution is sicklied o'er with the pale cast of thought;
like Hamlet, or Conrad's Jim (or, as those critics would say who consider
Thackeray constitutionally unable to portray action, like Thackeray himself as novelist), he is unable to act at the crucial moment. He ends by
seeing Lovel carry off the girl, and is not without some relief at his
deliverance: 'Suppose I had gone in? But for that sudden precaution,
there might have been a Mrs. Batchelor. I might have been a bullied father
of ten children. (Elizabeth has a fine high temper of her own)' [152].

This figure is recurrent in Thackeray's works, both as narrator and as a
character evidently having the author's sympathy. He is always watching
the girl he loves wooed and won by someone else; and often even promoting

the match. Dobbin worships Amelia, but pushes George Osborne into marrying her, and even after George's death continues to disqualify himself as a lover by contributing to her concept of George as the saint to whom a life of widowhood must be devoted. As Dobbin is the outsider, the detached and socially clumsy side of Thackeray, George Osborne, the unworthy winner of the prize, is another side of him, the side that was accused of being a snob. There is the same relation between Warrington and Pendennis, though Pen is more sympathetically portrayed than Osborne. Warrington falls in love with Laura, and is morally worthy of her; but he, like Thackeray, has made an unsuccessful early marriage, which has put him out of the race.

> 'You are on the bank, old boy, content to watch the waves tossing in the winds, and the struggles of others at sea,' Pen said. 'I am in the stream now, and by Jove I like it ... Eh, *vogue la galère*, I say. It's good sport, Warrington – not winning merely, but playing.'
>
> 'Well, go in and win, young 'un. I'll sit and mark the game,' Warrington said, surveying the ardent young fellow with an almost fatherly pleasure ... 'As for me, I am disabled. I had a fatal hit in early life.' [P 571–2]

Warrington promotes the marriage of the girl he loves to someone else, and Esmond is relieved when Beatrix engages herself to the Duke of Hamilton. So (with Thackeray) Dobbin, Warrington, Esmond, and Batchelor become voyeurs, watching the love of Amelia, Laura, Beatrix, Bessy – or, if it comes to that, Jane Brookfield – for some unworthy suitor.[5] The wistfully self-abnegating attitude of this figure – who is never sure whether the grapes beyond his reach are sweet or sour, nor even if they are in fact beyond his reach – is exasperating as well as pathetic, for there is an element of cowardice in it. Apparently he does not dare to be smirched with the evil or buffeted with the pains of the world, the inevitable consequences of participation. But his hesitance is understandable enough, and in fact his withdrawal makes it easier for him to be 'good,' at least in the negative sense, than for those who are 'in the stream.' When

5 See Russell A. Fraser, 'Shooting Niagara in the Novels of Thackeray and Trollope' *Modern Language Quarterly* XIX (1958) 141–6

Charlotte Brontë called Thackeray 'Mr. Warrington,' he was only half pleased, and corrected her, 'No, you mean "Arthur Pendennis"' [Letters II 784n]. Charlotte Brontë deplored Thackeray's propensity to see two sides of a question, taking it to be moral irresponsibility; and when she complains of the worldly side of him, 'Why should he lead so harassing a life? Why should his mocking tongue so perversely deny the better feelings of his better moods?'[6] she sounds like Laura talking of Pendennis.

Warrington's 'fatherly' attitude is typical of another noticeable trait of Thackeray's narrators – their age. To Thackeray himself the pose of the old fogey was a natural attitude. His own situation, married to a woman in an insane asylum, cut him off from many of the normal relations of life and forced on him the role of non-participant; it also made him feel old in experience. He was used to thinking of himself as older than his years. He talks of himself as 'a grave old gentleman,' and wrote in 1854, 'Now I am near 43 and no Grandfather can be more glum' [Letters III 359]. Trollope said of him in 1859:

> He was then forty-eight years old, very gray, with much of age upon him, which had come from suffering, – age shown by dislike of activity and by an old man's way of thinking about many things, – speaking as though the world were all behind him instead of before.[7]

He considered himself beyond the passions and aspirations of youth: 'At 47,' he wrote to a friend, 'Venus may rise from the sea, and I for one should hardly put on my spectacles to have a look' [Letters IV 115]. Nevertheless, he has a keen memory for Taglioni, the beauty of his own youth, 'when the zest of life was certainly keener; when tavern wine seemed to be delicious, and tavern dinners the perfection of cookery' [N 6].

This attitude, which pervades his letters, is communicated to his narrators and characters. At the age of thirty-nine, with only *Vanity Fair* of his major novels completed, he was already writing in the person of

6 Letter to James Taylor, 1 January 1851: *The Brontës: Their Lives, Friendships and Correspondence* 4 vols. *The Shakespeare Head Brontë* ed. Thomas James Wise (Oxford 1932) III 193

7 *Thackeray* (London 1879) 49–50

Dr Solomon Pacifico on 'The Pleasures of Being a Fogey,' and discussing the advantages of reminiscence over experience. Many of his central male characters, and some of the female (the worldly ones, Blanche and Beatrix), feel old before their time. Dobbin, on returning from India, 'had now passed into the stage of old-fellow-hood. His hair was grizzled, and many a passion and feeling of his youth had grown grey in that interval' [VF 737]. Pendennis feels he has been made prematurely old by his commerce with the world, and the George Warrington who takes over the narration of *The Virginians* (the grandfather of the Warrington of *Pendennis*) describes himself as a middle-aged gentleman, and is no more moved by the vision of sirens than Thackeray by Venus anadyomene – though he recalls the time when he was, and can to this extent identify with the youth he describes.

> The last time Ulysses rowed by the Sirens' bank, he and his men did not care though a whole shoal of them were singing and combing their longest locks. Young Telemachus was for jumping overboard; but the tough old crew held the silly, bawling lad. They were deaf, and could not hear his bawling nor the sea-nymph's singing. They were dim of sight, and did not see how lovely the witches were ... You see Lector Benevolus and Scriptor Doctissimus figure as tough old Ulysses and his tough old boatswain, who do not care a quid of tobacco for any siren at Sirens' Point; but Harry Warrington is green Telemachus. [The narrator, incidentally, is Harry's twin brother!] ... The song is not stale to Harry Warrington, nor the voice cracked or out of tune that sings it. But – but – oh, dear me, Brother Boatswain! Don't you remember how pleasant the opera was when we first heard it? [V 184–5]

Pendennis as the narrator in *The Newcomes* and *Philip* is another middle-aged gentleman who is considering events which happened in his youth: 'This narrative, as the judicious reader no doubt is aware, is written maturely and at ease, long after the voyage is over, whereof it recounts the adventures and perils' [N 296].

This is typical of the temporal relation in which the narrator stands to the events he relates in Thackeray's novels. *Denis Duval*, for instance, is written some fifty years after the events chronicled in the first chapters, and Denis describes himself sitting in his arm-chair surveying in memory the stormy past, and 'scared and astonished sometimes; as huntsmen look at the gaps and ditches over which they have leapt, and wonder how they are alive' [XVII 256].

Thackeray similarly comments on his own preference for the nostalgic, reminiscential vision in a Roundabout paper:

> The good-natured reader who has perused some of these rambling papers has long since seen (if to see has been worth his trouble) that the writer belongs to the old-fashioned classes of this world, loves to remember very much more than to prophesy, and though he can't help being carried onward, and downward, perhaps, on the hill of life, the swift milestones marking their forties, fifties – how many tens or lustres shall we say? – he sits under Time, the white-wigged charioteer, with his back to the horses, and his face to the past, looking at the receding landscape and the hills fading into the grey distance. [XVII 460]

This evocation of the forward motion with the backward vision is a vivid image for the kind of irony implicit in Thackeray's vision. His use of the aged narrator who recollects in tranquility gives him an opportunity not only to survey the action with superior wisdom, and to foresee the end in the beginning, but to bring into action all manner of contrasts implicit in the viewpoint of a detached and experienced narrator on involved and experiencing participants. The ardours of youth are exposed to the cool judgment of age, as in Yeats' poem 'The Scholars':

> Bald heads forgetful of their sins,
> Old, learned, respectable bald heads
> Edit and annotate the lines
> That young men, tossing on their beds,
> Rhymed out in love's despair
> To flatter beauty's ignorant ear.

The varying perspectives of age on youth fascinated Yeats too, and he also developed the image of himself as the 'sixty-year-old smiling public man,' who is constantly aware of his age as 'a sort of battered kettle at the heel.' There is a peculiar richness in the vision of the old man who, though sometimes intolerant or placid, has yet known what it is to be young.

This is the typical perspective in *Pendennis*: 'Ah, we are speaking of old times,' says the narrator wistfully, '– when people were young – when *most* people were young. Other people are young now; but we no more' [667]. It is not just youth and age and past and present which are contrasted, but idealism and cynicism, illusion and disenchantment, inflated aspirations and solid common sense: and all connected by the pervasive sense that here we have not just crabbed age judging wild youth, but an older man looking back in mingled sympathy and scorn on his own past.

This is the chief source of vitality in the description of Pen's romantic passion for Emily Costigan. Only a narrator of considerable experience and detachment would be capable of picturing this couple for us: 'A young lady of six-and-twenty, whose eyes were perfectly wide open, and a luckless boy of eighteen, blind with love and infatuation' [P 78]. The whole progress of the relationship is informed by this contrast. Pen in his love sees himself as Byronic; he writes copious poetry in the middle of the night, he gallops round the country on his mare Rebecca (references to *Ivanhoe* are always signals of romantic self-dramatization in Thackeray's novels), he fights for his love in a graveyard; he is in fact the romantic lover, 'Sighing like furnace, with a woeful ballad / Made to his mistress' eyebrow.' Emily, whom he sees as a heroine, is by contrast entirely down-to-earth and prosaic: after her theatrical fervours she consumes mutton chop and brown stout; she is puzzled or bored by Pen's literary allusions; and she has an eye to financial advantage. When she comes to return his letters and poems, she ties up his effusions 'with a piece of string neatly, as she would a parcel of sugar' [143].

It is the detached and experienced narrator who can make the most of the humour of the situation, and occasionally he will cut off a character's raptures with a comment that defines his viewpoint: 'Of course here Mr. Pen went off into a rhapsody which, as we have perfect command over our own feelings, we have no right to overhear' [78]. Major Pendennis shares this function with the author. His management of the situation is masterly, and can be summed up in a scrap of dialogue:

'I *will* see her,' said Arthur. 'I'll ask her to marry me, once more. I will. No one shall prevent me.'

'What, a woman who spells affection with one *f*? Nonsense, sir.' [151]

The two worlds can be seen there, each exposed to the judgment of the other: the youth's is absurd, no doubt, to the eye of worldly wisdom, and the major's contemptible to the perception of passionate youth. Yet both have a constituent of truth. The love that can overlook difference of class and education is a generous love; but on the other hand it is no more than good sense to foresee the danger of union with an inferior. Later in life Pen is ready to acknowledge his uncle was right: 'The period of my little illusions is over. You cured me of my first love, who certainly was a fool, and would have had a fool for her husband, and a very sulky discontented husband too, if she had taken me' [558]. But at this point Pen's attitude is again questionable, for though still only in his twenties he has already tipped over into cynicism and self-contempt.

That conflict between the starry-eyed and the worldly wise, which is in operation to some extent in all Thackeray's novels, is not resolved. He does not try to convince us that youth is foolish and age is wise, not that youth is the genuine experience and age merely a second-hand business of editing and annotating. 'A man can be alive in 1860 and 1830 at the same time, don't you see?' he explained in a Roundabout paper [XVII 440]. Or, as he puts it in *The Virginians*, when Harry Warrington has gone through the progress of a passion similar to Pen's, 'I never know whether to pity or congratulate a man on coming to his senses' [v 583]. 'Ah, poor Pen!' he reflects, when Pen is in the midst of the bitter experience of wondering what he could ever have seen in the Fotheringay, 'the delusion is better than the truth sometimes, and fine dreams than dismal waking' [234].

It is the same with the old question of whether Thackeray was a sentimentalist or a cynic. He is neither, except in so far as he is both. 'Under the mask satirical,' he said of himself, recalling the self-portrait in *Vanity Fair*, 'there walks about a sentimental gentleman who means not unkindly to any mortal person' [Letters II 539]. And he was just as capable of peeling off the 'sentimental' face to reveal another mocking countenance underneath. So he was always mentioning (but never fulfilling) his intention to change the yellow covers of his part numbers for a 'fresher tone':

> When this book is concluded, I shall change the jaundiced livery which my books have worn since I began to lisp in numbers, have rose-coloured coats for them with cherubs on the cover, and all the characters within shall be perfect angels. Meanwhile ... [v 364]

Meanwhile on this issue too he has a foot in both camps, and in the battle of love against the world which he is perpetually dramatizing he is as ready to expose an Amelia or a Helen as a real cynic like Lord Steyne; and yet he acknowledges at the same time their virtues of tenderness on one side and penetration on the other.

Thackeray's 'reminiscential vision,' as Taube calls it, has no doubt become a critical commonplace: at the beginning of the century Chesterton called him the novelist of memory, and he had called himself an old fogey almost all through his career. But it is fruitful to explore the particular complexity that arises from this vision. For Thackeray's characteristic viewpoints, with their built-in contrasts and maintained tensions – that of the satirist and self-mocker, that of the outsider envying the participant, and of the snob anxious about his own status, as well as of the old man castigating the folly of youth but seeing his own youth in it – constitute a view of reality. The contradictions in each standpoint act like two flat images which spring to three-dimensional life when one is superimposed on the other.

'If the secret history of books could be written, and the author's private thoughts and meanings noted down alongside of his story, how many insipid volumes would become interesting, and dull tales excite the reader!' [518]. That sentence is often quoted as evidence of the importance of the biographical element in Thackeray's novels. In context it refers to Pendennis's novel, *Leaves from the Life-Book of Walter Lorraine*, which, from what we can gather, is indeed a somewhat 'insipid volume.' What we have in *Pendennis* itself, however, is Thackeray's attempt to write that 'secret history.' The subject of the novel is not only the nature of experience – growing up, growing older, changing, coming to terms with the

No. IX. PRICE 1s.

THE HISTORY

OF

PENDENNIS.

HIS FORTUNES AND MISFORTUNES,
HIS FRIENDS AND HIS GREATEST ENEMY.

BY

W. M. THACKERAY,

Author of "Vanity Fair," the "Snob Papers" in PUNCH &c. &c.

LONDON: BRADBURY & EVANS, 11, BOUVERIE STREET.

J. MENZIES, EDINBURGH; T. MURRAY, GLASGOW; AND J. M'GLASHAN, DUBLIN.

'Here, on one side, is Self and Ambition and Advancement; and Right and Love on the other': *The Newcomes* 502. Cover for the original parts of *Pendennis* past as well as living forwards into the future, and through it all maintaining a struggle to be true to oneself — but also the progress from experience to expression. It is the story of a man who tries to be a gentleman and also an artist.

Thackeray's view of life as perpetual tension is expressed clearly enough in his allegorical cover design for *Pendennis*. The young man hesitates between the siren on one side, with her satyrs and their worldly temptations of crown and coach, and on the other the domestic angel, with her arguments of duty to family, education, and the church. With certain alterations it is an allegory that would fit any of Thackeray's novels: the sexes would need to be changed for *The Newcomes*, where Ethel would be between Farintosh and Lady Kew on one side and Clive and the colonel on the other; Esmond would stand much as Pen does, but Beatrix the siren would be dark-haired and Rachel the angel blond; in *Vanity Fair*, as I read it, the reader would be the one standing in the central position, choosing his place in relation to Becky and Amelia. For Arthur Pendennis, most of all, life consists of a set of tensions that cannot be resolved: he might say with Sir Thomas Browne, 'Let me be nothing, if within the compass of myself I do not find the battail of *Lepanto*, Passion against Reason, Reason against Faith, Faith against the Devil, and my Conscience against all.' The resolution of the tension is a piece of wishful thinking which Thackeray himself indulges in occasionally, as in the title page to the second volume of *Pendennis*, which shows the repentant Arthur embracing the domestic mother figure; but for the most part Thackeray's view of the moral life is like that of Browning's Bishop Blougram:

> No, when the fight begins within himself,
> A man's worth something. God stoops o'er his head,
> Satan looks up between his feet — both tug —
> He's left, himself, i' the middle: the soul wakes
> And grows. Prolong that battle through his life!
> Never leave growing till the life to come!

Browning's strife, however, takes place vertically, whereas Thackeray follows through the implications of his view of life as continuous conflict by setting his contestants on a horizontal plane, and making no such clear location of good and evil as Browning presents.

His allegory, as it applies to *Pendennis*, is both of man trying to live a decent life amidst the moral and psychological tensions of existence, and of the artist trying to represent them truly; of the man's problems in grasping reality, and of the artist's in turning it into art. The novel is an autobiography not so much in a historical sense as an intellectual one, for in it the writer, like his protagonist, is exploring the complex relation between truth and artifice, reality and illusion. There is a complex set of relations here, because Thackeray's own problem in rendering Arthur Pendennis is mirrored in Pen's rendering of Walter Lorraine, so that we have a secret life within a secret life.

One stream of Thackeray criticism which started in his own lifetime has insisted that he can't think – that, as Roscoe put it, 'there is a total absence in his books of what we usually call ideas.'[8] But what Thackeray's books lack is answers, not ideas; *Pendennis* is a novel of ideas; it asks Pilate's question, 'What is Truth?' And Thackeray was too wise to try to provide a glib solution.

The novel makes its first impact as the story of a boy who is growing up, and a man who is growing older. The main action starts at the period when 'Pen had just made his public appearance in a coat with a tail, or *cauda virilis*, and was looking most anxiously in his little study glass to see if his whiskers were growing, like those of more fortunate youths his companions' [20]. The connected images of beard and clothes belong to two major concerns of the novel, time and artifice. The imagery of whiskers and hair recurs through the novel as a reminder both of the merely physiological process of growing older, and of the social roles that a man must choose as well as grow into. Once Pen's long-expected beard begins to grow he pampers and perfumes it, unlike Warrington, whose bristly black whiskers are evidence of his unpretentious maturity against Pen's

8 'W.M. Thackeray, Artist and Moralist' in *Poems and Essays* (London 1860) II 274

'scented auburn hair' [650]. Pen's hair is shaved off during his purgative illness after his affair with Fanny (who keeps a lock of it), and its re-growth is a sign of his regeneration. Martha Coacher, the oft-jilted spinster who is growing desperate, keeps giving locks of her hair, tied up with blue ribbon, to the various men she has tried to capture: 'Thrice before had she snipped off one of her auburn ringlets, and given them away. The possessors were faithless, but the hair had grown again' [95]. Shaving becomes a ritual for the man who cares more for what the world thinks of him than for what he is in himself, and we have recurrent pictures of Morgan performing the rite on the Major. When Foker pre-pares to sally forth to conquer Miss Amory, he commands his valet:

> '*Cherchy alors une paire de tongs – et – curly-moi un pew,*' Mr. Foker said, in an easy manner; and the valet, wondering whether his master was in love or was going masquerading, went in search of the articles, – first from the old butler who waited upon Mr. Foker, senior, on whose bald pate the tongs would have scarcely found a hundred hairs to seize, and finally of the lady who had the charge of the meek auburn fronts of the Lady Agnes. And the tongs being got, Monsieur Anatole twisted his young master's locks until he had made Harry's head as curly as a negro's; after which the youth dressed himself with the ut-most care and splendour, and proceeded to sally out. [497]

The curling, the bald pate, and the false fronts are images used to define the members of the Foker family, both in their ages and the façade that each wants to present to the world, as his brown wig and false teeth are the emblems of the major.

The clothes imagery, too, is recurrent from the day Pen adopts his 'coat with a tail, or *cauda virilis,*' for the society satirized in *Pendennis* is that of the dandy, where, as in *Sartor Resartus,* the clothes make the man.[9] Again, Warrington's sartorial shabbiness shows up Pen's excessive concern with appearance, even in the days when he professes to be dis-

9 Martin Fido discusses the significance of theatrical and sartorial imagery in ' *The History of Pendennis*: a Reconsideration' *Essays in Criticism* XIV (1964) 363–79.

enchanted with the world. When Warrington accuses him of subjecting himself to a hairdresser and being 'scented like a barber ever since,' Pen defends himself.

'Violets smell better than stale tobacco, you grisly old cynic.' But Mr. Pen was blushing whilst he made this reply to his unromantical friend, and indeed cared a great deal more about himself still than such a philosopher perhaps should have done. Indeed, considering that he was careless about the world, Mr. Pen ornamented his person with no small pains in order to make himself agreeable to it, and for a weary pilgrim as he was, wore very tight boots and bright varnish. [589]

Along with that introduction of the boy with his anxious concern about his appearance and his manhood, we have his schoolmaster's report, delivered immediately after a harangue on the 'deadly crime' of mis-construing Greek, that 'he is a good boy, rather idle and unenergetic, but an honest gentlemanlike little fellow, though I can't get him to construe as I wish' [23]. Pen's 'goodness' is in question through the novel, as is his claim to the title of gentleman, but it is his honesty that is the major concern. For all his shortcomings and his failures, he deserves his place as hero, for his story is one of the young man growing older but trying to maintain a steady course in a world of tensions and changes, and trying to be honest as the member of an artificial society.

The chief tension developed in the novel is of course that between the Major and Helen, with their rival candidates for Pen's hand, Blanche and Laura. This operates at so very obvious a level, and the old opposition between love and the world is so standard, that the theme might be uninteresting but for Thackeray's subtle handling of it. Helen and the Major, the two incarnations of the rival impulses in Pen, are themselves marvellous pieces of characterization, and the clinging galling tendrils of the one are as vividly evoked as the tempting rationality of the other. But beyond this, Thackeray subtly demonstrates how their influence exceeds their obvious limitations: Pen sees through and patronizes both of them, but his irony and sophistication do not free him from the alternate dominance of what each of them represents.

Thackeray's world is the fallen world, in which goodness must consist not in itself but rather in the *knowledge* of good and evil; hence that continuing tension, and the fallen quality of good itself as represented by Helen, and the redeeming qualitites of the Major. The strife between them is for Pen a matter not just of ethics, but of perception. They are the Scylla and Charybdis between which he must steer, for to be fully identified with either is to deny the reality of the other. The Major's humour, sound sense, and keen eye to the main chance are characteristics that Pen must develop too, and his uncle zealously undertakes his education in things as they are: 'Mr. Pen's new guide, philosopher, and friend ... had his eyes, what he called, open. He took pity on this young greenhorn of a nephew, and wanted to open his eyes too' [109]. Pen, with his superior intelligence, soon feels he has outgrown his uncle, and sneers at the old fogeys in the Bays's Club window, but the Major has more influence over him than he knows, and he almost capitulates to his world by selling himself for a seat in parliament gained by blackmail. It takes this experience before he is fully aware how much those 'open' eyes of the Major have been 'dimmed by the constant glare of the pavement of Pall Mall' [206], and he exclaims in his moment of enlightenment, 'Great Heavens, sir! ... are you blind? Can't you see?' [908].

As he has to develop his uncle's keen perception without the withering selfishness that inhibits it, so he has also to learn the truth of his mother's world of the emotions without being engulfed by it. Helen's sentiment and romantic illusion are blindness too, the result of keeping her eyes shut to the glare of the Major's world; and she is as incensed when Pen and Laura don't conform to her happy-ever-after fairytale as the Major when Pen throws up a dowry and a seat in parliament. Her love, too, in its way is as selfish as the Major's ambition – as Pen's brief affair with Fanny shows – for it demands a return as exclusive as itself.

Between these two worlds of illusion, Pen tries to grasp at reality. He sees on the one hand goodness and love, and their fatal tendency to moral tyranny and emotional cannibalism, and on the other worldly success, with its tawdry accompaniments of compromised integrity and carelessness for others. So, in his statement to Warrington of his political and religious position, he tries to locate himself in some central position of knowledge, waiting 'for time and truth to develop' [796], leaving dogma

D

and reform to those who are arrogantly confident of their own rectitude. 'I acknowledge what *is*,' he declares [798]. But that very declaration, because of its assumption that he knows 'what *is*,' is a contradiction of his tentative position. His realism here is only that limited form which is the opposite of 'idealism,' the false realism which acknowledges the seamy side of reality not reality itself. So although Thackeray is not unsympathetic to Pen's attitude, he exposes that 'general scepticism and sneering acquiescence in the world as it is' [800] in the following chapter, 'Which accounts perhaps for Chapter LXI.' Here it becomes clear that Pen's manifesto was not a neutral statement of his position, but an attempt at self-justification after he has sold himself to his uncle's world. And here the narrator argues from Warrington's point of view:

> If the fight for the truth is taking place, and all men of honour are on the ground armed on the one side or the other, and you alone are to lie on your balcony and smoke your pipe out of the noise and the danger, you had better have died, or never have been at all, than such a sensual coward.
>
> 'The truth, friend!' Arthur said imperturbably; 'where is the truth? Show it me. That is the question between us. I see it on both sides.' [801]

Thackeray too sees it on both sides, but he sees also that it is a mean evasion to make that tension an excuse for mere passivity. Somewhere the balance has been disturbed, the conflict is momentarily over, and Pen's zeal to acknowledge reality has become a jaded acquiescence in expediency. He has to learn that he has leaned too far on the side of the siren, and he does with relief renounce Blanche to marry Laura. But the conflict is still not ultimately resolved, for even at the moment he is most confident of Laura's goodness he has his reservations:

> 'I was thinking, my dear, that nature in making you so good and loving did very well: but – '
> 'But what? What is that wicked but? and why are you always calling it up?'
> 'But will come in spite of us. But is reflection. But is the sceptic's

familiar, with whom he has made a compact; and if he forgets it, and indulges in happy day-dreams, or building of air-castles, or listens to sweet music, let us say, or to the bells ringing to church, But taps at the door, and says, 'Master, I am here. You are my master; but I am yours. Go where you will you can't travel without me. I will whisper to you when you are on your knees at church. I will be at your marriage pillow. I will sit down at your table with your children. I will be behind your death-bed curtain." That is what But is,' Pen said. [915–16]

And his statement that she is one of those who are exempt from the fall – 'Love you know; but the knowledge of evil is kept from you,' he tells her – sounds as much like indictment as praise.

Laura, however, has had her fall, in her own eyes at least, and this is what makes her superior in moral consciousness to Helen, as Pen is to the Major. Her love for Warrington makes her aware of her own moral arrogance when she, like Helen, had haughtily dismissed Fanny Bolton as a fallen woman, with a Pharisaical confidence in her own superior virtue: 'Oh, how wicked and proud I was about Arthur, ... how self-confident and unforgiving! I never forgave from my heart this poor girl, who was fond of him, or him for encouraging her love; and I have been more guilty than she, poor, little, artless creature!' [866]. Her sin has not been a heinous one, but at least, like Pen, she has something to reproach herself for, whereas Helen had always seen herself as more sinned against than sinning. The union of Laura and Pen is not an identification, for to some extent the tensions that existed between Helen and the Major are prolonged in this marriage rather than resolved; but the gap has lessened, and there is a possibility of love and communication between them that never existed for their mentors. They have at least approached the truth that exists between the tensions, if not attained it.

Pen's grasp at reality, which occupies more aspects of his life than his choice between the Major's world and Helen's, involves the acknowledgement of an essential ingredient of falsehood in every truth, and of an element of truth in every falsehood. He is constantly presented with alternatives, 'not knowing either, or the amount of truth in either, or being certain of the truth anywhere' [799], and his life becomes a series of problems to be solved; and they usually turn out to be not just problems in positive and negative quantities of good and evil, truth and falsehood, but problems in proportion. One of these that faces him not only in his own life but in his estimation of the lives of others is the question of how to love. His love for the Fotheringay was an undeniable emotional reality, and yet based in illusion, for, as he acknowledges later, she was not in truth what he took her to be. His love for Blanche, on the other hand, is synthesized almost from first to last, and yet for a while he believes it will do very well as a substitute for the real thing. How much illusion is necessary in love? Some, surely: the reader cannot but feel that Blanche has a right to resent her fiancé's jaded love-making:

> 'Look, my little Blanche,' said Pen, taking her hand, and with his voice of sad good-humour; 'at least I stoop to no flatteries.'
> 'Quite the contrary,' said Miss Blanche.
> 'And tell you no foolish lies, as vulgar men do. Why should you and I, with our experience, ape romance and dissemble passion? I do not believe Miss Blanche Amory to be peerless among the beautiful, ... but I think you are – well, there, I think you are very sufficiently good-looking.'
> '*Merci*,' Miss Blanche said, with another curtsy. [836–7]

Pen's various alternative ways of loving are mirrored and echoed in the loves of minor characters. Old Bows, who cherishes a hopeless love first for Emily Costigan and then for Fanny Bolton, has throughout a clear grasp both of their failings and of his own stupidity for loving where there is a minimum of desert and no hope of success. His love is a fatal combination of 'regard and contempt' [141]. And Pen has something to learn from the old man as together they lean over the bridge at Chatteris, discussing the woman they both hopelessly love:

> 'It's a habit, like taking snuff, or drinking drams ... I've been taking her these five years, and can't do without her ... Some day she'll marry, and fling me over, as I do the end of this cigar.'
> The little flaming spark dropped into the water below, and disap-

peared; and Pen, as he rode home that night, actually thought about somebody but himself. [164]

There is no illusion in Bows's love: his is a knowledge of the truth that withers and embitters him. The love of Madame Fribsby, on the other hand, seems to have been nearly all illusion: her two months of marriage early in life, to the compulsive bigamist Amory, have left her with a stock of tears, sighs, and happy pride in her own tragic past: '"*Mong cure a boco souffare*," she said, laying her hand on the part she designated as her *cure*. "*Il est more en Espang, madame*," she said, with a sigh' [187]. In fact, she lives a contendedly broken-hearted existence, her chief occupation being the benevolent enterprise of promoting other people's marriages.

Between these two extremes Pen himself goes through an evolution, as demonstrated by the ironic reversal of the relation between him and Foker. In Pen's early entanglement with the Fotheringay, Foker acts as 'a young man of the world,' and Major Pendennis's right-hand man in the campaign to extricate Pen from his imprudent love-affair. 'I'm not clever, p'raps,' he tells the Major: 'but I *am* rather downy; and partial friends say I know what's o'clock tolerably well. Can I tell you the time of day in any way?' [118]. But later in their careers, it is Pen who tells Foker, 'We are no longer children, you know, you and I, Harry. Bah! the time of our romance has passed away. We don't marry for passion, but for prudence and for establishment' [582]; while Foker, wildly in love with the girl that Pen is magnanimously intending to marry for her money, tells him, 'I can't stand it, Pen. I couldn't bear to hear you talking about her, just now, about marrying her only because she's 'money. Ah, Pen! *that* ain't the question in marrying. I'd bet anything it ain't' [583]. And while Pen throws the rosebud Blanche gave him into the gutter, Foker waters and cherishes his.

The social dimension of Pen's search for the truth takes the form of the problem of how to be a gentleman. And again, there is a whole range of possible answers. Arthur's own status is doubtful, as is clear from all the flummery about his being 'the prince of Fairoaks,' and from his cheap patronage of Fanny, the porter's daughter. His claim to be a gentleman is tested in his relation to a whole crowd of minor characters who are also candidates for the title. Mirobolant, though a cook, travels with his piano, wears a decoration, and, as the Chevalier de Juillet, considers it a point of honour to challenge Pen to a duel for naming his profession; although 'the idea of having insulted a cook, or that such an individual should have any feeling of honour at all, did not much enter into the mind of this lofty young aristocrat, the apothecary's son' [328]. Morgan the valet disapproves of Mirobolant for his pretension ('Them French cooks has as much pride and hinsolence as if they was real gentlemen' [458], he comments), but himself has ambitions of graduating from the status of gentleman's gentleman to the real thing. Smirke, the curate tutor who aspires to the hand of 'a lady of rank and good fortune,' is firmly reminded by Arthur, ' My tutor, I say *my tutor*, has no right to ask a lady of my mother's rank of life to marry him' [193]. Old Costigan, with his fencing, and his constant talk about his honour and his royal Irish ancestry, allows his daughter to support him by her acting but not to use the family name lest she should sully it. The young Arthur is ready enough to make this blustering old inebriate his father-in-law; but when he has become the more sophisticated man-about-town he selects instead Sir Francis Clavering, whose claim to true gentility, for all his baronetcy and his rich wife, is flimsier than anyone's, since he is quite bankrupt of integrity. The two potential fathers-in-law are vivid embodiments of the kinds of compromise Pen would have to make in stepping into their shoes. Clavering's blackmailer Altamont (whom Pen would presumably have inherited along with the baronet's other assets) is not even sure who he is – 'I'm John Armstrong, Amory, Altamont, – and let 'em all come on,' he declares belligerently [971]; but he is at least convinced *what* he is, when the footman tries to evict him: '"Hullo! keep your hands off a gentleman," he said, with an oath which need not be repeated' [481]. There is, in fact, a good deal too much protesting on the subject. On the other hand, the two men who do not make a noise about the matter, Warrington and Strong, are undeniably gentlemen, though one smokes an unpleasant-smelling pipe and cooks his own mutton chop and the other blacks his own boots and associates with a blackmailer – who does not, however, blacken him.

And yet to aspire to be a gentleman is not necessarily a mean enterprise,

though in a snobbish world it is apt to be an illusory one; and to consider
the subject entirely without illusion, as Shandon does, is to become a
cynic. He composes the prospectus for the *Pall Mall Gazette*, which claims
to be 'written by gentlemen for gentlemen' [410], while he is serving a
sentence for debt in the Fleet, and he throws in calculatedly stirring
references to Waterloo and the Duke of Wellington. 'I never knew the
duke to fail,' he explains, slyly. The infusion of snobbery in the republic
of letters is of course a major butt of satire in *Pendennis*. The title of the
magazine is itself a piece of snobbery, part of the rivalry for titled support
between the publishers Bacon and Bungay: Shandon pours scorn in his
prospectus on 'Grub Street publishing *Gazettes* from Whitehall' – as 'a
dig at Bacon's people,' he tells Bungay [408]. Later, when he is asked,
'Why *Pall Mall Gazette*?' he replies with irrefutable logic, 'Because the
editor was born at Dublin, the sub-editor at Cork, because the proprietor
lives in Paternoster Row, and the paper is published in Catherine Street,
Strand' [439]. His cynicism on the subject is a counterpart to Bows'
bitter self-contempt in love, or Pen's stale sneering about taking the
world as he finds it.

Among the questions forced on Pen with the endless process of changing
in time is 'What is experience itself?' The very word is used in two senses
that are in tension with each other. In one sense experience is something
as present and palpable as a physical sensation, like a cold shower or a kick
on the shin; but such experiences, accumulated in time and reflected upon
when the sensation is over, become remote and unavailable, and are
replaced by that collective 'experience' which goes with change in
character. And the change may comprehend anything from lost innocence
to acquired wisdom. Pen's love for the Fotheringay was the most genuine
and undeniable emotional experience of his life, and yet it is not only
founded on illusion but tainted and dissipated later, when he learns, with
the bitterness of disillusion, to regard it as youthful folly. He has to go
through the anguish of losing that experience before he can inherit his
yesterday, as Jean Sudrann has put it.[10] It is the same with Fanny Bolton,

10 See her article, the best critical treatment of Thackeray's handling of time,
'The Philosopher's Property: Thackeray and the Use of Time' *Victorian
Studies* x (1967) 376

though here Pen's mind telescopes into a few weeks the process which had before stretched over the years during which Emily Costigan became Lady Mirabel and the boy Arthur became the man Pendennis:

> He laughed at himself as he lay on his pillow, thinking of this second cure which had been effected upon him. He did not care the least about Fanny now: he wondered how he ever should have cared: and according to his custom made an autopsy of that dead passion, and anatomized his own defunct sensation for his poor little nurse. What could have made him so hot and eager about her but a few weeks back? Not her wit, not her breeding, not her beauty – there were hundreds of women better looking than she. It was out of himself that the passion had gone: it did not reside in her. She was the same; but the eyes which saw her were changed; and alas, that it should be so! were not particularly eager to see her any more. He felt very well disposed towards the little thing, and so forth ... I'm not sure that he was not ashamed of the very satisfaction which he experienced. It is pleasant, perhaps, but it is humiliating to own that you love no more. [670–1]

So the reality which Pen so eagerly grasps at changes as he clutches it, or fades into illusion and is real no more. There is one truth for the present, but too frequently another for the past. And then, to add to the confusion, there is another past and another present which some men invent for themselves – and believe in, to the extent that they are not lying when they recount them. We hear of Costigan when he attempts to tell his life history that he 'was not only unaccustomed to tell the truth – he was unable even to think it – and fact and fiction reeled together in his muzzy, whiskified brain' [59]. Altamont is similarly bewildered about the facts of his own experience when he tries to determine whether he actually lost or was cheated of his 'five hundred and sixty gold napoleons, by Jove':

> 'What could I do? Everybody was against me. Caroline said I had lost the money: though I didn't remember a syllable about the business ... And I can't tell you at this minute whether I was done or not,' concluded the colonel, musing. 'Sometimes I think I was: but then Caroline was so fond of me. That woman would never have seen me

done: never, I'm sure she wouldn't: at least, if she would, I'm deceived in woman.' [551–2]

Even a simple soul like Altamont has to grope for the truth among complex qualifications. Perhaps a drinker, gambler, and philanderer cannot be expected to have a very strong grasp on reality, but more respectable and sophisticated folk than the Costigans and Altamonts are similarly confused. Archer, whom Warrington characterizes as otherwise 'both able and honest' [390], creates the most elaborate fabrications about the celebrities of his acquaintance, embellished with startlingly authentic detail; like the story of his wife's Blenheim spaniel which fell victim to the Chinese ambassador's cook:

'The beast of a cook ... seized upon the poor little devil, cut his throat, and skinned him, and served him up stuffed with forced meat in the second course.'

'Law!' said Mrs. Bungay.

'You may fancy my wife's agony when she knew what had happened! ... The Lord Mayor, who did me the honour to dine, liked the dish very much; and, eaten with green peas, it tastes rather like duck.'

'You don't say so, now!' cried the astonished publisher's lady.

'Fact, upon my word.' [742]

Clavering is another man who cannot look reality in the face. To the accusation that he married for money he replies defensively, 'It don't make it any the pleasanter to hear because it's true, don't you know' [282]. His debts, moral and financial, do not touch him: 'As long as he could renew a bill, his mind was easy regarding it; and he would sign almost anything for to-morrow, provided to-day could be left unmolested' [552]. A grasp of reality consists partly in the ability to know the difference between past and present, but it is a matter of integrity to relate them properly too; to separate the two completely, as Clavering does, is to acknowledge no responsibility.

So fact and fiction reel together in more minds than Costigan's. Blanche Amory is of course the most extended study in this kind of confusion. She composes her life like a three-volume romance, busily synthesizing emotions that can be distilled into *Mes Larmes*, the book of poems lamenting the thorns of life on which she bleeds. Her epistolary style is exemplary: 'I have shed bitter, bitter tears over your letter! To you I bring the gushing poesy of my being – the yearnings of the soul that longs to be loved ...' etc., etc. [923]. Even her name is a nom de plume, since she adopted Blanche in preference to the more humdrum Betsy of her mother's choice. 'You are always reading and dreaming pretty dramas, and exciting romances in real life,' Pen tells her [920]. And his engagement to her represents his acquiescence in a world of artifice that has insufficient foundation in reality. The chapter in which he goes down to the country and proposes to her is called 'Phillis and Corydon,' and is the culmination of the pastoral motif by which 'the Sylphide' has been exposed.[11]

'And do you really like the country?' he asked her, as they walked together.

'I should like never to see that odious city again. Oh, Arthur – that is, Mr. – well, Arthur, then – one's good thoughts grow up in these sweet woods and calm solitudes, like those flowers which won't bloom in London, you know. The gardener comes and changes our balconies once a week. I don't think I shall bear to look London in the face again – its odious, smoky, brazen face! But heigho!'

'Why that sigh, Blanche?'

'Never mind why.'

'Yes, I do mind why. Tell me, tell me everything.'

'I wish you hadn't come down;' and a second edition of *Mes Soupirs* came out.

'You don't want me, Blanche?'

'I don't want you to go away. I don't think this house will be very happy without you, and that's why I wish that you never had come.'

Mes Soupirs were here laid aside, and *Mes Larmes* had begun. Ah! what answer is given to those in the eyes of a young woman? What

11 Loofbourow has discussed the connection of the pastoral parody with the pursuit of artifice in *Pendennis* in *Thackeray and the Form of Fiction* (Princeton 1964) 57–60.

is the method employed for drying them? What took place? O ring-doves and roses, O dews and wildflowers, O waving greenwoods and balmy airs of summer! [825–6]

That is a marvellous passage, with its use of the clichés of pastoralism, its suggestion of love-making by rote, and its sly references to the merely literary nature of Blanche's self-dramatization; with its evocation, in fact, of 'two battered London rakes, taking themselves in for a moment, and fancying that they were in love with each other, like Phillis and Corydon!'

In getting over the Fotheringay and Fanny, Pen sees it as a sign of maturity in himself that he is ready to acknowledge a proportion of illusion in life, and so with Blanche he enters into wilful self-delusion. But now he has gone too far, and has reason to question himself angrily, when he finds that he is trapped: 'Why was I not more honest, or am I not less so?' [932]. It is another version of the Major's irritable reflection on Pen: 'If ... he speaks the truth, as the rascal will, it spoils all' [690]. There is such a thing as being too honest, too penetrating: and again Thackeray shows how there is a certain point at which self-knowledge tips over into cynicism, as when Pen notes within himself, 'with a fatal keenness of perception,' that Foker's love for Blanche gives an impulse to his own bored courtship [585]. It is only when, more by luck than good manage-ment, he has managed to get himself released from his engagement that he realizes not only that Blanche adopts a façade, but that there is no sub-stance behind it: 'For this young lady was not able to carry out any emo-tion to the full; but had a sham enthusiasm, a sham hatred, a sham love, a sham taste, a sham grief, each of which flared and shone very vehe-mently for an instant, but subsided and gave place to the next sham emotion' [939].

Pendennis is about the artist as well as the man, or rather, about the artist *as* man. Thackeray was not given to talking portentously about the creative process, and the poet as prophet, and so on, and of course *Pendennis* itself is a major document in the long dispute on the status of literature that made Thackeray to some extent an outlaw among his own colleagues. Even in his obituary on Thackeray, where one would expect the *nil nisi bonum* principle to be in operation, Dickens complained, 'I thought that he too much feigned a want of earnestness, and that he made a pretence of undervaluing his art, which was not good for the art that he held in trust.'[12] Thackeray was too conscious of his shortcomings as a man to feel that he could become godlike and infallible as an artist. In a passage suggesting that we have been 'too prodigal of our pity upon Pegasus,' the author admits,

> I for one am quite ready to protest with my friend, George Warrington, against the doctrine which some poetical sympathizers are inclined to put forward, viz., that men of letters, and what is called genius, are to be exempt from the prose duties of this daily, bread-wanting, tax-paying life, and are not to be made to work and pay like their neighbours. [450]

He usually uses the word 'genius' with a touch of irony that suggests more the pretension to the quality than the quality itself: when a man draws his singing robes about him, he is as accessible to folly and conceit as when he wears his workaday clothes, and perhaps even more so.

And yet Thackeray is far from being flippant about the artist's business. His reservations only emphasize that art is *not* easy. For if honesty and a firm grasp on reality are difficult for the man, they become immensely complicated for the artist, who has to render experience into art. There is a new dimension to the problem, which becomes as it were a trigonometrical rather than a geometrical one. 'I ask you to believe that this

---

12 'In Memoriam' *Cornhill Magazine* IX (1864) 130. Reprinted in *Thackeray: The Critical Heritage* ed. Geoffrey Tillotson (London and New York 1968) 321. Dickens' most hostile comment on Thackeray as an artist is perhaps his portrait of him as the snobbish painter, Henry Gowan, who thus airily denigrates his profession:
> 'I am not a great impostor. Buy one of my pictures, and I assure you, in confidence, it will not be worth the money. Buy one of another man's — any great professor who beats me hollow — and the chances are that the more you give him, the more he'll impose upon you. They all do it.'
> 'All painters?'
> 'Painters, writers, patriots, all the rest who have stands in the market.'
> (*Little Dorrit*, chapter 26)

person writing strives to tell the truth,' writes Thackeray in his preface. And 'Pen' the writer, like 'Pendennis' the denizen of the world, has the same underlying principle. 'I pray Heaven I may tell the truth as far as I know it,' he prays at the outset of his literary career [418], and in face of Shandon's expedient philosophy he reiterates that the writer's business is '*ruat coelum*, to tell the truth' [445].

And yet Pen, like Thackeray, has constantly to question himself about the complex relation between experience and expression, and the artifice involved in turning the one into the other. He has to argue out for himself Sidney's conclusion in the *Apologie for Poetrie*, 'Now, for the Poet, he nothing affirmes, and therefore never lyeth.' For one thing, he sees plenty of evidence of lies among the surrounding crowd of his colleagues, whom he nevertheless cannot dismiss, as Sidney could, as merely 'versifiers who neede never aunswere to the name of Poets.' But, for another, he feels more of the fallible man than the prophetic poet within himself; and the relation between his life and his art, from his human perspective, is too close for him to be unaware of the proportion of humbug in the transaction between them. However genuine his initial impulse to write, he keeps finding that his productions degenerate into insincerity and deceit. The poems which, as a young man in love with Emily, he 'Rhymed out in love's despair / To flatter beauty's ignorant ear,' he afterwards adapts for Blanche, and Blanche herself sets his words to music and sings them to attract another suitor. He tries as an artist to arrest his feelings in time, but in the very act of pouring out his anguish on paper he is performing a therapy that erases it from his mind: for 'when a gentleman is cudgelling his brain to find any rhyme for sorrow, besides borrow and to-morrow, his woes are nearer at an end than he thinks for' [167]. As a young man at Oxford, Pen makes capital of his *grande passion*, passes about his verses, and as a result is 'pronounced a tremendous fellow' [218]; and then in London he uses the tricks he has learned in his trade to revise and adapt the novel that he had written about and during his youth at Chatteris.

Tears fell upon the leaf of the book, perhaps, or blistered the pages of his manuscript as the passionate young man dashed his thoughts down. If he took up the books afterwards, he had no ability or wish to sprinkle the leaves with that early dew of former times: his pencil was no longer eager to score its marks of approval ... How pompous some of the grand passages appeared; and how weak others were in which he thought he had expressed his full heart! ... And what meant those blots on the page? As you come in the desert to a ground where camels' hoofs are marked in the clay, and traces of withered herbage are yet visible, you know that water was there once; so the place in Pen's mind was no longer green, and the *fons lacrymarum* was dried up. [518]

The result of his perusal of his old manuscript, and the faint renewal of the experience recorded in it, is the reflection that 'if Bungay won't publish it, I think Bacon will' [520]. Warrington's comment on this decision suggests that there may be prostitution in the writer's act of selling his sensibility.

'That's the way of poets,' said Warrington. 'They fall in love, jilt, or are jilted; they suffer and they cry out that they suffer more than any other mortals: and when they have experienced feelings enough they note them down in a book, and take the book to market. All poets are humbugs, all literary men are humbugs; directly a man begins to sell his feelings for money he's a humbug. If a poet gets a pain in his side from too good a dinner, he bellows "Ai, Ai," louder than Prometheus.' [520]

Pen defends himself valiantly against this suggestion, maintaining that the poet has as good a right to sell his sensibility as a lawyer has to sell his legal experience; nevertheless Warrington, on this occasion as on others, is to some extent the voice of Pen's conscience.

Thackeray wrestles with the problem of honesty in the artist elsewhere – significantly enough, in his discussion of Sterne:

A perilous trade, indeed, is that of a man who has to bring his tears and laughter, his recollections, his personal griefs and joys, his private thoughts and feelings to market, to write them on paper, and sell them for money ... How much of the paint and emphasis is necessary for the fair business of the stage, and how much of the rant and rouge is put on for the vanity of the actor? His audience trusts him: can he trust himself? How much was deliberate calculation and imposture – how much was false sensibility – and how much true feeling? Where did the lie begin, and did he know where? and where did the truth end in the art and scheme of this man of genius, this actor, this quack? [XIII, 665–6]

Sterne's defenders would be less exasperated at Thackeray's criticism if they realized he was applying the same strictures to himself. For Thackeray and Pendennis, actor and quack are necessarily facets of the artist, and honesty consists partly in the admission of them, and in the ability to define the limits of their influence.

Pen finds himself constantly involved in hypocrisy in this process by which his life and his art alternately scratch each other's back. For all his determination to act and write truly, 'ruat coelum,' he cannot resist the sort of histrionic poses that Blanche goes in for: his empty gesture of throwing his manuscript on the cinders, after he has ascertained that the fire is out, deserves Warrington's scorn: 'Oh, Pen, what a humbug you are! ... and, what is worst of all, sir, a clumsy humbug. I saw you look to see that the fire was out before you sent *Walter Lorraine* behind the bars' [522]. And Warrington himself will handle the manuscript only with the tongs.

Pen the artist goes through the same evolution as Pen the man, and the exchange between the young author and the literary roué Shandon sounds very like the exchange between the young lover and Major Pendennis:

'I would rather starve, by Jove, and never earn another penny by my pen' (this redoubted instrument had now been in use for some six weeks, and Pen spoke of it with vast enthusiasm and respect) 'than strike an opponent an unfair blow, or, if called upon to place him, rank him below his honest desert' ... 'Gad,' said [Shandon], 'you've a tender conscience, Mr. Pendennis. It's the luxury of all novices, and I may have had one once myself; but that sort of bloom wears off with the rubbing of the world.' [446]

Even the shaving metaphor reappears in this context, and Warrington picks it up again in his comments on Pen's first fine careless rapture: 'There's a certain greenness and freshness in it which I like somehow. The bloom disappears off the face of poetry after you begin to shave' [522]. And Shandon is right in his private surmise that 'a few years hence perhaps the young gentleman won't be so squeamish' [446], though Pen never fully capitulates to Shandon's literary cynicism as he never fully acquiesces in the Major's worldliness. Many of Thackeray's colleagues, at least, considered that the description of the literary world in *Pendennis* was itself 'an unfair blow.'

Pendennis is both explicitly and implicitly a novel about a writer. There is a sort of allegory in the history of Pen's loves that has a bearing on the development of the artist as well as of the man. The novel can be read rather like another version of *The Tales of Hoffman*,[13] where the sequence of the poet's loves has a significance to his art. All Pen's women have something to do with his profession; three of them are artists themselves in one way or another.

It is significant that Pen's first wild passion is for an actress: he falls in love with the Fotheringay when he sees her on the stage as Mrs Haller, and he is smitten first of all by the appurtenances of illusion that surround her and her profession: 'How beautiful she looked! Her hair had fallen down, the officers threw her flowers. She clutched them to her heart. She put back her hair, and smiled all round. Her eyes met Pen's. Down went the curtain again: and she was gone' [48]. Although Pen then meets her in her native identity of Emily Costigan, she is not divested of that footlight glow, and in his mind her real domestic existence is only an extension of her brilliant stage prescence. Pen is here the budding artist, enamoured of illusion, and building real emotion on that precarious foundation. Emily herself, however, is perhaps the sanest character in the novel (though that

---

13 Theodore Reik sees a significant pattern in Hoffmann's loves in the Offenbach opera, in 'The Three Women in a Man's Life' *Art and Psychoanalysis* ed. William Phillips (Cleveland 1963) 151–64; and it is not difficult to see in Pen's loves another less tragic version of the artist's attraction to the doll (Emily, articulated by Bows), the siren (Blanche and Fanny) and art (Laura).

kind of sanity has its mental limitations too), for she knows, to the last detail of a guinea piece against a trinket of costume jewellery, the difference between illusion and reality, and never gets them confused. Her talent on the stage, aside from her native endowments of a beautiful voice and figure, is a merely mechanical business of absolute obedience to her director. There is nothing of herself in her performance, which is the reason for the ultimate lifelessness of her art. Pen is later to become a better artist because his own life is in his work, but he pays the price of some measure of his honesty, and the best that he can do is to admit that he plays roles. Emily does not need to, however, because she is able to keep her roles so entirely separate from one another. She is not even aware, as more self-conscious people are, of the humbug in social forms, and so is able to be the one character in the novel who is perfectly sincere. She treats the end of her engagement to Arthur in a matter-of-fact, down-to-earth manner that exasperates even Bows, who stands to gain by Arthur's loss; but she is not even conscious of his irony:

'Then papa writes, and says ... the match had best be at an end.'

'And, of course, you enclose a parting line, in which you say you will always regard him as a brother,' said Mr. Bows, eyeing her in his scornful way.

'Of course, and so I shall,' answered Miss Fotheringay. 'He's a most worthy young man, I'm sure. I'll thank ye hand me the salt. Them filberts is beautiful.' [142]

Arthur's next love, Blanche, is another actress, but unlike Emily she does her role-playing in her life, and forgets the difference between the two. Blanche is the essential element of dishonesty that the artist becomes involved in if he cannot separate his art from his life, and though like Pen he must encounter it, he must not succumb to it.

Fanny Bolton (her singing and her relation with Bows connect her both with Blanche the siren and with Emily the doll) is another temptation to the artist, who has now advanced beyond the boy enamoured of illusion at Chatteris. With Emily, Pen was the adorer and adopted the inferior position at her feet. With Fanny, the positions are changed, and the Prince of Fairoaks looks down at his worshipping handmaid. He has had some measure of success, and suffered some measure of disillusion, and he requires more fuel. '"What a nice little artless creature that was," Mr. Pen thought at the very instant of waking after the Vauxhall affair: "what a pretty natural manner she has; how much pleasanter than the minauderies of the young ladies in the ball-rooms"' [606]. Pen is attracted to two things in Fanny: her apparent innocence and her admiration of himself. On the one hand she is his own public, and he cannot but be moved when she sighs that his novel is 'so beautiful! ... And Walter, oh, how dear he is!' [627–8]. And on the other he sees in her artlessness the raw material of art, and is tempted, with the diabolic impulse of the artist, to form her, to make her his creature. It is the kind of artistic egoism which Browning depicts in the Duke of Ferrara, who prefers a portrait behind a curtain that only he may lift to the living wife, and which Meredith explores in Willoughby Patterne, whose peculiar sensuality requires his women to be as pure as chickens from the egg. Thackeray was aware that the attraction of the little girl, to which so many nineteenth-century writers succumbed (including Dickens, Ruskin, and even James, besides the Romantics), was both aesthetically and erotically suspect. This is the allegory implicit in the literal and social level of Pen's relation with Fanny, in which the aristocrat is suspected of seducing the low-born maiden. There is danger to the artist as well as his subject in such a temptation, and it is predictable that Pygmalion should almost become a victim of his Galatea, who in her way is as artful as he.

The only one of Pen's loves who practises no airs and graces is Laura. He seldom sees her, as he sees Emily, as anything but what she is. At the ball at Clavering Park, Laura, with her healthy bloom and vigorous dancing, represents the real and the natural. She is contrasted there with the artificial Blanche, whose wriggling white shoulders and rolling eyes are part of her constant striving for effect. Blanche's bearing, we hear, seems to say, 'Come and look at me – not at that pink, healthy, bouncing country lass, Miss Bell, who scarcely knew how to dance till I taught her' [323]. Again there is an implicit contrast between the two proposal scenes: when Pen first asks Laura to marry him she appears indeed as a country lass, picking roses in the garden, and wearing practical country garb; she is no jaded city flirt like Blanche, who deceives herself and others with a false pastoralism adopted for the occasion. Unlike Fanny Bolton, too, Laura is intelligent and critical of Pen both as man and writer, and her influence is nearly always to make him look at himself and his work honestly, and to be embarrassed at his own posturing. Laura is in fact his truth, the reality that must be the basis of his art. Under her influence, instead of selling himself to become a politician, following a business he does not believe in for some paltry status, and allowing himself to be 'choked with red-tape,' Pen is persuaded to 'stop at home, and write books – good books' [864]. And, as her name implies, Laura becomes the crown as well as the inspiration of the artist's labours.

So the quest for truth, the preoccupation of the author as well as his protagonist, is pursued through its various facets, the problems that face the man and the artist of how to love, how to be a gentleman, and how to write honestly. Thackeray's theme is articulated not only in the aspirations and actions of his hero, but also through the numbers of minor characters who embody the variety of alternative answers. Pen as lover is set between such figures as Bows, Madame Fribsby, and Foker; as gentleman he is measured against a series of candidates from valet to baronet; as artist he is compared with those who mingle fact with fiction in their own lives as well as with professional writers whose integrity varies from Shandon's to Warrington's. And, as man and artist too, he works out the rival claims of emotion and ambition and truth and falsehood in the sequence of his loves. The profusion of minor characters is part of the unity of the novel. As at a serious level Warrington, the writer, gentleman and lover of Laura, is a parallel to and constant moral yardstick for Pen, so at a comic level even a minor figure like Mirobolant, the vocational cook, chevalier and aspirant to Miss Amory's hand, acts as a parody of Pen's aspirations. The novel is neater and more coherent than a first glance at its profusion and variety would suggest.

Pendennis is by no means a perfect novel: there are ways in which its reach exceeds its grasp. For all his careful handling of the Fanny affair, Thackeray seems to have panicked about it after it was over, overdoing the exoneration of Pen, and introducing artificial comedy in her marriage to Huxter; Pen's deliverance from Blanche is a little too easy; and there is a strained series of last-act revelations in the disposal of Altamont. But, these reservations aside, it is a fine novel. To call it a novel of ideas, though as a careful exploration of time and truth it certainly is one, is to underestimate it. It has its passages, like the talks between Pen and Warrington, of straight Shavian disputation, but these only provide a focus for what is fully incorporated in character and action. The regular *roman à these*, like *Caleb Williams* or *Sybil*, is comparatively a bore, because it remains a diagram rather than a picture. But *Pendennis* has life as well as ideological structure, because its narration is animated by that tone of personal experience, and its ideas fully incarnated in a vivid troop of psychologically convincing as well as thematically appropriate characters.

3

Moral Ambiguity:
Henry Esmond

WHATEVER THACKERAY'S RESERVATIONS ABOUT HIS STATUS AS an artist, as a moralist he took himself seriously. He was prepared to joke about the tendency of his novels to put his readers to sleep, but not so readily about the system of values they present. By 1847, at the outset of his career as a major novelist, he was aware of something like a vocation, as he explained to his *Punch* colleague, Mark Lemon:

> What I mean applies to my own case & that of all of us – who set up as Satirical-Moralists – and having such a vast multitude of readers whom we not only amuse but teach ... A few years ago I should have sneered at the idea of setting up as a teacher at all, and perhaps at this pompous and pious way of talking about a few papers of jokes in Punch – but I have got to believe in the business, and in many other things since then. And our profession seems to me to be as serious as the Parson's own. [Letters II 282]

Having once 'got to believe in the business,' Thackeray is a zealous convert to Sidney's doctrine of the sugared pill of instruction plus entertainment; in his explicit statements at least, he is always as much concerned with the quality of the pill as of the sugar. His judgments of others' work as well as his own usually have a moral rather than an aesthetic basis. And when, in his lectures on the English humourists, he comes to define his term, his emphasis is more on the humourist's didactic responsibility than on his ability to make his readers laugh:

> The humorous writer professes to awaken and direct your love, your pity, your kindness – your scorn for untruth, pretension, imposture – your tenderness for the weak, the poor, the oppressed, the unhappy. To the best of his means and ability he comments on all the ordinary

actions and passions of life almost. He takes upon himself to be the week-day preacher, so to speak. [XIII 469–70]

It is not surprising that he was immediately on the defensive when the *Times* review of *The Newcomes* qualified its general praise of him by the statement, 'He is a great humorist, and we only regret that he is not a great moralist also.'[1] He wrote to Whitwell Elwin,

> I think please God my books are written by a God-loving man, and the morality – the vanity of success &c of all but Love and Goodness – is not that the teaching of Domini Nostri? [Letters III 467]

That is indeed the most explicitly developed morality in Thackeray's novels. As he told his daughters, 'the frontispiece of Pendennis is verily always going on in my mind' [Letters IV 28]: the battle between the worldly siren and the domestic angel, with the latter apparently victorious, continued to be the basic structure of the novels. Amelia, not Becky, is rewarded with the loving husband and the happy ending; Pendennis rejects Blanche for Laura; Esmond is united with Rachel, not Beatrix; George Warrington wins the loving Theo after he has escaped the wiles of the millionaire's daughter, Lydia Van den Bosch; Philip is the happier for his union with the tender brown-haired Charlotte after he has been jilted by the social-climbing blond Agnes Twysden.

But we need only think of the ending of *Vanity Fair* to remember that Thackeray's more comprehensive vision saw 'Love and Goodness,' at least as manifested in the fallen world, as vanity too; Dobbin's pursuit of what he sees as love and goodness is ultimately as illusory as Becky's struggle for social success. Those apparent resolutions in favour of the angels are not really resolutions at all. There are no real 'happy endings' in the novels – Pendennis comes the nearest to achieving one, and we saw how his was qualified by that 'but' remaining in his mind. In spite of Pen's love for Laura, and in spite of Thackeray's reverence for goodness, they both have their reservations, resulting from a sad knowledge of the way of the world. And in spite of Thackeray's strong stand on the moral outcome of his fables, his real moral strength lies in just those reservations

1 29 August 1855

– that is, in his ability to see and embody what is attractive in evil, and what is destructive in good.

The ironic nature of his moral vision aroused the distrust and hostility of contemporary critics, and this, in turn, made him overstate his championship of love and goodness. Roscoe complained, 'It grates on our ears to hear English ladies talking as they do sometimes of "that charming wicked little Becky,"' and went on to summarize his objection to Thackeray, and that of the other critics who 'only regret that he is not a great moralist,' 'We do maintain that there is a sin against good taste and right moral influence in mingling too intimately real vice and the ridiculous; they may be alternated, but not mixed, still less almost chemically combined, after Mr. Thackeray's fashion.'[2] That vice should not be made appealing was Thackeray's own maxim in 1839, when he wrote *Catherine* with the rather dreary object of inducing a 'wholesome nausea' for his subject; but the Thackeray who wrote the major novels knew that vice can be attractive and virtue uninteresting or even pernicious, and that moral integrity, as well as literary realism, consisted in showing them as such. He had developed the ability to embody the intricate combinations of good and evil, and his moral vision becomes sharper, and not more blurred, for the increased subtlety. For if he creates a compound in which the elements are 'almost chemically combined,' he is still aware, as the careful reader is still aware, of the nature of those elements. An examination of some of Thackeray's 'good' characters, and one of his 'bad' ones, will show how his own somewhat simplified statement of his morality is qualified and expanded in the novels.

As the ironic intonation in his use of the word 'genius' is a reminder that for Thackeray the artist is but a man, so a similar ring in his adjectives 'good' and 'virtuous' is an indication that even his saints are but sinners.

One of his recurrent satiric butts is the self-righteous character who feels his virtue should be rewarded in hard cash, like Burns' Holy Willie, who prays, 'Lord, remember me and mine / Wi' mercies temporal and divine.' There is a long list of characters in his novels, particularly

2 'W.M. Thackeray, Artist and Moralist' in *Poems and Essays* (London 1860) II 299–300

women, who make capital out of their morality. *Vanity Fair*, as he summarized it in a letter, is about a set of people who are 'greedy pompous mean perfectly self-satisfied for the most part and at ease about their superior virtue' [II 309]. Miss Crawley, the godless old heiress, is beset by people who are trying to get her money under the guise of saving her soul. The Anglican clergyman's wife, Mrs Bute Crawley, who 'thought herself one of the most virtuous women in England' [499], rushes to Miss Crawley's bedside when she is sick, and proceeds so to frighten her with apprehensions about her body and her soul that she almost succeeds in killing her:

> Thus, for instance, Mrs. Bute, with the best intentions no doubt in the world, and wearing herself to death as she did by forgoing sleep, dinner, fresh air, for the sake of her invalid sister-in-law, carried her conviction of the old lady's illness so far that she almost managed her into her coffin. [VF 231]

A parallel figure, who similarly confounds bodily with spiritual welfare, the evangelical Lady Southdown, administers quack medicine and quack religion alternately to her protegées, and 'would order Gaffer Jones to be converted, as she would order Goody Hicks to take a James's powder' [VF 414]. She too is after Miss Crawley's money, as is her hypocritical son-in-law, Pitt.

In *Esmond*, it is the Tushers, *père et fils*, with their smug conviction of their own good deserts and their shrewd eye to the main chance, who belong to this category. The whole of *The Newcomes* exposes the Newcome kind of 'goodness' – a goodness which consists in a prudent avoidance of scandal and in lip-service to popular morality, covering a complete callousness about the concerns of others. The part of 'Consummate Virtue' is personified in Mrs Hobson Newcome, who is always finding moral lapses in the people whose wealth or social position she envies. Her counterpart in *The Virginians* is, again, the hero's aunt by marriage: 'My Lady Warrington, one of the tallest and the most virtuous of her sex, who had goodness forever on her lips and "Heaven in her eye" ... had the world in her other eye, and an exceedingly shrewd desire of pushing herself in it' [828]. The attack is continued, in *Lovel the Widower*, on

Lady Baker, 'who, to be sure, might do duty for a villain, but she considers herself as virtuous a woman as ever was born' [57]. The original of Lady Baker is Lady Kicklebury of *The Kickleburys on the Rhine*, on whose species Thackeray, in the person of Michael Angelo Titmarsh, had early declared war, with a resumé of his reasons:

'She has no idea but that everything she says, and thinks, and does is right. And no doubt she never did rob a church: and was a faithful wife to Sir Thomas, and pays her tradesmen. Confound her virtue! It is that which makes her so wonderful – that brass armour in which she walks impenetrable – not knowing what pity is, or charity; crying sometimes when she is vexed, or thwarted, but laughing never; cringing, and domineering by the same natural instinct – never doubting herself above all. Let us rise, and revolt against those people, Lankin. Let us war with them, and smite them utterly. It is to use against these, especially, that Scorn and Satire were invented.'

'And the animal you attack,' says Lankin, 'is provided with a hide to defend him – it is a common ordinance of nature.' [x 264–5]

Thackeray's attack is not just on the Pecksniffian hypocrite like Barnes Newcome or Mrs Bute, who, under their whited exteriors, must be quite conscious of their own mercenary motivation; it is aimed also at those exasperating people whose complete confidence in their own merit makes them unapproachable, simply not amenable to any suggestion that there may be other opinions worth considering. Here the emphasis shifts from the satirical towards the psychological, and the issues become more serious. There is a general attack on dedicated do-gooders in *Philip*:

If somebody or some Body of savants would write the history of the harm that has been done in the world by people who believe themselves to be virtuous, what a queer, edifying book it would be, and how poor oppressed rogues might look up! Who burns the Protestants? – the virtuous Catholics to be sure. Who roasts the Catholics? – the virtuous Reformers ... Who scorns? Who persecutes? who doesn't forgive? – the virtuous Mrs. Grundy. She remembers her neighbour's peccadilloes to the third and fourth generation. [103]

To be unforgiving is the proper vice of the virtuous. 'Those who know a really good woman are aware that she is not in a hurry to forgive' [VF 506], Thackeray says of Mrs Bute. But his exposure of this quality is not limited to the creation of such minor characters as Mrs Bute or Lady Kicklebury or Mrs Hobson Newcome. These, we can see, are not really good at all, for all their possible absence of vices, for they lack the positive virtues which Thackeray valued – humility, generosity, selflessness, and above all love. But that treatment of the hypocrite who masks his avidity with morality and of the do-gooder who is overly confident of his own rectitude blends into a more comprehensive irony, which encompasses the truly loving souls like Amelia, Helen Pendennis, Rachel Esmond, and Colonel Newcome. Much of what is said about the 'virtuous' characters applies also to them. 'The wicked are wicked no doubt, and they go astray and they fall, and they come by their deserts: but who can tell the mischief which the very virtuous do?' [N 246]. This is said à propos of Mrs Hobson Newcome; but it can apply not only to her kind, but to the major saintly characters too. The moral pattern of all Thackeray's novels suggests that goodness is defined in terms of the pursuit of love rather than of worldly success, and by this definition Amelia and her kind are good, for they are all loving beings to whom social prestige is more or less indifferent. In the sorting of good and bad they have been set aside as the sheep, while Becky, Blanche, Beatrix, and Barnes are the goats; but the sheep are still not exempt from a closer scrutiny, and they suffer a more subtle ironic exposure.

Amelia is deliberately distinguished from the 'virtuous' species to which Mrs Bute belongs, for she does not harbour malice or revel in the peccadilloes of others. When she meets Becky in Pumpernickel, she is ready to forget the part Becky had played in alienating her husband's affections: 'As she had never thought or done anything mortally guilty herself, she had not that abhorrence for wickedness which distinguishes moralists much more knowing' [VF 835]. There is a double irony in operation here, however; the attack on the Unco' Guid still stands, but Amelia's readiness to re-establish intimacy with Becky is, in the event, more like lack of judgment than Christian forgiveness – Dobbin, for instance, knows enough to beware of Becky.

But there can be no doubt that Thackeray genuinely valued Amelia's qualities of tenderness and gentleness. If he recognizes that Dobbin is a spooney for allowing himself to be tyrannized over and made to fetch and carry by Amelia ('This history has been written to very little purpose if the reader has not perceived that the major was a spooney,' he says [844]), Thackeray can still sympathize with him and to some extent identify with him. In a letter – appropriately to Mrs Brookfield, who was partly his model for Amelia – he wrote: 'I rank myself among the spoonies. Soft-heartedness seems to me better than anything better than stars and garters great intellect blazing wit &c' [Letters II 469].

Yet for all the emphasis on Amelia's soft-heartedness, her selfless adoration of her husband and her son, her forgiving nature, her qualifications for being a true gentlewoman, sufficient attention is given to her faults. 'Of course you are quite right about Vanity Fair and Amelia being selfish,' Thackeray wrote to his mother. 'My object is not to make a perfect character or anything like it' [Letters II 309]. And her faults are closely related to her virtues. Her forgiving temper has its origin in silliness, her trust in an inability to discriminate: 'It needs not to be said that this soft and gentle creature took her opinions from those people who surrounded her, such fidelity being much too humble-minded to think for itself' [322]. Her capacity to feel is sometimes seen as a watery sentimentality, a tendency to react emotionally in excess of the real stimulus: 'The very joy of this woman was a sort of grief, or so tender, at least, that its expression was tears' [489]. Thackeray suggests the morbid element in her devotion to George when he tells us, 'the business of her life was – to watch the corpse of Love' [217]. And the seemingly selfless dedication of her whole existence to her love for him becomes itself selfish, like any over-indulgence in emotion; her parents find, for instance, that she can spare no attention or energy for their catastrophe while she is so wrapped up in her own.

The parallel with Becky, which is one of the structural principles of the book, shows up Amelia's callousness: in Number XI, the part concerned with Becky's and Rawdon's prosperous existence on nothing a year, we are told also of Amelia's hard-heartedness towards Dobbin. Becky cheats financially, and her creditor, the poor trusting Raggles, has to suffer;

Amelia cheats emotionally, by never acknowledging her debts to Dobbin, and makes him suffer just as surely and unjustly as Raggles does. Similarly, when we have been told of Becky's callousness about her adoring son, who was 'worshipping a stone' [478], the image is recalled in Dobbin's thoughts of Amelia:

Amelia's letter had fallen as a blank upon him. No fidelity, no constant truth and passion, could move her into warmth. She would not see that he loved her. Tossing in his bed, he spoke out to her. 'Good God, Amelia!' he said, 'don't you know that I only love you in the world – you, who are a stone to me – you, whom I tended through months and months of illness and grief, and who bade me farewell with a smile on your face, and forgot me before the door shut between us!' [551]

Amelia, the gentle and uncalculating, is, however, well aware of the chain by which she holds Dobbin, though she does not always choose to admit it. Ingenuous as she appears, she is quite conscious of the nature of their relationship, and capable of taking steps to maintain it: 'She didn't wish to marry him, but she wished to keep him. She wished to give him nothing, but that he should give her all. It is a bargain not unfrequently levied in love' [853]. The emphasis has shifted, in fact, from her absorbing love for George to her lack of love for Dobbin. And even her love for George is vanity, another of her gushings of emotion in excess of the cause. George is unworthy of her love, as she sees but will not acknowledge; and after his death she deliberately deludes herself, by excluding from her mind much of her knowledge of him and his behaviour, so that she can devote herself to a picture of a dead husband which is not even a true likeness. Dobbin finds our her real deficiency in love at the end, and the most complete exposure of her is in his words:

'I know what your heart is capable of: it can cling faithfully to a recollection, and cherish a fancy; but it can't feel such an attachment as mine deserves to mate with, and such as I would have won from a woman more generous than you. No, you are not worthy of the love which I have devoted to you. I knew all along that the prize I had

set my life on was not worth the winning; that I was a fool, with fond
fancies, too, bartering away my all of truth and ardour against your
little feeble remnant of love.' [852–3]

It is the wicked Becky who works towards Amelia's salvation by her
exposure of George's worthlessness. By this time Amelia has already
almost lost Dobbin because his eyes have been opened to her. He marries
her in any case, but it is a marriage made in Vanity Fair and not in heaven;
Dobbin's love for her is revealed as vanity, just as hers for George had
been vanity. Thackeray explained this in a letter to a reviewer after the
novel was completed: 'If I had made Amelia a higher order of woman
there would have been no vanity in Dobbin's falling in love with her,
whereas the impression at present is that he is a fool for his pains that he
has married a silly little thing and in fact has found out his error'
[Letters II 423].

So good constantly changes its face, and love becomes the deluded
deification of a false idol, and triumph turns to ashes. Dobbin achieves his
lifelong goal, and is at best 'a fool for his pains,' at worst united with his
own destruction:

He has got the prize he has been trying for all his life. The bird has
come in at last. There it is with its head on his shoulder, billing and
cooing close up to his heart, with soft outstretched fluttering wings.
This is what he has asked for every day and every hour for eighteen
years. This is what he pined after. Here it is – the summit, the end –
the last page of the third volume. Good-bye, colonel – God bless you,
honest William! – Farewell, dear Amelia – Grow green again, tender
little parasite, round the rugged old oak to which you cling! [871]

It is possible, then, to see Amelia as the weak but tender character who
is more sinned against than sinning; for it is true that she never per-
petrates a deliberate act of malice, and that she always means well. But a
closer scrutiny of her goodness in operation reveals that, in her very
passivity, she wreaks havoc in the lives of the people nearest to her. As a
daughter she is insensitive: she is unaware of her father's extremity, and
she quarrels with her mother, whom she causes to pray, 'Oh, Amelia, may

God send you a more dutiful child than I have had' [587]. As a sister, by her undiscriminating trust she introduces into her brother's house the woman who is possibly to be his ruin. She is no doubt both adoring and mistreated as a wife to George; but Amelia, like others of Thackeray's suffering saints, has a way of creating her own martyrdom. It is her nature as well as George's infidelity that makes her unhappy after a week of marriage, for she constantly puts herself in a posture of subjection that invites brutality. Often enough it seems as though the fault is not in her stars but in herself that she is characteristically 'in a sainted agony of tears' [625]. She is certainly a devoted mother to Georgy, but there is a preview of the final parasite image in the account of 'how his mother nursed him, and dressed him, and lived upon him' [447]. Her very tenderness and submissiveness develop aggressiveness and a sense of superiority in her child; and although we are meant to be touched by her grief when Georgy is taken from her, we are also meant to contrast the kind lad Rawdon, the son of a selfish and neglectful mother, with the snobbish young Georgy, whom his mother's indulgence has modelled in his father's obnoxious image. We hear no more of her relation to her daughter Janey than that she is jealous of her in her father's affections. Finally, as the beloved of Dobbin, she is selfish and unobtrusively tyrannical, and as his wife, at last, she is the 'tender little parasite' who, at least potentially, can destroy 'the rugged old oak' to which she clings. And this is the woman that the literary histories still claim to be presented as Thackeray's ideal of Victorian womanhood! Rather he was showing a sentimental Victorian public, which did indeed venerate such qualities as Amelia's, exactly what kind of an idol it was worshipping.

It is on the saintly qualities of Helen Pendennis, the prototype of the mother in his novels, that Thackeray is most insistent. She is one of those women, we hear, 'in whose angelical natures there is something awful, as well as beautiful, to contemplate; at whose feet the wildest and fiercest of us must fall down and humble ourselves, in admiration of that adorable purity which never seems to do or to think wrong' [P 18]. Such is the description of her at the outset. And after her death, and her long influence over the fortunes of her son, and all the scenes in which she has been seen in a light that is far from saintly, we are still told that 'Penden-

nis's mother was worshipped in his memory, and canonized there, as such
a saint ought to be. Lucky he in life who knows a few such women! A kind
provision of Heaven it was that sent us such; and gave us to admire that
touching and wonderful spectacle of innocence, and love, and beauty'
[791]. The effusions, in fact, are often embarrassing, when read in isolation. But they do not appear in isolation, and the voice of the narrator who
tells us that she 'ought' to be canonized in her son's memory is no more
the authentic voice of the novel (though Thackeray himself in some moods
might have claimed that it was) than are the dry tones of the ironist that
alternate with it. So, after the introduction of her as one of the angelic
kind, he goes on: 'That even a woman should be faultless, however, is an
arrangement not permitted by nature ...' [18].

The one flaw in her character, he explains, is an exaggerated pride in
her family, especially in her son, whose virtues, graces, and talents she
considers unsurpassed. Being offered her worship, Pen accepts it, as
Georgy did Amelia's, as his due. And again the effect, as we are told
explicitly at the outset, is detrimental to his moral character: 'This un-
fortunate superstition and idol-worship of this good woman was the cause
of a great deal of the misfortune which befell the young gentleman who
is the hero of this history, and deserves therefore to be mentioned at the
outset of his story' [19]. Laura, whose moral discrimination is much
keener than Helen's, is able to see how bad the mother's worship has been
for her son: how it has made him self-satisfied and selfish, supercilious and
finally cynical. One of the major themes of the novel is the process of
Pen's recognition of that self, which his mother has helped to build, as his
own worst enemy.

Helen has, also, the familiar shortcomings of the virtuous. She lacks a
sense of humour; and she is, as Amelia is not, unforgiving, and even
ready, in a sexual matter at least, to believe Pen more wicked than he is.
Her exaggerated sense of moral outrage and her gross injustice to Fanny,
when she thinks Pen has had an affair with her – these are the sins that
grow directly out of her goodness and love.

Thackeray vividly dramatizes, in individual scenes in the book, how
Helen's goodness becomes exasperating in a way that only righteousness
and love can. Her eagerness to promote Pen's happiness by pushing him

into Laura's arms almost looks like procuring: she eagerly leaves them alone together, she wakes Pen early to send him out into the garden after Laura – and watches the scene from behind the window-curtains. Her love for her son has a suffocating quality about it:

> [Her] wounded bosom yearned with love towards him, though there was a secret between them, and an anguish or rage almost on the mother's part, to think that she was dispossessed somehow of her son's heart, or that there were recesses in it which she must not or dared not enter. She sickened as she thought of the sacred days of boyhood when it had not been so – when her Arthur's heart had no secrets, and she was his all in all. [716]

This is the kind of absorbing and clinging love that makes its object want to tear and rend at its entanglements; and in fact immediately following this passage there is a repetition of the image of a woman's love as the 'pretty fond parasite' that twines round the oak.

There is something about certain kinds of tenderness and vulnerability that prompts in others the irresistible impulse to be rough and to wound. Thackeray shows this with a clarity which his explicit moralizing sometimes seems to belie. Helen's death scene may appear an orgy of sentimentality; but it is as well to note the psychological realism of it:

> Pen remarked that his mother's voice and her whole frame trembled, her hand was clammy cold as she put it up to his forehead, piteously embracing him. The spectacle of her misery only added, somehow, to the wrath and testiness of the young man. He scarcely returned the kiss which the suffering lady gave him: and the countenance with which he met the appeal of her look was hard and cruel. 'She persecutes me,' he thought within himself, 'and she comes to me with the air of a martyr.' 'You look very ill, my child,' she said. 'I don't like to see you look in that way.' And she tottered to a sofa, still holding one of his passive hands in her thin, cold, clinging fingers. [730]

The modern reader's gorge rises at the whole scene depicting Helen's lingering agonies and long-drawn-out prayers. But we should notice that

Pen's gorge rises too, even if only momentarily: it is an indication that Thackeray knew what he was doing.

There is a tendency in casual criticism of Thackeray's work to notice two things – that he explicitly praises the goodness of such characters as Amelia and Helen, and that as characters they are exasperating – and to conclude from this that Thackeray has failed in what he set out to do. But Thackeray was in far greater control of his novels than this suggests. He is perfectly aware of the discrepancy; it is for him a discrepancy that exists in life. There *is* goodness in such characters as Amelia and Helen, and, though it is a kind of goodness less appealing to us than to a Victorian, we should make no mistake about the fact that such people are more trust-worthy than the serpents like Becky and Blanche: they will not lie to you, or cheat you of your livelihood. At the same time, the demands that they make on those they love are of a nature to prompt a rebellion that can be the more cruel for being the less justified. Thackeray's wicked characters inflict suffering on those they encounter; but the good ones inflict guilt. And it is matter for speculation whether poverty and neglect are harder to bear than 'agenbite of inwit.'

It is easier to see Thackeray's intention in his depiction of Rachel, Lady Castlewood, in *Esmond*, for we expect a bias in her favour in a narrative by the man who loves her and eventually marries her. The view of her which Esmond gives in the body of the novel contrasts with what we are told of her by her Virginian daughter in the preface, as well as with what we hear of her from other characters in the novel. Besides this, we have the further commentary provided on her years later by Beatrix, in another novel. The ironic framework for the presentation of Rachel is clear; but it is not essentially different from that in *Vanity Fair* and *Pendennis*, where a sentimental commentary alternates with an ironic one.

Esmond depicts Rachel as a saint, and she is indeed humble, religious, selfless and – usually – loving; though, being more intelligent, she is made of perceptibly sterner stuff than Amelia and Helen. He himself can see some of her faults; but for the most part we can recognize his description as partisan, and much of our information about her must be gained from others. Although Harry apparently believes her to be a loving wife,

E

Castlewood confides to Harry that, since the time of the smallpox, 'my wife's as cold as the statue at Charing Cross.'

> 'I tell thee she has no forgiveness in her, Henry. Her coldness blights my whole life, and sends me to the punch-bowl, or driving about the country ... I'm killed by the very virtue of that proud woman. Virtue! give me the virtue that can forgive; give me the virtue that thinks not of preserving itself, but of making other folks happy.' [HE 128]

Rachel, like other 'virtuous' women, takes a certain satisfaction in her husband's misdemeanours – his drinking, his coarseness and stupidity, and his keeping a mistress; for it gives her some justification for transferring her love from him to Harry. The manifestation of her sense of intellectual and moral superiority to her husband drives him to a kind of despair:

> 'She neither sins nor forgives. I know her temper – and now I've lost her: by Heaven I love her ten thousand times more than ever I did ... I am not good like her, I know it. Who is – by Heaven, who is? I tired and wearied her, I know that very well ... I felt she didn't belong to me: and the children don't. And I besotted myself, and gambled, and drank, and took to all sorts of devilries out of despair and fury.' [153]

Such is the saint as a wife, when she is married to the wrong person. As a mother she follows the usual pattern of loving mothers by being over-indulgent, especially to her son. This Esmond himself sees: 'I am inclined to fancy, my mistress, who never said a harsh word to her children ... must have been too fond and pressing with the maternal authority; for her son and her daughter both revolted early' [351]. She is also jealous – jealous of her son's love for others, and of others' love for her two daughters. And, as with her husband, her very goodness drives Beatrix to wickedness. Esmond, contemplating the daughter's selfishness and ambition, considers "'Tis a marvel to think that her mother was the purest and simplest woman in the whole world, and that this girl should have been born from her' [351]. Thackeray, however, presents this as no marvel at all, but rather as the natural course of events. In Beatrix's weaker and more introspective moments she can give another account of the effect of her mother's goodness on her: 'Oh, how good she is, Harry ... Oh, what a saint she is! Her goodness frightens me. I'm not fit to live with her. I should be better, I think, if she were not so perfect' [355]. The self-righteousness and pride of the mother became selfishness and ambition in the daughter.

The ironic tension that we find in *Esmond* between Harry's fervent admiration for Rachel's moral rectitude and our knowledge of the psychological damage this rectitude can cause when in operation is humorously expressed years later in the dry comments of the detached and worldly-wise old Beatrix in *The Virginians*. She speaks about Rachel to her grandson:

'My mother has always described hers as an angel upon earth,' interposed George.

'Eh! That is a common character for people when they are dead!' cried the baroness; 'and Rachel Castlewood was an angel, if you like – at least your grandfather thought so. But let me tell you, sir, that angels are sometimes not very *commodes à vivre*. It may be they are too good to live with us sinners, and the air down below here don't agree with them. My poor mother was so perfect that she never could forgive me for being otherwise. Ah, mon Dieu! how she used to oppress me with those angelical airs!'

George cast down his eyes, and thought of his own melancholy youth. [v 560].

In *The Newcomes* there is a minor character who seems to be there specifically to point a moral to over-moral mothers. Lady Walham, young Lord Kew's mother, again is invested with saintly qualities. She herself has lived a life of rigid purity, and has tried to impose her standards on her son – and she has signally failed. We meet Kew as a good-humoured prodigal, very like young Frank Castlewood in *Esmond*. We meet his mother when she comes to his bedside after he has been shot in a duel. It is an encounter that makes her examine her conduct to see how far she has been to blame, and she discovers in herself the vices which Thackeray shows as the other side of the coin of virtue.

Very likely her mind was narrow; very likely the precautions which she had used in the lad's early days ... had served only to vex and weary the young pupil, and to drive his high spirit into revolt. It is hard to convince a woman perfectly pure in her life and intentions, ready to die if need were for her own faith ... that she ... may be doing harm. [N 485–6]

This mother does achieve self-knowledge, and an awareness of the harm she has caused, and she repents of the excess of morality that has driven her son to dissipation. It is she, and not the prodigal, who has most need to repent.

While she is debating her moral choice in her mind, the narrator, in preaching vein, considers 'that battle betwixt Evil and Good.' 'Here, on one side, is Self and Ambition and Advancement; and Right and Love on the other. Which shall we let to triumph for ourselves – which for our children?' [502]. In *The Newcomes* and his other novels Thackeray explores the irony that the parent who chooses the one is likely to determine the child's predilection for the other.

The most sympathetic of all Thackeray's good characters is a man, Colonel Newcome. He is less subject to attack as a creation because the writer is both more explicit about his faults and less insistent on his saintliness. He is a lovable character, like his heroes and literary forbears, Dr Primrose, Sir Roger de Coverley, and Don Quixote. But in many ways he follows the same pattern as the female parents. He is so morally upright that he cannot forgive any deviousness, and he damages his son's cause by his irascibility with Barnes in much the same way as Kent damages Lear's cause by attacking Oswald. So we are told of the colonel's vindictiveness towards the other side of the Newcome family, 'what is sheer hate seems to the individual entertaining the sentiment so like indignant virtue, that he often indulges in the propensity to the full, nay, lauds himself for the exercise of it' [838].

His love for Clive is not of the suffocating kind that prompts rebellion; it is rather so undemanding that he ties Clive to him with a net of obligations which influences him to choose for his father's sake rather than for his own. The colonel decides that art is an inferior occupation and Ethel not good enough for his son, and a combination of circumstance and grateful deference to his father makes Clive give up painting and marry Rosey. 'Between his two best beloved mistresses, poor Clive's luckless father somehow interposes ... In place of Art the colonel brings him a ledger; and in lieu of first love, shows him Rosey' [851]. The result for Clive is a dreary and frustrating existence, in a profession that bores him and with a wife who is little more than a doll. 'With the best intentions in the world,' he exclaims of his father, 'what a slave's life it is that he has made for me!' [853].

Although the colonel is on the side of love and honour against the world and expediency, his eagerness for his son's happiness and prosperity makes him, by a kind of inversion, vicariously worldly. In the days of his prosperity, when he too is in the banking business and displaying at dreary soirées his grandiose lack of taste, he becomes pompous and almost snobbish; so that it takes his misery, and the inevitable poverty which follows his ill-advised transactions in a world he knows nothing of, to restore our sympathy for him.

George Orwell, speaking of Agnes Wickfield in *David Copperfield*, calls her 'the real legless angel of Victorian romance, almost as bad as Thackeray's Laura.'[3] Laura as she appears in *Pendennis* is pleasant enough, and her sense, in contrast to Blanche's sham sensibility, and her shrewd judgment, against Helen's tendency to hysteria, as well as her sense of humour, make her a substantial character who is, if moral, still a tolerable heroine and a likeable person. It is the Laura who is the wife of the narrator in *The Newcomes* and *Philip* who is hard to take.

To call her a legless angel is an apt description, for indeed in these novels she is not a complete person: she is an allegorical figure, an attitude rather than a character. She plays Sentiment to Pendennis's Cynicism; and in fact she has some shrewd things to say to a writer whose concern for style can eclipse the concern for morality, and to the habitual ironist whose detachment can become, like Mr Bennet's in *Pride and Prejudice*, a deadening evasion of responsibility:

'You dare not have opinions, or holding them you dare not declare

3 'Charles Dickens' *Dickens, Dali and Others* (New York 1946) 73

them, and act by them. You compromise with crime every day because you think it would be officious to declare yourself and interfere.
You are not afraid of outraging morals, but of inflicting ennui upon
society, and losing your popularity ... It is not right to "put your oar
in", as you say in your jargon (and even your slang is a sort of cowardice, sir, for you are afraid to speak the feelings of your heart): – it is
not right to meddle and speak the truth, not right to rescue a poor
soul who is drowning – of course not.' [AP 174–5]

It is an extension of the old argument between Pen and Warrington, the
debate on the relative merits of moral commitment and detached analysis.
And of course Thackeray himself has not found the answer, and so
combines his championship of the tender-hearted against the self-seekers
with a cool assessment of the qualifying faults of the one group and the
redeeming virtues of the other. But although he can combine the two
attitudes in his commentary, in trying to personify them in the domestic
relations of Mr and Mrs Arthur Pendennis he has failed to make them
interesting characters who belong in a realistic novel. The Laura of *The
Newcomes* and *Philip* is an attitude insufficiently embodied.

So far as she is realized as a character, she is shown as morally sententious (she refuses to forgive Clara for her sin even before she has committed
it), and of course rather suffocatingly affectionate to her children. There is
some ironic exposure of her, as we would expect. When she expresses her
indignation at the worldly and grasping Twysdens even her husband can
suggest an inversion: 'Regarding this blue-eyed mother and daughter,
Mrs. Laura Pendennis was in such a state of mind, that she was ready to
tear their blue eyes out' [AP 174]. And Thackeray pointed out that the
narrator's usual assumption about her goodness proves Pen's uxorious-
ness rather than Laura's infallibility.

As part of the attempt to define Thackeray's good characters, it is
worth examining one of his bad ones. Becky, of course, is the obvious
choice, though Beatrix would also be appropriate for a consideration of the
intelligence and vitality that are among the redeeming features of some of
the determined self-seekers in Thackeray's world. Blanche and Barnes,
who are also among the goats rather than the sheep in that they care more

for social success than for domestic felicity, are otherwise not in Becky's class. Blanche lacks a grasp on reality, and Barnes is mean and malicious.

It is of course a mistake to suppose that Thackeray was of Becky's party without knowing it. It is clear that this siren, beautiful and enticing as she is, is also a monster who will have no scruple about devouring those in her way. But in understanding her badness we must understand the limits of it too. The people she is most likely to harm are in the main the ones who most deserve it. As the most resourceful and convinced member of Vanity Fair, she is also its own proper punishment. It is the people like George Osborne that she can gauge and deal with, in the course of her career, according to their deserts. She gets his number when he is magnanimously praising and patronizing Dobbin:

> 'There's not a finer fellow in the service,' Osborne said, 'nor a better officer, though he is not an Adonis, certainly.' And he looked towards the glass himself with much *naiveté*; and in so doing, caught Miss Sharp's eye keenly fixed upon him, at which he blushed a little, and, Rebecca thought in her heart, '*Ah, mon beau monsieur*! I think I have *your* gauge' – the little artful minx! [VF 57–8]

Dobbin, on the other hand, is more or less immune from her, though she gauges him accurately and promptly too – unlike Amelia, who is obtuse about him and his love for her:

> Little Amelia, it must be owned, had rather a mean opinion of her husband's friend, Captain Dobbin. He lisped – he was very plain and homely-looking: and exceedingly awkward and ungainly ... As for Rebecca, Captain Dobbin had not been two hours in the ladies' company before she understood his secret perfectly. She did not like him, and feared him privately; nor was he very much prepossessed in her favour. He was so honest, that her arts and cajoleries did not affect him, and he shrank from her with instinctive repulsion. [293]

Becky and Dobbin inhabit different worlds, and she cannot harm him. In fact he is the one person who gives her a sense of another world, not all hypocrisy and selfishness, to which she might have belonged: '"Ah," she thought, "if I could have had such a husband as that – a man with a heart and brains too! I would not have minded his large feet'''[853]. This is no doubt an unlikely hypothesis, but at least she can see Dobbin's qualities; and he does inspire her one genuinely selfless act. Becky's discernment exceeds Amelia's not only in her perception of evil but in her perception of good. She may not be more moral than her friend, but she certainly has far more moral discrimination.

Dobbin is one of the few people in the novel who sees and carefully judges Becky for what she is. Both Rawdon and Steyne, in their different ways, admire her cleverness; but for the most part, the crowd of Vanity Fair assesses her and dislikes her not for what she is or does, but only as she is a threat to them. The servants in the Sedley household and in Miss Crawley's ménage, Lady Bareacres, and the ladies at Gaunt House all react to her out of themselves, from envy and jealousy. Even Lady Jane, who, at least as a mother, stands as the golden mean between Becky and Amelia, exposes herself as well as Becky by her distrust. When Becky and Rawdon visit the family at Queen's Crawley for the second time, 'Lady Jane and Becky did not get on *quite* so well at this visit as on occasion of the former one, when the colonel's wife was bent upon pleasing ... Perhaps Sir Pitt was rather too attentive to her' [572].

Not only is the harm she does qualified by the fact that it is often deserved (not that she consciously administers rewards and punishments: to be the scourge of Vanity Fair is her function but not her conscious purpose), but she is also the vehicle of a considerable amount of good. With her cleverness, her sense of humour, and her vitality, she has the ability to make other people's lives gay and vivid. Amelia adds to her parents' troubles, but Becky is able to revitalize the dreary family at Queen's Crawley when she is governess there, to delight Miss Crawley to give everybody an invigorating if delusory sense of his own potential It is a temporary effect, certainly, but one that Amelia cannot achieve at all. She is a dead weight where Becky is buoyant. And to minister to people as Becky does requires a kind of devotion. Of course she ministers to the Crawleys for her own ultimate gain, but in the course of her campaign she shows a selflessness of which Amelia is incapable. She never so much deserves the epithet 'indefatigable' as when she is tending Miss Crawley in her illness, and soothing both the patient and old Sir Pitt and Rawdon, the father and son who are rivals for her attention:

> She passed as weary a fortnight as ever mortal spent in Miss Crawley's
> sick-room; but her little nerves seemed to be made of iron, and she
> was quite unshaken by the duty and the tedium of the sick-chamber.
> She never told until long afterwards how painful that duty was;
> how peevish a patient was the jovial old lady; how angry; how sleep-
> less; in what horrors of death ... Sharp watched by this graceless bed-
> side with indomitable patience ... During the illness she was never
> out of temper; always alert; she slept light, having a perfectly clear
> conscience; and could take that refreshment at almost any minute's
> warning. And so you saw few traces of fatigue in her appearance. Her
> face might be a trifle paler, and the circles round her eyes a little
> blacker than usual; but whenever she came from the sick-room she
> was always smiling, fresh, and neat, and looked as trim in her little
> dressing-gown and cap, as in her smartest evening suit. [164]

And, where Amelia often fosters the faults in those she loves, Becky
brings out the best in people. Rawdon's love for her gives him moral
definition, almost his existence. Before his marriage he is a formless
lump of unawakened allegiances and undirected energy. But Becky
awakens in him 'the admiration, the delight, the passion, the wonder, the
unbounded confidence, and frantic admiration with which, by degrees,
this big warrior got to regard the little Rebecca,' and these faculties give
him direction and meaning, and inspire him to exert himself:

> When she sang, every note thrilled in his dull soul, and tingled
> through his huge frame. When she spoke, he brought all the force
> of his brains to listen and wonder. If she was jocular, he used to
> revolve her jokes in his mind, and explode over them half an hour
> afterwards in the street, to the surprise of the groom in the tilbury
> by his side, or the comrade riding with him in Rotten Row. [190]

One can, of course, argue the matter to and fro. If most of the people
Becky damages are those who deserved it, and if she makes up to Amelia
in the end for her earlier malice, there are still the innocents like Briggs
and Raggles whom she ruins. And if she is able to charm and delight, those

under her spell are often the more cast down once they are disenchanted. The arguing to and fro is no doubt part of Thackeray's intention, too. He means us to debate Amelia's and Becky's relative merits, to take account of debits and credits on both sides, to avoid glib judgments. He is not only a realist who sees human beings as they are, neither wholly good not wholly evil, but a shrewd moralist who, by maintaining an ethical as well as a realistic vision, puts us through a process of sharpening our moral perception.

'Ah! Vanitas Vanitatum! Which of us is happy in this world? Which of us has his desire? or, having it, is satisfied?' Becky belongs to that theme as well as Amelia, but no more than Amelia. When the saintly Lady Steyne says Becky sings like an angel, we hear, 'Now there are angels of two kinds, and both sorts, it is said, are charming in their way' [620]. As agents of good and evil, there is little to choose between them.

Some of his critics have found fault with Thackeray because he seems to say one thing about a character, while they discover for themselves other and contradictory things. But what they discover is only what Thackeray has shown them, and shown intentionally. If they find a character who is called an angel on one page behaving very much like a fallible or vicious human being on another, it is because Thackeray saw the aspiration to be a saint, like the aspiration to be a lord, as a very human characteristic. Certain qualities in certain characters have for him a sanctity which he is concerned to acknowledge. They mean well and, after all, this is preferable to meaning ill. But in a fallen world, as he constantly shows, tenderness is often misdirected and can become stifling, and good itself can be perverted to the performance of evil.

'I'm killed by the very virtue of that proud woman'; 'I should be better, I think, if she were not so perfect'; 'With the best intentions in the world, what a slave life's it is that he has made for me!' So speak a husband, a daughter, and a son of some of Thackeray's saints. In his novels those who are well-meaning cast a blight on those they mean well by, and the goodness of the parents is inexorably visited on the children. No wonder that in *The Rose and the Ring* (which, being a fairy tale, is the only one of Thackeray's stories that has a really happy ending) the Fairy Blackstick decides at the christenings of the hero and heroine, 'My poor child, the best thing I can send you is a little *misfortune*' [x, 326] – and the misfortune which is to be so good for them consists in their losing their parents in infancy, and being battered about in a selfish and loveless world until they have become good enough for each other!

HENRY ESMOND

I have saved Henry Esmond, among Thackeray's 'good' characters, for the last, because he seems to me to be a special case. Thackeray's qualifications about his goodness are expressed not so much in terms of his effect on others, as in terms of his own inner perception and motivation; and to discover these involves a certain amount of detective work, and some scrutiny of Thackeray's use of the limited point of view. The other saints tend to be mainly passive beings, more characteristic in their suffering and their tears and their deaths than in their doing: and when they do take the initiative they are likely to suppress a letter, like Helen, or lead their friends into financial disaster, like Colonel Newcome. It is easier to see the limitations of such goodness. But Henry Esmond is both active, and noble in his action. Where then is the qualification? It would seem that here at last we have a good man. And though critics have frequently found him dull, and somewhat sententious, they have seldom thought him anything but the '*noble cœur*' of Father Holt's description.[4] Attention has in fact been focussed on the relative merits of Esmond's women: Beatrix had her day when the novel was read as a historical romance,[5] and Rachel, who shocked some contemporary readers, has since Tilford's re-examination[6] most fascinated modern ones. But the moral claims of Esmond himself have usually been taken for granted. Thackeray after all called him 'a handsome likeness' of himself [Letters II 815].

But we know enough of Thackeray to realize that an element of the

4 An exception is William H. Marshall, in his article 'Dramatic Irony in *Henry Esmond*' *Revue des langues vivantes* XXVII (1961) 35–42, where he points out how strong is the motive of self-justification in Esmond's account of himself.
5 See Ray *Thackeray: The Age of Wisdom, 1847–1863* (London 1958) 190
6 See 'The "Unsavoury Plot" of *Henry Esmond*' *Nineteenth-Century Fiction* VI (1951) and 'The Love Theme of *Henry Esmond*' *PMLA* LXVII (1952)

self-portrait, even a 'handsome' one, is no guarantee of extraordinary goodness. And what emerges from an examination of Esmond is that for Thackeray there *is* no extraordinary goodness, if the motive as well as the effect is taken into account. Like Pendennis, and Clive and Ethel, and Kew, and all of Thackeray's prodigals, a human being can only do his best, without much hope of outstanding merit, in a world whose claims are not reducible to simple moral alternatives.

The point of view is of major importance in *Henry Esmond*, because it is the main vehicle of Thackeray's irony. The events of the narrative show the protagonist to be a noble character, but the fact that they are narrated by Henry himself introduces an ambiguity, just as the same situation does, say, in *Pamela*. But the point of view in Thackeray's novel is more complicated than in Richardson's, for Esmond recounts his life in the third person – that is, he tells the story without appearing to do so. His own motives for this procedure would no doubt be conscientious enough, had he formulated them: he might be trying to distance himself from the experience in order to be less biassed in his reporting; or he might use the third person from motives of modesty, to avoid the appearance of boasting. But to boast without the appearance of boasting is perhaps more vain than the unmuffled blowing of one's own trumpet; and as the attempt to attain the truth by distancing can be more delusive than a frankly subjective account, so such modesty is closely related to a deep self-centredness.

The reader should not allow himself to be put off his guard by that third person, or to suspend his usual practice of weighing a statement according to who makes it. For it makes a considerable difference that we are hearing Esmond's story from Esmond himself. His account is very definitely biassed in his own favour, both in the information that he gives and, even more, in the information that he withholds.

A crucial question in our moral assessment of Henry is 'did he know Rachel was in love with him?' If he does not know, comparatively little blame can attach to him. But a man of honour does not remain in a household where he knows his presence is destroying a marriage, or make a woman the confidante of his passion for her daughter if he is aware that she loves him herself. The older Esmond evidently learned from her stealing of the gold sleeve button that Rachel had been in love with him at least since immediately after her husband's death; but on the key issue of the extent of his younger self's knowledge, Esmond is silent. He does however manage to suggest his innocence by omitting to record his inner thoughts at certain times.

There are constant hints, and even direct statements made by other characters, of the love between Harry and Rachel. Both Mohun and the dowager Isabel suggest that he is having an affair with 'the pretty Puritan' [145, 182]. 'Mother's in love with you, – yes, I think mother's in love with you,' says Frank [224]; 'You and mamma are fit for each other. You might be Darby and Joan,' says Beatrix [341]; and so on. It is noticeable that Esmond very seldom shows his own reaction to these suggestions, either in his immediate reply or in his commentary. He apparently chooses not to understand them, or not to take them seriously.

It becomes necessary to postulate that Harry maintains a sort of wilful ignorance about the question, or some intermediary state where he can have the advantage of both the blamelessness of ignorance and the satisfaction of knowledge. In the crucial scene of Harry's reunion with Rachel at Walcote, for instance, she is almost explicit about the sexual nature of her love for him: 'I would love you still – yes, there is no sin in such a love as mine now; and my dear lord in heaven may see my heart; and knows the tears that have washed my sin away' [215]; but she is not *quite* explicit, and this leaves just a possibility for Harry not to know. Certainly his answer, 'I think the angels are not all in heaven,' is singularly inept for a man who has just heard a confession of adulterous love.

The novel is of course mainly about Esmond's emotional and domestic life, of which his military and political activities are extensions rather than interruptions. It is worth examining in some detail his part in the two main emotional situations of the book, which take the shape of two, interlocking, triangle relationships. In the first Harry is one of the two men in the affections of a lady, and in the second he is himself the apex of the triangle, while mother and daughter are rivals for his love.

The first is a courtly love situation: the lord of the castle, or 'Castlewood,' is Harry's beloved patron, and Harry is the lady's faithful worshipper and 'knight,' who longs for a dragon to slay so that he might prove his devotion: 'it pleased him to think that his lady had called him "her knight," and often and often he recalled this to his mind, and prayed that he might be her true knight, too' [105]. All the usual tensions of conflicting loves and loyalties are in operation in this situation, with the added irony that the 'knight' seems ignorant of his role as lover. It seems that the narrating Esmond, too, is not aware of the full significance of the situation, for his account of what happens in the marriage is heavily biassed.

He describes the deterioration of the marriage with an authority which his limited knowledge does not warrant; and according to his analysis the main fault lies with the husband. What happens by his account is that Francis, Lord Castlewood, first shows his moral weakness to his adoring wife when he deserts her at the time of the smallpox, and that he ceases to love her when she loses her beauty. Then he further betrays her by taking a mistress. So, as he ceases to love Rachel, she finds how little worthy he was to be loved himself. Once a woman has found out her idol's feet of clay, 'what follows?' asks Esmond, and confidently answers his own question: 'They live together, and they dine together, and they say "my dear" and "my love" as heretofore; but the man is himself, and the woman herself: that dream of love is over, as everything else is over in life' [75]. Esmond speaks with the detachment of a mere observer of the situation, when in all probability he is the cause of it. Similarly, when Harry returns from Cambridge to find a 'secret care' preying upon his mistress, he finds no difficulty in diagnosing her sorrow – 'his affection leading him *easily* to penetrate the hypocrisy under which Lady Castlewood generally chose to go disguised' [119]. '*No doubt*,' he says, the sorrow is the loss of her husband's love [115].[7] The reader, however, can divine that it is more likely the lack of Harry's. There is much that is penetrating about his analysis of the situation; but he still does not tell us the whole truth.

If we consider the situation from the husband's point of view, it emerges that it is he who has lost his wife's love, not she who has lost his; and we can infer that the reason is that Rachel has transferred her adoration to Harry. As we have seen, Castlewood has some cause to feel that it is his wife who is to blame. There are several hints that, after that complex

7 The italics are mine.

incident of the smallpox, when she betrayed to herself if not to others her love for Harry, Rachel actually denies her husband sexually. He constantly talks of her coldness, and in his cups he contrasts her previous warmth of love with what she has become: 'hands off, highty-tighty, high and mighty, an empress couldn't be grander' [104]. If he takes a mistress, he might have some excuse: 'Her coldness blights my whole life, and sends me to the punch-bowl, or driving about the country' [128], he justifies himself. And his assertions are to some extent dramatically confirmed by Rachel's bahaviour to him, for she frequently rejects his demonstrations of affection. When she announces her decision to spend her legacy on sending Harry to Cambridge, her husband, after a moment of sulkiness, bursts out impulsively, '"By G–d, Rachel, you're a good woman!" says my lord, seizing my lady's hand, at which she blushed very much, and shrank back, putting her children before her' [103]. When Francis abuses Rachel as a jilt, Esmond says piously, 'so a man dashes a fine vase down and despises it for being broken' [129]. His narration, then, always suggests that it was the husband who deserted the wife; but we have evidence that it was just as likely the wife who deserted the husband.

In this courtly love triangle the lady is the most aware of what is going on, and has most to conceal. Even the husband seems to know more of Rachel's feelings for Harry than Harry, or even the mature Esmond, does himself. Harry would convince us that Rachel 'never thought of or suspected the admiration of her little pigmy adorer' [72]; but Castlewood knows better than this: 'Why, when you was but a boy of fifteen I could hear you two together talking your poetry and your books till I was in such a rage that I was fit to strangle you' [153]. And he has his momentary deep suspicions of Harry, even when he is on a false scent in suspecting Mohun: the young man tries to exonerate Rachel by saying she was thinking of him, not of Mohun, when she fainted at the news of 'Harry's' accident.

'But my lord, *my* name is Harry,' cried out Esmond, burning red. 'You told my lady, "Harry was killed!"'

'Damnation! shall I fight you too?' shouts my lord, in a fury. 'Are you, you little serpent, warmed by my fire, going to sting – *you?* –

No, my boy, you're an honest boy; you're a good boy.' (And here he broke from rage into tears even more cruel to see.) [156]

'Honest, honest Iago' comes momentarily to mind.

Harry himself tells us singularly little of *his* reactions when his patron voices such a suspicion, although his blushes show his consciousness; and it must surely be a subject that would be much in his thoughts. Does the boy miss the constant hints about Rachel's love for him as completely as his silence suggests? Is even the mature Esmond, who has for years been married to Rachel, ignorant of the implications of the blushes and suggestive words and gestures which he reports? It seems more likely that the boy Harry knows a good deal more than his older self is prepared to admit; that he is closer to being the 'little serpent' than at first appears; and that Esmond is omitting to tell us a good many things which he knows, or at least suspects, well enough, but which might make his young self appear in a discreditable light.

The next triangle situation is still more complex, when we consider the part the hero plays in it. The situation appears to be that he is hopelessly pursuing a disdainful Beatrix, while confiding in her mother and relying on a maternal sympathy from her. But, as we know from the last sentence of the book, where he mentions the gold button, the mature Esmond at least must be fully aware of Rachel's sexual love for him at this time. And he is again reticent about this awareness.

At one point it does sound as though he admits to a full knowledge of the suffering he is causing Rachel:

This passion [for Beatrix] did not escape – how should it? – the clear eyes of Esmond's mistress: he told her all; what will a man not do when frantic with love? To what baseness will he not demean himself? What pangs will he not make others suffer, so that he may ease his selfish heart of a part of its own pain? Day after day he would seek his dear mistress, pour insane hopes, supplications, rhapsodies, raptures, into her ear. [249]

This sounds as though he knows the full extent of the suffering which he is causing Rachel; and, with some part of him, indeed he must do. But he immediately annuls what looked like an admission by suggesting that 'compassion' is the only pang he is causing her. And he is all too ready to believe her when she re-asserts the purely maternal nature of her love for him:

> 'I am your mother, you are my son, and I love you always,' she said, holding her hands over him; and he went away comforted and humbled in mind, as he thought of that amazing and constant love and tenderness with which this sweet lady ever blessed and pursued him. [250]

Only towards the end of the book, where Harry the protagonist and Esmond the narrator begin to merge into a single consciousness, does he seem ready to admit a knowledge of her sexual jealousy: after his tête-à-tête with Beatrix, 'Esmond's mistress showed no signs of jealousy when he returned to the room where she was. She had schooled herself so as to look quite inscrutably, when she had a mind' [398].

Beatrix's part in the triangle is also more complex than a single reading makes apparent. For Esmond again appears greatly to underestimate his place in her feelings. As he says that Rachel cared little for the worship of her 'pigmy adorer,' when she was just betraying an adulterous love for him, so he says deprecatingly of his place in Beatrix's estimation:

> Beatrix thought no more of him than of the lackey that followed her chair. His complaints did not touch her in the least; his raptures rather fatigued her; she cared for his verses no more than for Dan Chaucer's, who's dead these ever so many hundred years; she did not hate him; she rather despised him, and just suffered him. [249]

But we should be as wary in one case as the other of taking Esmond's words at face value. Beatrix is by no means as unattainable as he likes to suggest. Harry makes himself unacceptable by wooing her in the guise of 'the knight of the Woeful Countenance,' when what she wants is an impetuous lover who will sweep her off her feet. In her long self-examination, at Harry's last abject proposal, she says that he was 'ever too much of a slave to win my heart' [397], but that had she found the man she loved she would have followed him in rags. It is not for his poverty or his bar-sinister that she rejects him, but for his lack of resolution.

Esmond seems to have a knack of proposing in such a way as to determine a refusal. Even Rachel, who confesses to loving him, meets his first proposal that she should go away with him to Virginia with a sad refusal: 'You never loved me, dear Henry–no, you do not now' [215]. The manner of his proposals evidently gives Beatrix the same conviction. And perhaps in being refused Harry feels the same mixture of satisfaction and chagrin that Pen experienced after his half-hearted proposal to Laura: 'Was he pleased, or was he angry at its termination? He had asked her, and a secret triumph filled his heart to think that he was still free. She had refused him, but did she not love him?' [P 348].

Beatrix often gives Harry opportunities to win her. In the scene where Rachel leaves the two alone so that Beatrix can break the news of her engagement to the Duke of Hamilton, Beatrix leads instead to the subject of Harry's feelings for her. But he moons in his usual manner about his despair, and she tries to provoke him into being more demonstrative and determined: 'I feel as a sister to you,' she tells him:

> 'Isn't that enough, sir?' And she put her face quite close to his – who knows with what intention?
> 'It's too much,' says Esmond, turning away. [358]

Esmond may be telling us of the hopelessness of his love; but the image here is one of the woman who, within the bounds of propriety, is wooing the man, while the man is rejecting her. That he never really wanted her to accept him is suggested by his relief when he knows of her engagement.

> 'I have been hankering after the grapes on the wall,' says he, 'and lost my temper because they were beyond my reach; was there any wonder? They're gone now, and another has them – a taller man than your humble servant has won them.' And the colonel made his cousin a low bow.
> 'A taller man, cousin Esmond!' says she. 'A man of spirit would have scaled the wall, sir, and seized them! A man of courage would have fought for 'em, not gaped for 'em.' [362]

Such a hint suggests that, even at this stage, if Harry had been really resolute he could have made her break off her engagement: he could have become the man she would follow in rags. But his reply shows not only lack of resolution, but a good deal of pique as well: 'A duke has but to gape and they drop into his mouth.' Beatrix at this can only reply, with justifiable exasperation, 'Yes, sir ... a duke *is* a taller man than you.'

When Harry brings her news of the Duke's death in a duel, she momentarily believes – and perhaps even hopes – that it was Harry who killed him (she afterwards owns, 'I was frightened to find I was glad of his death' [397]). Harry corrects her, telling her sententiously, 'he died by the bloody sword which already had drank your own father's blood' [385]. History is repeating itself in more than just the fact of Mohun's being the slayer both times. Here the daughter is guiltily glad of her fiancé's death, as the mother had been guiltily glad of her husband's; and we can infer that for both it is wishful thinking when they believe that Harry, as their lover, had killed his rival. There are even parallels in the imagery and the gestures of the two women:

> The Lady Castlewood went back from him, putting back her hood, and leaning against the great stanchioned door which the gaoler had just closed upon them. Her face was ghastly white, as Esmond saw it, looking from the hood ...
> 'And this, Mr. Esmond,' she said, 'is where I see you; and 'tis to this you have brought me!' [166]

That is Rachel in the gaol, when she casts off Harry for what she chose to think was his responsibility for the death of her husband, but steals his sleeve button to wear over her heart. The parallel when Harry encounters Beatrix after the duke's death suggests a similar ambivalence:

> 'The duke is not alive, Beatrix,' said Esmond.
> She looked at her cousin wildly, and fell back to the wall as though shot in the breast: – 'And you come here, and – and – you killed him?' [385]

Beatrix, the cynosure of all eyes, the sun that eclipses all other luminaries, etcetera, can be seen as a lonely and rejected woman. If Harry puts Rachel to the torture by making her watch him with Beatrix, so he torments Beatrix by making her watch him with her mother. Neither loves Beatrix, it seems, as much as she loves them. 'Is it mamma your honour wants, and that I should have the happiness of calling you papa?' she asks Harry banteringly [357]; but the tone is only half playful, and leaves the impression that the spectacle of the absorption of these two in one another gives her more pain than she is prepared to admit. She foresees their marriage long before either of them, and by her own confession (she is franker than Rachel) she is not immune from jealousy [398]:

> 'She loves you, sir, a great deal too much; and I hate you for it. I would have had her all to myself; but she wouldn't. In my childhood, it was my father she loved ... And then, it was Frank; and now, it is Heaven and the clergyman. How I would have loved her! From a child I used to be in a rage that she loved anybody but me; but she loved you all better – all, I know she did.' [356]

And when she is banished from the prince's presence by a conspiracy between her brother, her mother, and Harry, she has the last word, and it is not calculated to make us think the better of the 'saintly' Rachel: 'I always said I was alone; you never loved me, never – and were jealous of me from the time I sat on my father's knee. Let me go away, the sooner the better; I can bear to be with you no more' [435]. Far from being proud, self-sufficient, and disdainful, as Esmond seems to depict her, Beatrix, as she appears in an alternative picture, is finally a pathetic figure. She is not deficient in love, like Becky, but she cannot reconcile her love with her pride. When in *The Virginians* she dies an old woman, in her delirium she is still complaining of her mother's rejection of her, and calling on Henry to kill his royal rival [v 881].

Beatrix tells Harry, explicitly and repeatedly, that he is the only man who has touched her heart [364], that 'you might have had me' [365], even that she loves him [397]. But he continues to regard her as beyond his reach, and persists in offering the wrong price to buy her – military glory, diamonds, the restoration of the Stuart dynasty – when what she wants is to be not bought but taken. As he prefers to believe that Rachel's love for him is only maternal, so he prefers to think Beatrix is unattainable, and that she loves the world better than him. But at the same time, perhaps, he has a secret satisfaction in the half-knowledge that he could take either woman whenever he wishes. He loves to be on his knees and yet worshipped at the same time.

There is a similar ambivalence in his behaviour with the family title. There is no doubt that his action in forgoing the title, to which he has a just and legal claim, in gratitude to the family that befriended him, is generous and heroic. And yet how he enjoys the situation! In a moment of genuine self-examination, he admits that he is 'perhaps secretly vain of the sacrifice he had made, and to think that he, Esmond, was really the chief of his house, and only prevented by his own magnanimity from advancing his claim' [184–5].

As he enjoys underestimating his place in the feelings of women, while having a secret knowledge of his own importance, so he enjoys being thought a bastard in society, while having a secret knowledge that he is legitimately head of the family. He likes to be on his knees before Beatrix, with a knowledge that he is the stronger; and he likes to be patronized by Frank, knowing that the right to patronize is really his.

> What Harry admired and submitted to in the pretty lad, his kinsman, was (for why should he resist it?) the calmness of patronage which my young lord assumed, as if to command was his undoubted right, and all the world (below his degree) ought to bow down to Viscount Castlewood. [225]

When this viscount finds that he actually owes his title to his cousin, 'the fond boy with oaths and protestations, laughter and incoherent outbreaks of passionate emotion ... wanted to kneel down to him, and kissed his hand' [411]; that Esmond somewhat enjoys this reversal is evident later in the scene when he adroitly turns the conversation in a manner that will put Frank on his knees to him again.

The subtle masochism which Harry shows in his emotional life has its parallel in his social attitude, which is that of the inverted snob. In his way, he is a refined Bounderby, parading his menial origin while enjoying his actual power. His encounter with Swift has been taken as just another instance of Thackeray's animus against the Dean, who of course appears in no very gracious light. But it is characteristic of Esmond, too, that he should first lead Swift to believe he is a menial, and a 'poor broken-down soldier' (as he has before called himself pigmy adorer, lackey, and bastard), and then humiliate him with his mistake when they are both guests at the table of General Webb, with Esmond taking the precedence [378–9].

This is part of a regular pattern of reversals in Harry's relations with the various people he encounters. It seems that he, and other characters too, can never love but where they adore, and never serve but where they are devoted. But part of that steady infiltration of knowledge and 'strange series of compromises' that is England's history and Harry's too [372],[8] involves the realization that certain figures whom he had taken to be superhuman are merely human after all;[9] at the end the novel's personnel consists largely of an array of fallen idols.

The first of Harry's idols is Father Holt, the apparently omnipotent and omniscient Jesuit priest. He leaves Harry before the boy is quite confirmed in his faith, and so loses him to the succeeding influence of Rachel; and when Harry meets him years later in Flanders, he is able to see through the priest's pose of infallibility.

> A foible of Mr. Holt's, who did know more about books and men than, perhaps, almost any person Esmond had ever met, was omniscience; thus in every point he here professed to know, he was nearly right, but not quite ... Esmond did not think fit to correct his old master in these trifling blunders, but they served to give him a knowledge of the other's character, and he smiled to think that this was his oracle of early days; only now no longer infallible or divine. [268]

This divinity is to be further debased; not only is he not omniscient, he is so far from being omnipotent that eventually he shows as virtually impotent, a man whose every enterprise must end in failure. This is the

8 George J. Worth, in 'The Unity of *Henry Esmond*,' reads the novel as a *bildungsroman* and traces the education of the hero, who learns, in politics and religion as well as in love, to reject the glamorous alternative for the stable one. *Nineteenth-Century Fiction* xv (1961) 345–53.

9 Henri-A. Talon who, in 'Time and Memory in Thackeray's *Henry Esmond*,' also describes Esmond's growth to maturity and wisdom, points out how his progress enables him to take stock of some figures he had once thought divine. *Review of English Studies* XIII (1962) 147–56

final vision of him as he is forced to cheer for the victory of his opponents at the succession of the Hanovarians:

> The poor fellow had forgot to huzzah or to take his hat off, until his neighbours in the crowd remarked his want of loyalty, and cursed him for a Jesuit in disguise, when he ruefully uncovered and began to cheer. Sure he was the most unlucky of men: he never played a game but he lost it; or engaged in a conspiracy but 'twas certain to end in defeat. [461]

Rachel is Harry's next divinity: 'she had come upon him as a *Dea certe*' [17], we are told of their first meeting; and when Harry kneels to her the child Beatrix says, aptly enough, 'He is saying his prayers to mamma' [18]. Rachel too falls from her pedestal, though she never falls as low as Father Holt. After the reunion at Walcote, Harry tells us how the goddess of his youth was 'goddess now no more, for he knew of her weaknesses ... but more fondly cherished as woman perhaps than ever she had been adored as divinity' [210].

Rachel herself has a human idol who falls in her estimation as others do in Harry's. Her husband is 'first and foremost, Jove and supreme ruler' [72]. It is still early in the novel when she recognizes his feet of clay: 'Then, perhaps, the pair reached that other stage which is not uncommon in married life, when the woman perceives that the god of the honeymoon is a god no more; only a mortal like the rest of us – and so she looks into her heart, and lo! *vacuae sedes et inania arcana*' [75]. But Rachel is a woman who can love only where she worships, and when her husband topples from his pedestal there is no question of her cherishing *him* more fondly as a man; instead she finds another idol, Harry, to put in his place.

In spite of what Harry says of his increased love for Rachel as a woman, it seems that he too must worship where he loves; for once he has found Rachel to be no more than human he transfers his adoration to Beatrix; and the mother, like the moon, fades at the advent of Beatrix's sun [241]. Harry is by no means blind to Beatrix's moral failings. His love for her is strongly sensual, but it is also worship, as in this definitive scene: 'Having finished her march, she put out her foot for her slipper. The colonel knelt down: "If you will be Pope I will turn Papist," says he; and her holiness gave him gracious leave to kiss the little stockinged foot before he put the slipper on' [336]. His deification of Beatrix was sensual, and she loses her beauty and her divinity in his eyes simultaneously: 'The roses had shuddered out of her cheeks; her eyes were glaring; she looked quite old ... As he looked at her, he wondered that he could ever have loved her' [459].

An idol for many of the characters in the book is the Stuart Pretender whose cause they support. Esmond himself is early disillusioned about royalty, and converted from his belief in divine right. But we see in more detail the process of the other Jacobites' disillusion. The women, particularly, are ready to worship the hereditary heir to the throne, and make a ritual of their preparations for his arrival: ''Twas then Beatrix knelt down and kissed the linen sheets. As for her mother, Lady Castlewood made a curtsy at the door, as she would have to the altar on entering a church, and owned that she considered the chamber in a manner sacred' [409]. Progressively his worshippers find out the human failings of their deity. Frank, aggrieved at the prince's undignified behaviour, admits 'he is not like a king' [411]. The prince is early subject to Esmond's irony:

> The heir of one of the greatest names, of the greatest kingdoms, and of the greatest misfortunes in Europe, was often content to lay the dignity of his birth and grief at the wooden shoes of a French chambermaid, and to repent afterwards (for he was very devout) in ashes taken from the dustpan. 'Tis for mortals such as these that nations suffer, that parties struggle, that warriors fight and bleed. [418]

And Esmond also tells us of Rachel's loss of faith: 'how deep her mortification was at finding the hero whom she had chosen to worship all her life (and whose restoration had formed almost the most sacred part of her prayers), no more than a man, and not a good one' [420].

Among all these toppling idols there is only one, Esmond himself, who retains his pedestal. Often enough he even usurps the pedestals of others as they fall. When Rachel ceases to idolize her husband, and finds '*vacuae sedes*,' Harry is set up in the empty shrine; and later, when she knows of his sacrifice of the title, she kneels at his feet: '" Don't raise me," she said, in a wild way, to Esmond, who would have lifted her. "Let me kneel – let me kneel, and – and – worship you"' [332].[10] As surely as the other idols fall, Harry rises, in the estimation both of the worshippers and of the idols themselves. Francis is aware of Harry's superior moral claim to his position: 'By George, Harry! you ought to be the head of the house ... You had been better Lord Castlewood than a lazy sot like me' [155]. When young Frank tells Harry of his discovery that the prince 'is not like a king,' he simultaneously decides 'somehow, Harry, I fancy you are like a king' [411]. Harry has already taken Father Holt's measure, and found him to be no more than human, when Holt discovers Harry's true worth, and breaks out into expressions of admiration and regret that such a *'noble cœur'* should be lost to the Jesuit cause [272]. After Harry repudiates the prince, breaks his sword, and ends the Esmonds' allegiance to the Stuart cause, the prince himself is almost ready to acknowledge the inversion of their roles as idol and worshipper:

> 'Thus to lose a crown,' says the young prince, starting up, and speaking
> French in his eager way; 'to lose the loveliest woman in the world;
> to lose the loyalty of such hearts as yours, is not this, my lords, enough
> of humiliation? – Marquis, if I go on my knees will you pardon me?'
> [458]

If all the other mortals who have been raised to godhead are thrown down, why is the man who tells the story the only one to be spared? Is Thackeray telling us that Esmond's kind of goodness, and his alone, is worthy to be worshipped? Or has this mortal deity been saved for dramatic irony to depose?

There are some external references for a view of Esmond quite different from that suggested by the surface events of his account. The preface is written by his daughter, another woman who idolizes him, but even she admits that he was unforgiving, and that his reputation in Virginia was that 'he liked to be first in his company' [10]. But it is from Beatrix that we have the most penetrating analysis. 'You are a hypocrite,

10 John W. Dodds, quoting this passage, also points out Esmond's evident enjoyment of such demonstrations. *Thackeray: A Critical Portrait* (London 1941) 168

too, Henry, with your brave airs and your glum face,' she tells him [356]. She can see through his pose of grave self-deprecation: 'Of all the proud wretches in the world Mr. Esmond is the proudest, let me tell him that'; and, still more shrewdly, she divines his secret longing, which he realizes in his memoirs, to appear in the role of a divinity: 'I won't worship you and you'll never be happy except with a woman who will' [363].

If we take Esmond's memoirs at face value, we have a picture of a man who may be grave and melancholy, but who is possessed of the virtues of courtesy, honesty, courage, wisdom, love, and humility. He renounces a title from pure generosity; and though he contributes to the failure of a marriage, and causes some suffering to a woman who loves him by confiding in her while he woos her daughter, he does these things unwittingly. He hopelessly loves an unworthy woman, but finally learns to reject her and marry the elder and more worthy one. Through his life he grows to wisdom and maturity, not only in knowledge of the world, but emotionally and morally as well. There is something god-like about so much virtue and self-abnegation.

If, on the other hand, we read the novel as a sustained piece of dramatic irony, we notice not so much the god-like attributes as the wish to appear god-like. His humility is inverted pride, and his self-abnegation an elaborate glorification of self. He renounces a title because he finds more satisfaction in the debt than the ownership. He keeps two women at his feet by maintaining a pose of being at theirs, and he takes a secret pleasure in his knowledge of their adoration while pretending to be unaware of it. And, far from growing to maturity, he finally fulfils the infantile impulse to marry his mother.

My interpretation has suggested the second reading because critical emphasis has usually been the other way. But I do not mean to exclude the first: there is again that double focus which is part of the complexity of Thackeray's moral vision. As usual, Thackeray's interest turns on the psychology that is the basis of the morality: Esmond's suffering is real, even if there is part of him that enjoys it, and his actions are noble, even if he has himself a rather exaggerated sense of their nobility. Generosity *is* akin to selfishness, and humility to pride, and knowing and not knowing one's place in another's feelings is of the essence of any deep relationship.

Esmond (as he would be the first to say himself) is no hero; but he is certainly not a wicked man either, only a human being whose very goodness is necessarily tainted by a somewhat selfish enjoyment of appearing selfless. But judge every man according to his ulterior motives, and who should 'scape whipping?

4

Manners and Morals:
The Newcomes

'FIRST THE WORLD WAS MADE: THEN, AS A MATTER OF COURSE, Snobs.' This is Thackeray's version of Genesis in *The Book of Snobs*, the work which established him as virtually the world authority on the subject. Through his career that initial vision of snobbery as the human condition expands into the greater concept of the world of Vanity Fair, and is carried on through the quest for the true gentleman in *Pendennis*, to the study of respectability in all its forms in *The Newcomes*.

Acknowledged expert though he is in this field, Thackeray has not escaped criticism for his absorption with class distinctions and social pretension. Bagehot spoke with some exasperation of his endless accumulation of 'petty details to prove that tenth-rate people were ever striving to be ninth-rate people';[1] and G.M. Young's image of Thackeray is of a passenger in a railway carriage 'whose joy is darkened by one anxiety – he is not quite sure if his ticket entitles him to travel first class.'[2] And Sadleir, of course, disregarding Thackeray's disarming anticipaton of the charge in *The Book of Snobs*, denounced him as being himself a snob. But, as Thackeray himself might have told such critics, 'You must not judge hastily or vulgarly of Snobs: to do so shows that you are yourself a Snob' [BS 261].

Of course snobbery is not all that Thackeray's novels are about: they are far more than just lively studies of middle-class manners. His minutely realized social milieu is the context for individual dramas which have implications far beyond the business of mere status-seeking. But it is in this area, in his portrayal of the social universe, that much of the comedy and page-to-page vitality of his novels reside. Becky putting George Osborne in his place by offering him only one finger when he magnani-

1 'Sterne and Thackeray' *Literary Studies* (London 1891) II 144
2 'Thackeray' *Victorian Essays* (London 1962) 82

mously decides to shake her hand, on nonplussing Lady Bareacres by an apparently innocent reference to her pawned diamonds at the dinner in Gaunt House: these are scenes which make the world of Vanity Fair sparkling and memorable. And though Thackeray's chosen setting is always that World, 'wherever there is a competition and a squeeze,' the effect is not repetitive, for he manages to make every snob also an individual. 'I have,' he claims proudly, 'an eye for a Snob' [BS 261]; and indeed his ability to portray the finer shades of class distinction, to dramatize the minutiae of social one-upmanship, is what gives his world that marvellously authentic texture. Chesterton pointed out that the novel as a genre shows our increased interest in the ways in which men differ,[3] and Trilling suggests 'the novel is born in response to snobbery.'[4] Thackeray' preoccupation with class distinctions puts him right in the centre of the tradition.

And, behind all his vivid dramatization of social climbing, inside all his incarnated snobs, there is a solid structure of ideas. Thackeray is a shrewd social commentator, even if, writing in the hungry forties, he did not choose manufacturers and factory operatives for his characters.[5] Jos Sedley, the Collector of Boggley Wollah, with his curry and his shuddering 'native,' and his blustering about tiger-hunts, is an essay on what was wrong with the British Empire; and the single tableau of Lady Bareacres, waiting in her horseless carriage with her diamonds sewn into her stays, in its way can tell us as much of the state of the English aristocracy as Disraeli's somewhat painstaking analysis in *Sybil*.

'It is among the RESPECTABLE classes of this vast and happy empire that the greatest profusion of Snobs is to be found' [BS 286], Thackeray declares. And so it is the vicissitudes of middle-class existence that he chronicles. He can range above and below this world that he knows so well, with some

3 *The Victorian Age in Literature* (London 1913) 98
4 'Manners, Morals and the Novel' in *The Liberal Imagination* (New York 1950) 209
5 Ray has claimed that *The Book of Snobs*, as an analysis of Victorian society, deserves a place on the shelf beside *Culture and Anarchy* and *Past and Present*. 'Thackeray's *Book of Snobs*' *Nineteenth-Century Fiction* x (1955) 22–33

insight into the aristocracy – in *Vanity Fair* he even penetrates, in Becky's train, into the very shrine of George IV – and with glimpses into 'those mysterious haunts, which lie couched about our splendid houses like Lazarus at the threshold of Dives' [x 108]. But for the most part his lords are seen in relation not so much to each other as to the middle-class society which adulates them; and his lower orders are usually of the servant class. Most of Thackeray's characters can be imagined as living or visiting in the house of, say, Sir Brian Newcome, the banker of dubious family origin, but who has money, and an earl's daughter for a wife: Lord Steyne would be bored, no doubt, and Captain Costigan, though he would feel quite at home, would be hustled out as soon as decently possible; but neither would be extravagantly out of place there. And there would be room below or above stairs for Morgan, Briggs, Horrocks, Mrs Bonner, and the rest. It would be difficult, by contrast, to conceive of any likely pretext that would summon all Dicken's characters into any single setting; though Dickens is capable of showing the symbolic connection between Miss Havisham and a convict, between Lady Dedlock and Jo the crossing-sweeper, between Sir John Chester and the brutal Hugh, the kind of belief that he requires is of a different order from that of Thackeray, who was content to show, in realistic terms, the world as he knew it – a world in which the upper classes had very little to do with the lower, however their position might depend on them. Thackeray's characters are all gentlemen, or think themselves gentlemen; failing that, they are gentlemen's gentlemen.

The middle-class world that Thackeray chose to write about is repre-sentative enough, we understand, of the rest of the world. He suggests the same struggles and status-seeking going on upwards in the higher levels of the aristocracy and downwards among the servants. So we are shown Hannah Hicks, a landlady's maid-of-all-work, who herself has 'a young lady from the workhouse, who called Hannah, "Mrs. Hicks, mum," and who bowed as much in awe before that domestic, as Hannah did before Miss Honeyman' [N 120]. And so *ad infinitum*.

Thackeray was preoccupied with class as he saw the world around him was preoccupied with it. If a character's position on the social ladder does not always determine what he is, it is at least always relevant. Relations are constantly seen in terms of class gradations, so that even a short novel like *Lovel the Widower*, which has the old Cinderella plot of the low-born maid's marrying the master, becomes a little social history. The heroine, a governess, is courted by a literary dilettante, by a withered sprig of the nobility, by a doctor, by the butler, and by her master the sugar merchant: the worlds of art, the aristocracy, the professions, domestic service, and trade are at her feet. Within the domestic hierarchy itself, we have the maid in love with the butler who is in love with the governess who sets her cap at the master. And Lovel's mother and successive mothers-in-law represent between them the decayed aristocratic, the middle-class evangelical, and the shabby-genteel.

Whole plots are based on the progress of the characters up and down the gradations of the social ladder. Becky's career is the obvious example: the main plot interest of *Vanity Fair* is in how the illegitimate daughter of a Bohemian painter rises to frequent the houses of the great. Becky climbs the ladder, misses a step, and only just manages to find a precarious hold many rungs down. Even Amelia's story, in which the emphasis is psychological rather than social, is tied closely to her position in the world; and, in the structure of the novel, the parallels between the two heroines, or anti-heroines, are seen in terms of their relation to their source of income.

No novelist makes a man's income seem more significant than Thackeray – the amount of it, how he gets it, how he spends it, and what his own circle in society thinks of how he gets and spends it. Thackeray shows men adopting social personae, and expending all their energy in living up to them. They are always asserting themselves in terms of their status – whether it derives from their birth or their money or the number of their titled acquaintance – as though their very existence depended on it, as though it *were* their existence. A snob is '*he who meanly admires mean things*' [BS 269]: it is this inversion of values that Thackeray the social historian portrays, and Thackeray the satirist and moralist exposes. He depicts that elaborate confusion between status and function, between appearance and essence, with a show of being an impartial chronicler, often with the explicit assumption that these things are as they must and should be. But his irony is constantly implying the essential values that society has debased, and showing up the sham that has come to be accepted as the reality.

The social ladder is the context and partly the subject of Thackeray's novels. At the top there is still the aristocracy of hereditary rank, represented by powerful figures like Lord Crabs, Lord Steyne, Lady Rockminster, Lady Kew, the Baroness Bernstein, and Lord Ringwood. They are powerfully conceived, at least, and even pervasively influential in themselves – there is a touch of the devil, or the fairy, or the witch about many of them. But there is also the sense that their power has been curtailed. They are noticeably old, survivals from a world which does not quite exist any longer; and though they are usually sure-footed and resourceful, they are momentarily uncertain of themselves. Lady Kew does not ultimately succeed in ruling Ethel Newcome; Lord Ringwood at last fails to be as despotic as he means to be. The younger generation usually inherit their weaknesses without their strengths. Young Lord Kew is the most sympathetic of them; but there is nothing particularly commanding about him; and he virtually abdicates from the aristocracy by adopting his mother's bourgeois evangelical morality. Lord Steyne's son is insane, and hereditary madness threatens his grandchildren. Foolish young lisping lords like Cinquebars in *A Shabby-Genteel Story*, completely despicable though universally fawned upon, recur in the novels as degenerate figures:

A sallow, blear-eyed, rickety, undersized creature, tottering upon a pair of high-heeled lacquered boots, and supporting himself upon an immense gold-knobbed cane, entered the room with his hat on one side and a jaunty air ... The little man had no beard to his chin, appeared about twenty years of age, and might weigh, stick and all, some seven stone. [III 364]

The same figure returns as the alcoholic Captain Baker of *Lovel the Widower* at the end of Thackeray's career; the type is perhaps best realized in Lord Farintosh, the nobleman whom Ethel almost marries in *The Newcomes*, and who is mentally if not physically deficient.

Below the aristocracy in the hierarchy of birth are the baronets, and the

F

country gentry like the Crawleys. Often enough they are degenerate too, as witness the compulsive gambler Sir Francis Clavering in *Pendennis*, and the elder Sir Pitt, who is coarse, miserly, malicious, and litigious to the extent of burdening his estate with lawyers' fees and damages. But they are wily and adaptable as a class, and many of them are able to change from their eighteenth-century or Regency prodigality and independence of moral judgment to a kind of compromise with nineteenth-century evangelicalism. In other words, they become niggardly hypocrites, like Pitt Crawley the younger, Sir Miles Warrington in *The Virginians*, or Sir John Ringwood in *Philip*. Such men are models for Hobson Newcome, the parvenu banker, in his endeavour to buy himself into country-gentleman-hood.

Birth and money are a powerful combination, but where birth is lacking, money alone can be of considerable effect, and there is another whole system of gradations based on income. So we have the Sedley-Osborne history in *Vanity Fair*, and its effect on the union of the younger genera-tion, Amelia and George. The old stockbroker Sedley, who had sponsored the new financier Osborne and stood godfather to his son, goes bankrupt on the return of Napoleon. Osborne turns against him, and years later moralizes on the difference between them to his grandson:

> 'You see ... what comes of merit and industry, and judicious specula-tions, and that. Look at me and my banker's account. Look at your poor grandfather Sedley, and his failure. And yet he was a better man than I was, this day twenty years – a better man I should say by ten thousand pound.' [VF 773]

For Osborne, value and price are synonymous terms.

Of course it makes a difference, even within the business and trading classes, *how* you make your money. Dobbin, the grocer's son, in a school populated by the sons of wholesalers, is sneered at and called 'Figs' because his father is in the retail trade. Banking is perhaps as respectable a way of making money as any, and the Newcomes are a 'most respectable family.' But it is questionable whether making money as such is respect-able at all. The doctrine that money is the greatest good is fervently practised in Society, but not preached. The banking Newcomes know enough to leave their business identities behind them in the City each night, and merely to enjoy the returns of their industry without mentioning them in their social gatherings. In boasting of his wealth old Osborne brands himself as *nouveau riche*, and his son, with the same instincts as the Newcomes, is disgusted at the social solecism:

'Curse the whole pack of money-grubbing vulgarians! I fall asleep at their great heavy dinners. I feel ashamed in my father's great stupid parties. I've been accustomed to live with gentlemen, and men of the world and fashion, Emmy, not with a parcel of turtle-fed tradesmen.' [VF 246]

But George is of course ready enough to spend the money which he does not like to hear mentioned.

The relationship between the hereditary members of Society and those who try to buy themselves into it is an uneasy one, particularly in the generation of the elder Osborne. 'I am a plain British merchant, I am,' he finds it necessary to assert, claiming a kind of superior reality for his status over that of the nobility:

'[I] could buy the beggarly hounds over and over. Lords, indeed! ... Why, I'll lay my life I've got a better glass of wine, and pay a better figure for it, and can show a handsomer service of silver, and can lay a better dinner on my mahogany, than ever they see on theirs – the cringing, sneaking, stuck-up fools.' [VF 538]

Nevertheless, he toadies shamelessly to them, and even takes a kind of satisfaction in being patronized by his own son and grandson. George Osborne is on easier terms with Society, and considers himself a gentleman. Society does not, however, grant him this status without qualification, and a penniless ne'er-do-well of a baronet's son like Rawdon Crawley still considers him an upstart, and wins his money from him at billiards almost as a favour.

'I've no pride about *me*, Pen,' says Major Pendennis in confidence to his nephew, on the subject of marriage. 'I like a man of birth certainly, but dammy, I like a brewery which brings in a man fourteen thousand a year' [P 508]. The mercenary marriage motive is a favourite subject of Thackeray, and it forms a major theme in *The Newcomes*. 'A comfortable thing it is to think that birth can be bought for money,' reflects the writer of the *Book of Snobs*, as he relates how Lady Blanche Stiffneck is made to stoop to marriage with the banker's son, young Pump and Aldgate. 'I like to see those two humbugs which, dividing, as they do, the social empire of this kingdom between them, hate each other naturally – making truce and uniting – for the sordid interests of either' [BS 297]. The blood-money marriages depicted in the novels are far from idyllic. The amiable Lady Clavering, who pronounces Hackney 'Ackney' but has many lakhs of rupees to her credit, lives a miserable life with an aristocratic wastrel of a husband who gambles away her fortune; Lady Anne Newcome, an earl's daughter who married a banker out of 'duty' to her family, calmly disparages the *ton* of her brother-in-law, her son, and her husband when she is speaking to her daughter: '*Que voulez-vous*, my love? The Newcomes are honourable: the Newcomes are wealthy: but distinguished; no. I never deluded myself with that notion when I married your poor dear papa' [N 203]. The children of such marriages, we are told, are likely to be lacking in love for their parents. Nevertheless, there can be a certain vitality in them, as witness the lively Foker in *Pendennis*, whose maternal and paternal grandfathers were respectively an earl and a brewer.

It is perhaps these hybrids who are to inherit the earth. At the ends of the novels it often looks as though the Fokers, the Kews, the Barnes and Ethel Newcomes, and the young de Floracs are to be the ones who will effectively pull the strings of society. But they usually suffer from the ambiguity of their claim to power. They lack both the habit of unscrupulous dominance of their aristocratic forebears and the bourgeois confidence of their moneyed ones. They pay some price in emotional stability for the success of this aspect of the Victorian compromise.

Failing both birth and money, a man's chances of penetrating into Society are still not quite hopeless. In fact the man with a small income and the right kind of self-confidence and push can do better than someone like Osborne. Major Pendennis, a half-pay officer whose father was an apothecary, manages to move in the very best society on the strength of an annuity, his military campaigns in India, a talent for genealogy, and a good deal of tact and diplomacy. With only as much confidence as he derives from being the second son of an impoverished baronet, Rawdon Crawley lives off the fat of the land when he is among 'those who are comfortably and thoroughly in debt,' for 'long custom, a manly appearance, faultless boots and clothes, and a happy fierceness of manner, will often help a man as much as a great balance at the banker's' [VF 268]. At a more securely respectable level, the Twysdens in *Philip*, by dint of turning dresses, hiring servants by the evening, starving themselves when there is no company, and swearing they pay a higher figure for their wine than they do, manage to preserve the illusion that their income is twice what it is, and to lure certain members of the nobility to attend their dinners at least once. These are the people who have learned the lesson of *The Newcomes*, that 'to push on in the crowd, every male or female struggler must use his shoulders' [95].

If you fail in your endeavour to go up in the world, there is at least some consolation in coming down in it. The family that has been expelled from the heaven of gentility has a certain bad eminence in the world of the shabby-genteel, and those who have seen better days sometimes manage to convince themselves that it is 'better to reign in hell than serve in heaven.' Mrs Baynes in *Philip* takes a certain satisfaction in competing with her fellow inmates in the seedy boarding house in Paris on the basis not of her present position but of her past glory. Miss Honeyman, the Brighton land*lady*, finds that 'the true pleasure of life is to live with your inferiors' – because there you can be 'the queen of your coterie.'

> If I cannot be first in Piccadilly, let me try Hatton Garden, and see whether I cannot lead the *ton* there. If I cannot take the lead at White's or the Travellers', let me be president of the Jolly Sandboys at the 'Bag of Nails', and blackball everybody who does not pay me honour. If my darling Bessy cannot go out of a drawing-room until a baronet's niece (ha! ha! a baronet's niece, forsooth!) has walked before her, let us frequent company where we shall be the first; and how *can* we be the first unless we select our inferiors for our associates? [N 118–19]

Another shadowy borderline like that between the genteel and the shabby-genteel is that between the two worlds above and below the stairs. Inhabiting the no-man's land between them are the governesses and lady companions, who may penetrate into their employers' world, like Becky and Bessy Prior, or, like Briggs, remain despised by their superiors and envied by their inferiors. There are various means by which servants try to effect an entry into their masters' world, but most are attended by disaster, as though such an attempt were a kind of hubris. Horrocks, the butler's daughter and housekeeper at Queen's Crawley, hopes to become Lady Crawley by being Sir Pitt's mistress, but at his death the self-righteous and unforgiving Mrs Bute casts her down from her pride in her trinkets and ribbons. Raggles the butler, who saves his wages and becomes a capitalist and the landlord of Becky's sparkling establishment in Curzon Street, is finally ruined by the family that had originally made his fortune. Mrs Bonner, the lady's-maid in *Pendennis*, who buys the affections of the young footman Lightfoot by setting him up as a publican with her savings, has reason to repent of their change in station when he treats her as callously as his master, Sir Francis Clavering, treats the woman *he* married for money.

Because that boundary between masters and servants is so fortified, those occassions on which the servants do get the upper hand over their masters have a peculiar power. Dorothy Van Ghent has pointed out the multiple symbolic and social implications of the scene between Jos Sedley and Isidor: the fat English milor, who is in a panic lest his moustaches cause him to be taken for a British officer by a victorious Napoleonic army, subjects himself to the razor of his Flemish valet. The very nadir of Becky's fortunes is after Rawdon has left her, and there is a 'little revolution in May Fair' [VF 689], during which her servants won't answer her summons, and then sit on the sofa and drink her maraschino in her presence. Nothing dramatizes Mr Sedley's downfall more clearly than the encounter with his son-in-law's valet:

> He took off his hat, however, with much condescension to Mr. Sedley, who asked news about his son-in-law, and about Jos's carriage, and whether his horses had been down to Brighton, and about that infernal traitor Bonaparty, and the war; until the Irish maid-servant came with a plate and a bottle of wine, from which the old gentleman

insisted upon helping the valet. He gave him a half-guinea, too, which the servant pocketed with a mixture of wonder and contempt. [VF 318]

Another great master-servant confrontation is that between Major Pendennis and Morgan. Although Morgan, by shrewd speculation, has become something of a capitalist, and actually owns the house in which his master rents lodgings, he still has to put up with the major's arrogance.

The old gentleman's foot-bath was at the fire; his gown and slippers awaiting him there. Morgan knelt down to take his boots off with due subordination: and as the major abused him from above, kept up a growl of maledictions below at his feet. Thus, when Pendennis was crying, 'Confound you, sir, mind that strap – curse you, don't wrench my foot off,' Morgan *sotto voce* below was expressing a wish to strangle him, drown him, and punch his head off. [P 877]

This is a memorable tableau. Here are all the English lower classes kept in subjection by what is now little more than a habit, and beginning to know it. The tension is at breaking-point; and Morgan does in fact succeed in breaking the habit of a lifetime by denouncing the major outright. Major Pendennis is equal to the situation, and for this time maintains his dignity though he loses his valet. But that pitched battle is powerfully dramatized. Although Thackeray never wrote a *Hard Times* or a *Sybil* or a *Felix Holt*, the great lesson of the Victorian age, 'we must educate our masters,' is embodied in his ironic inversions of the master-servant relationship, and might have been learned as readily from his as from the so-called 'social' novels.

The class distinctions continue, of course, down the ranks of the servants. Horrocks, with her pretensions of becoming a lady, has as a toady 'the little kitchenmaid on her promotion,' who is effusively delighted by Horrocks' cacophonous piano-playing, 'crying, "Lor, mum, 'tis bittiful," – just like a genteel sycophant in a real drawing-room' [VF 505]. Naturally the kitchenmaid deserts and betrays Horrocks at her downfall.

A further nicety in discrimination among servants is introduced by the fact that their status depends not only on their place in the domestic hierarchy from butler to skivvy, but on their employers' standing in the great world as well. 'Morgan Pendennis' talks in his Gentlemen's Gentlemen's club as though he and his master were a composite being, using the flunkey's – as opposed to the royal – "we." As one would expect in the major's valet, Morgan is scornful of the suggestion that status is to be defined merely in terms of birth and money:

> 'It ain't money, nor bein' a baronet, nor 'avin' a town and country 'ouse, nor a paltry five or six thousand a year ... that will give a pusson position in society, as you know very well. We've no money, but we go everywhere; there's not a housekeeper's room, sir, in this town of any consiquince, where James Morgan ain't welcome.' [P 780]

But servants in a bourgeois family are more inclined to be like Mr Osborne, and assert their identity in terms of money. So Mrs Blenkinsop, the Sedley's housekeeper, resents governesses because 'they give themselves the hairs and hupstarts of ladies, and their wages is no better than you nor me' [VF 75].

It is not a system of subordination in itself that Thackeray satirizes – so long as it has some more equitable basis than mere status without function. For a man like Lockwood in *Esmond* and *The Virginians*, service is an honourable and proud profession. But if the social system, by elaborating and ritualizing the subordination, turns every servant into an untouchable – then shame and contempt enter the transaction. The writer of *The Book of Snobs* takes a savage delight in a story from the *Court Circular* which tells how, in a conflagration in the royal palace, the king of Spain 'in great part was roasted because there was not time for the Prime Minister to command the Lord Chamberlain to desire the Grand Gold Stick to order the first page in waiting to bid the chief of the flunkeys to request the Housemaid of Honour to bring up a pail of water to put His Majesty out' [BS 281]. It is of the nature of the state of society – 'viz., Toadyism, organized' [BS 273] – that it turns every man into a flunkey. Miss Crawley knows this, and treats everyone about her as a menial, and they are all apparently delighted when she condescends to trample on them. Those who deify George IV as the First Gentleman of Europe – for Thackeray 'fat old Florizel' was the proper idol of the snob – are invited to 'go and see the figure of Gorgius in his real, identical robes, at the waxwork. – Admittance one shilling. Children and flunkeys sixpence. Go, and pay sixpence' [BS 271].

The social ladder has its vertical as well as its horizontal divisions. Cutting across the strata of birth and wealth are the categories of the professions, with their own pecking order and their own rivalries between one another: so 'the doctor's wife is sulky because she has not been led out before the barrister's lady' [BS 375], and the apothecary Clump profits in his profession by plying Dr Squills with choice madeira [VF 233].

The military world, with its rigid system of subordination, is a favourite milieu for Thackeray, and many of his major characters either are or have been in the army. With his usual minuteness he shows how Rawdon Crawley remembers the name of George Osborne's regiment 'after an effort, as became a guardsman' [VF 169]. In *Philip* he explores the situation where Mrs *Major* MacWhirter has to give precedence to her younger sister, Mrs *General* Baynes.

There is the same pretentiousness in the church as in the secular professions: parson and curate have the same relation as doctor and apothecary. Parsons, too, have to be on their promotion. Dr Tusher, in *Henry Esmond*, knows on which side his bread is buttered and acts accordingly: 'It being this man's business to flatter and make sermons, it must be owned he was most industrious in it, and was doing the one or the other all day' [HE 90]. His son Tom, following in his father's footsteps, finally gains his bishopric after a career like the Vicar of Bray's. Charles Honeyman, the fashionable preacher of Lady Whittlesea's Chapel, has to compete against other fashionable preachers:

> Honeyman has a right to speak of persecution, and to compare himself to a hermit in so far that he preaches in a desert. Once like another hermit, St. Hierome, he used to be visited by lions. None such come to him now. Such lions as frequent the clergy are gone off to lick the feet of other ecclesiastics. [N 320]

Parson Sampson, another minister who has allowed worldly pursuits to mitigate spiritual ones, is besieged in his very pulpit by Irish and Jewish bailiffs, in a chapter headed 'Sampson and the Philistines' [V 397].

The changing fashions from low to high church are part of the background of *The Newcomes*, where the self-righteous bluestocking Mrs Hobson Newcome elects to be low because the Brian Newcomes are high. The rivalry between denominations is also part of the social context: in *Pendennis* we are shown how Dr Portman and Mr Simcoe, of church and chapel respectively, vie with each other for the greatest share of the Chatteris population in their congregations. Among the minor characters of the novels there is a troop of ministers of various persuasions, whose names indicate the nature of their doctrines: 'the Reverend Saunders McNitre, the Scotch divine; or the Reverend Luke Waters, the mild Wesleyan; or the Reverend Giles Jowls, the illuminated cobbler' [VF 414], as well as the Reverend Samuel Whey, who is 'full of the milk-and-water of human kindness.'

Nor is there any great sanctity about the administrators of the realm: the political profession is another part of the world of pushing and squeezing. The two members for Queen's Crawley are elected by some seven voters; and even after this rotten borough is abolished with the reform bill, elections are far from equitable. Pen almost gains himself a seat in parliament, but gives it up when he finds that blackmail is the means of getting it. Colonel Newcome is degraded by the election in which he is returned as a member for Newcome, and never takes up his seat. Warrington, one of his staunch supporters, has no illusions about the house of Commons; the colonel, he says, 'knows no more about politics than I do about dancing the polka; but there are five hundred wiseacres in that assembly who know no more than he does' [N 873].

There is plenty of snobbery in the literary and artistic world which Thackeray knew and depicted. Bacon and Bungay, the tuft-hunting publishers in *Pendennis*, have their counterparts in Gandish and Smee, the rival painters in *The Newcomes*. Toadying and flattery are a part of their trade: 'Smee plastered his sitters with adulation as methodically as he covered his canvas. He waylaid gentlemen at dinner; he inveigled unsuspecting folks into his studio, and had their heads off their shoulders before they were aware' [N 217]. All this testifies that the literary and artistic professions, far from being a 'republic of letters,' or ruled by an aristocracy of merit, are part of the world of Vanity Fair. Doyle's initial illus-

The professions of Vanity Fair: *The Newcomes* 998

tration for the last chapter of *The Newcomes* shows how the labours of the painter, the writer, the lawyer, and the lover are equally presided over by a cynical ass-eared little fiend.

Supporting all this minute differentiation in terms of birth, of money, and professional status, there is a closely woven texture of image and gesture. A mere handshake becomes an elaborate exercise in social discrimination. It is not just a question of whether one does or does not shake hands with a certain person; but there is a whole range of possibilities in a handshake itself, which may include how many of the fingers are offered, whether the hand is gloved or not, whether the gloves are new or merely cleaned, or even dirty. Becky can readjust a whole relationship by offering George one finger to shake, transforming his attitude from patronage to deference. Lady Kew shows her estimation of Clive Newcome by offering him two fingers to shake; Sir Brian Newcome similarly condescends to Pendennis, who afterwards regrets that he had not the presence of mind 'to poke one finger against his two' [N 174]. Perhaps the most elaborate image of the kind is in *Pendennis*, where Pen, strolling arm-in-arm with his uncle down St James's Street, feels a thrill of elation because he is holding the left arm of the man whose right hand is embracing the single gloved finger of the Duke of Wellington:

> The duke gave the elder Pendennis a finger of a pipe-clayed glove to shake, which the major embraced with great veneration; and all Pen's blood tingled, as he found himself in actual communication, as it were, with this famous man (for Pen had possession of the major's left arm, whilst that gentleman's other wing was engaged with his Grace's right). [P 461]

Alternatively, people may be classified according to where they live. It would almost be possible to make a map of London from Thackeray's novels that would be zoned according to degrees of gentility. Clive New-come acknowledges himself to be not in Ethel's world: 'I live in Charlotte Street, Fitzroy Square: which is not within the gates of Paradise. I take the gate to be somewhere in Davies Street, leading out of Oxford Street into Grosvenor Square. There's another gate in Hay Hill: and another in Bruton Street ...' [N 618]. Russell Square is genteel enough for the Sedley family in their days of prosperity; but it is anathema to Yellowplush, the footman in high society who considers himself at home in Piccadilly and Belgrave Square.

There is frequent joking about the peerage and the *Court Circular*. In speaking about Sir Pitt, the writer apologizes for having to admit the presence of any bad qualities in anyone 'whose name is in Debrett' [VF 102]. He describes many people who buy their way into such publications. The Newcomes, refusing to take the hint that is contained in their name, buy themselves a genealogy, and are uncertain, when told with some *éclat* that they are descended from Edward the Confessor's barber-surgeon, whether to be proud of the antiquity of the family, or ashamed of its menial origin. Alfred Muggins, on the authority of *Fluke's Peerage*, appears as Sir Alured Mogynes Smythe de Mogynes, with further testi-monies of his family's ancient standing: 'Arms – a mullion garbled, gules on a saltire reversed of the second. Crest – a tom-tit rampant regardant. Motto – *Ung Roy ung Mogyns*' [BS 291]. Old Stiffneck, who boasts of

Becky condescends to George Osborne: *Vanity Fair* 172

having Orlando Furioso and Peter the Cruel among his forebears, adds with savage satisfaction, 'I quarter the royal arms of Brentford in my coat' [BS 297].

Court titles, and the flunkeyism involved in jostling for any proximity to royalty, are another favourite butt for satire. Lord Steyne's formidable list of titles includes 'First Lord of the Powder Closet and Groom of the Back Stairs.' Esmond tells the story of an officer who is proud to be the eldest son of the Hereditary Grand Bootjack of the Empire, 'and heir to that honour of which his ancestors had been very proud, having been

The landlady ministers to the valet: *Pendennis* 875

kicked for twenty generations by one imperial foot, as they drew the boot from the other' [HE 14].

Imagery of boots, shoes, and feet is appropriately frequent when Thackeray is on his subject of subordination. I have already mentioned the fully dramatized scenes in which Esmond idolatrously kisses Beatrix's foot before he puts on her slipper, and Morgan mutters imprecations at Major Pendennis's feet while he loosens his straps. Morgan's kneeling 'with due subordination' is doubly exasperating to him in that he has himself just been exacting the same ministrations from Mrs Brixham, the intimidated landlady whose mortgage he owns [P 877]. Lady Lyndon's utter subjection to her brutal husband is signalled by her readiness to pull off his boots and fetch his slippers [BL 299]; and George IV's mean absorption with subordination is indicated by the fact that he 'invented ... a shoe-buckle (this was in the vigour of his youth, and the prime force of his imagination)' [BS 270]. On the other hand, those who black their own boots demonstrate an admirable independence of petty class-consciousness. Colonel Strong is affectionately depicted thus occupied in *Pendennis*, and the idle Prince Giglio in *The Rose and the Ring* begins his reformation when he finds in the fairy bag

> a blacking-brush and a pot of Warren's jet, and on the pot was written,
>> Poor young men their boots must black.
>> Use me and cork me and put me back.
> So Giglio laughed and blacked his boots, and put back the brush and the bottle. [x 408]

One facet of Victorian society that Thackeray shows as vitiating morality is the fashion for virtue. Just as it is considered a moral asset to have money, so it becomes a capital asset to appear religious, sententious, sexually pure, and domestically affectionate. Thackeray, whose purpose it was to redefine the gentleman according to a moral rather than an aristocratic standard,[6] is understandably exasperated to find that morality itself, or at least the appearance of it, has become an item on the status-seeker's list. Barry Lyndon, a representative of the opposite extreme of the bad old days, is at least straightforward about his villainy, and Thackeray partly shares his disgust at 'your modern moral world' [BL 129]; Barnes Newcome, an the other hand, though as financially grasping and domestically brutal as Barry ever was, sows his wild oats discreetly, and gives lectures on 'The Poetry of the Affections' as part of his political campaign. Society's insistence on the appearance of virtue if not on the thing itself is imposed even on the novelist, who, since the days of Fielding, has not been 'permitted to depict to his utmost power a MAN. We must drape him, and

---

6 See Ray *Thackeray: The Uses of Adversity, 1811–1846* (London 1955) 13ff.

give him a certain conventional simper' [P xxxvi]. 'The Comic Muse, nowadays, does not lift up Molly Seagrim's curtain; she only indicates the presence of some one behind it, and passes on primly, with expressions of horror, and a fan before her eyes' [v 206].

A recurring scene that illustrates this obligatory hypocrisy is the funeral of the rich old relative. As the heirs are trained in the values of Vanity Fair they are of course glad of the death but, as they are trained in its conventions, they must put on a display of grief. The deaths of Miss Crawley, Sir Brian Newcome, Lady Kew, and Lord Ringwood all cause a secret thrill of joy among their survivors, who nevertheless wear their mourning with ostentation; and Sir Pitt Crawley is followed to his grave by 'the family in black coaches, with their handkerchiefs up to their noses, ready for the tears which did not come' [VF 530]. Miss Crawley, with her 'balance at her banker's which would have made her beloved anywhere' [VF 103], is a focus for the depiction of the confused system of values which imposes at the same time mercenariness and the rule that it must be concealed. In the elaborate ritual of adulation that goes on round her and her banker's account, her devotees are ready to assign any motive to their attention rather than the actual mercenary one. When young Pitt, professing to have scruples about her lack of religion, says piously, 'What is money compared to our souls?' his father, who is of Barry Lyndon's generation, shrewdly answers him, 'You mean that the old lady won't leave the money to you?' [112]. But the canting young Pitt has a successful strategy: 'It is by soothing that wounded spirit that we must lead it into the right path' [417]; and Miss Crawley is indeed soothed into leaving him her seventy thousand pounds.

One strength that Thackeray derives from his acute perception of the finest shades of social discrimination is his ability to evoke what one might call 'social emotion.' He can probe that sensitive spot in us that reacts minutely to the estimation of others. Many of his characters exist as sentient beings only in so far as their status in society is inflated or deflated. They can cringe and they can smirk, for their deepest emotions – embarrassment and smugness – are those that depend on their standing in the eyes of others. Love, and hatred, and the deeper emotions that are

'Miss Crawley ... had a balance at her banker's which would
have made her beloved anywhere': *Vanity Fair* 103

usually evoked by friends, family, and active enemies – these the snob
has ceased to feel intensely, and all that is left to him of emotional life is
his excruciating concern about the estimation of his acquaintances. It is
the same 'social emotion' that is expressed in 'The Lovesong of J. Alfred
Prufrock'; and, unlike the elemental feelings of love and hatred, it is
perhaps more pervasive in life than in literature. 'I protest the great ills of
life are nothing,' reflects Pendennis in *The Newcomes* – 'the loss of your

fortune is a mere flea-bite; the loss of your wife – how many men have supported it and married comfortably afterwards?' [N 529]. And so Thackery likes to show, rather than the tragic agonies, the nagging twinges of existence, the little humiliations which can become so excruciating in their constant recurrence. Such is the familiar discomfort of Mr Batchelor when he is mistaken for the footman by the odious Baker:

> 'Sir!' says I, and 'sir' was all I could say. The fact is, I could have replied with something remarkably neat and cutting, which would have transfixed the languid little jackanapes who dared to mistake me for a footman; but, you see, I only thought of my repartee some eight hours afterwards when I was lying in bed, and I am sorry to own that a great number of my best *bon mots* have been made in that way. [LW 132]

But although as a social realist Thackeray understands and can explore a man's quivering sensitivity to what other people think of him, as a moralist he has a perception of just that confusion of values that cares more for the appearances than for the reality. There is a sense in which the evolution of the Snob involves the extinction of the Man. The fully-developed snob has no moral sense, for he behaves and judges according to a scale of rank rather than value; his emotions too are subservient to considerations of status; all his faculties of wonder and admiration become atrophied, for every channel of perception is blocked by the one obsession: 'Art, Nature pass, and there is no dot of admiration in his stupid eyes; nothing moves him, except when a very great man comes his way, and then the rigid, proud, self-confident, inflexible British Snob can be as humble as a flunkey, and as supple as a harlequin' [BS 383]. His very senses are paralysed, for he cannot even enjoy a glass of wine unless it has been recommended by a lord.

That is the extreme of the type. Not many of Thackeray's characters are so fully snobs that they have ceased to be human beings. But many of them have had their humanity curtailed or warped by the organized toadyism that is society. Even Becky, for all her vitality, is so indifferent about her physical being that she is ready to give herself to a Jos Sedley or a Lord Steyne.[7] Beatrix, who is not without love, prostitutes herself to a prince whom she morally despises.

The snob can be seen as a very specialized animal, struggling for survival in a highly competitive environment. 'Animals ... turn and rend each other – that is all. Men, too, rend each other; but their greater or less intelligence makes the struggle far more complicated' – that is Balzac's background for *La Comédie humaine.*[8] Thackeray also invokes this social jungle, where the main motive is survival (it is, to be sure, a highly refined sort of 'survival' that he is talking about, with an elaborately developed system of determining 'the fittest'). But one of his strengths is his ability to define the limits within which a character is merely a social animal, out to get what he can for himself, and the point at which he becomes a moral being with a code of behaviour more complex than that dictated by the principle of survival. Even minor characters are given the chance of self-definition against the context of the social jungle. George Barnes decides to stand by his mother against his rich old grandmother, Lady Kew, with the rueful reflection, 'She always hated me ... but if she had by chance left me a legacy, there it goes' [N 498]. Thackeray can suggest, too, how personal and individual a matter morality is. The disreputable brawling old Captain Macmurdo, whom Rawdon recruits as a second in his projected duel with Steyne, is, by his own standards at least, an honourable and even gentle man:

> Old Mac was famous for his good stories. He was not exactly a lady's man; that is, men asked him to dine rather at the houses of their mistresses than of their mothers. There can scarcely be a life lower, perhaps, than his; but he was quite contented with it, such as it was, and led it in perfect good nature, simplicity, and modesty of demeanour. [VF 698]

George Orwell comments on this skill in moral definition: 'Major

7 A.E. Dyson points out that it is Amelia, not Becky, who is the sensual one of the pair. '*Vanity Fair*: An Irony Against Heroes' *Critical Quarterly* VI (1964) 11–31

8 'Introduction' to *The Human Comedy*, trans. Clara Bell, ed. George Saintsbury (London 1895) III 3

Pendennis is a shallow old snob, and Rawdon Crawley is a thick-headed ruffian ... but what Thackeray realizes is that according to their tortuous code they are neither of them bad men. Major Pendennis would not sign a dud cheque, for instance. Rawdon certainly would, but on the other hand he would not desert a friend in a tight corner.'[9]

That interaction between the individual's values and the values of the society to which he belongs occurs all through *The Newcomes*, where Clive, Ethel, Pendennis, as well as a numerous group of figures like Kew, Florac, Fred Bayham, and Jack Belsize, are all trying to define themselves within the context of the acquisitive, respectable Newcome world.

It is partly his powerful sense of social context that makes Thackeray good at showing his characters in the process of aging: Major Pendennis sinking from middle-aged Regency buck to querulous old man; Beatrix Esmond passing from enchanting girlhood to tarnished womanhood in *Esmond*, and then reincarnated as the irascible and possessive, but still shrewd and engaging, old Baroness Bernstein of *The Virginians*. This aging is not just a matter of accumulated years or even experience; Thackeray can suggest that people get old because they leave their worlds behind them, because in the new age in which they find themselves they are anachronisms, and their values and attitudes are superannuated. Old Barry Lyndon speaks bitterly of 'your modern moral world' because he knows it is no longer *his* world; Major Pendennis and Colonel Newcome, so different in their values in spite of their similar experience of India and the army, are alike in their wistful harking back to how different things were 'in my day,' and in the consciousness that to their heirs they are old fogeys. And the narrator himself, of course, with his nostalgia for the old coaching days and for the vivid sensations of his youth, can portray their situation with a deeply founded sympathy.

Every man is in his own way like Terribile, the perennial valet and model for the changing generations of art students in Rome: 'He has figured on a hundred canvases ere this, and almost ever since he was born. All his family were models; his mother having been a Venus, is now a Witch of Endor. His father is in the patriarchal line: he has himself done the cherubs, the shepherd boys, and now is a grown man, and ready as a

9 *Dickens, Dali and Others* (New York 1946) 28

warrior, a pifferaro, a Capuchin, or what you will' [N 469]. It is a succinct image of how a man's identity changes according to the generation that encounters him.

Henry Esmond is such a man. It was courageous of Thackeray to follow so highly concentrated a work as *Esmond* with *The Virginians* as a sequel, a novel that considers the same events and characters from a viewpoint of forty years later. Esmond himself as a writer was so scrupulous, so keenly self-conscious, and so deeply concerned in the relationships and issues in which he was involved, that it is something of a shock to find him and his political, moral, and sexual preoccupations exposed to the loosely sceptical assessment of his descendants. The divine Beatrix reappears as a cynical and crusty old woman; the sainted Rachel is discussed as having been almost old enough to be his grandmother [205]; and his grand act of self-abnegation is shown merely to have put the title and the family estate into the hands of a set of rakes and scoundrels.

The time sequence of the novels – distinct from their order of composition – from *Esmond* through *The Virginians*, *Vanity Fair*, *Pendennis*, and *The Newcomes* to *Philip*, gives Thackeray a span of almost two centuries in which to explore the ironies of heredity and the anomalies of the relationships between the generations. The novels are linked to each other by the characters and their descendents who cross the boundaries of the divisions between the novels, so that we have a vivid sense of the survival of one age into another, and of the continuity as well as the discontinuity of time. Old Lady Kew of *The Newcomes* is the sister of Lord Steyne in *Vanity Fair*, and brings into the midst of Victorian respectability the less scrupulous standards of Regency aristocracy. Her evangelical daughter-in-law rebels against her, but she manages nevertheless to assert herself to some extent with her grandchildren, Ethel and Kew, whose mixed parentage has made them more amenable to the union of blood with money and the compromise of virtue with expediency. Thackeray needs that wide span of time because of his vision of man as being not just himself, nor himself in his society, but a being partly determined by his past and his family's past. So we know more about George Warrington of *The Virginians* when we think of him as the grandson of Henry Esmond, and as himself the grandfather of George Warrington of *Pendennis*. The present too can be an illumination of the past, and one index of Henry Esmond's character is that of his daughter, 'Madam Esmond.' A family tree, like that of the Esmonds, Warringtons, or Newcomes, is an accumulation of relevant information about the characters who are immediately to concern us. The first names alone of the Crawley forbears – Pitt, Bute, and 'Charles Stuart, afterwards called Barebones Crawley' [VF 77] – suggest a family of time-servers whose allegiance has swung as regularly as a pendulum, and constitute a preview of the inheritance from the older Pitt to the younger, and of the fraternal disputes between young Pitt and Rawdon.

It is not just the relations of the generations and the ironies of heredity that Thackeray can evoke through his wide span of time. It gives him scope, too, for that kind of irony that consists in the contrast of the present dramatized moment with the whole spread of history. As Empson described it, 'the human mind has two main scales in which to measure time. The large one takes the length of a human life as its unit, so that there is nothing to be done about life ... The small one takes as its unit the conscious moment, and it is from this that you consider the neighbouring space ... delicacies of social tone, and your personality.'[10] Thackeray is a master at switching between these two time scales. He can alternate between a close-up view of the minute distinctions between individuals and their day-to-day aspirations, with a vivid evocation of feverish activity, and the timeless view in which distinctions are blurred and all activity seems pointless. It is the temporal equivalent of that ability to move in space from the panoramic view of the nations clashing at Waterloo to the detail of George's dead body that is to shake Amelia's little world. So Beatrix Esmond, the sun around whom so many satellites revolve, becomes just another courtesan in the undiscriminating spread of history; and Esmond's great enterprise, his attempt to restore the Stuart succession, becomes at the end of the novel just another plot that failed. Dobbin's final embrace of Amelia is seen briefly as the momentary consummation of a lifetime's longing, and then recedes into disillusion and finally insignificance in the wide vision that takes the lifetime as its unit: 'Ah! *Vanitas Vanitatum*! Which of us is happy in this world? Which of us has his desire?

10 *Seven Types of Ambiguity* (London 1930) 31

or, having it, is satisfied?' It is the appropriate refrain of the writer who sees a grain of sand not only as a world but as a grain of sand too; and who, if he holds eternity in an hour, also knows that the hour won't last forever.

THE NEWCOMES

There are various reasons why *The Newcomes* has always lagged so far behind *Vanity Fair* in popularity and critical attention. It is not as lively, the characters are less vividly animated, the incident and commentary are not as piquante. *Vanity Fair* contains more of the sparkling exaggerations of satire – showing, in effect, one Dobbin in a world of cheats and humbugs – and its satirical vision makes its theme more obvious, and more immediately interesting. The ratio of good to bad is perhaps more realistic in *The Newcomes*, which shows a number of characters who, if not good, are concerned with the problem of how to live according to conscience in a fallen world. But its scope is in certain ways the larger for this increased realism: its emotional appeal is greater, for ultimately we care less for the sirens and parasites like Becky and Amelia than for decent people like Clive, Ethel, and Colonel Newcome.

It is also slow to get going, and never achieves the pace of Thackeray's first novel. He takes his time to describe the various branches of the family, and to define the world in which Colonel Newcome is to grow old and his son is to grow up. Structurally, too, it does not hold together as tightly as *Vanity Fair*. With its vast number of characters, three of whom are rival claimants for the central position, and its spread of time and place, and its accumulation of detail, it is a novel that one easily gets lost in; James's description of it as a 'loose baggy monster' has stuck.[11] Nevertheless, it is not only endowed with life, but also thematically and artistically coherent, though its range and complexity tend to make its effect cumulative rather than immediate.[12]

It is in the third number that Thackeray defines his social theme:

11 See the preface to *The Tragic Muse*
12 Much of the material for my present treatment appeared first in my article, 'Theme and Form in *The Newcomes*' *Nineteenth-Century Fiction* XXIII (1968) 177–88.

To push on in the crowd, every male or female struggler must use his shoulders. If a better place than yours presents itself just beyond your neighbour, elbow him and take it. Look how a steadily-purposed man or woman at Court, at a ball, or exhibition, wherever there is a competition and a squeeze, gets the best place; the nearest the sovereign, if bent on kissing the royal hand; the closest to the grand stand, if minded to go to Ascot; the best view and hearing of the Rev. Mr. Thumpington, when all the town is rushing to hear that exciting divine; the largest quantity of ice, champagne, and seltzer, cold pâté, or other his or her favourite flesh-pot, if gluttonously minded, at a supper whence hundreds of people come empty away. A woman of the world will marry her daughter and have done with her; get her carriage and be at home and asleep in bed; whilst a timid mamma has still her girl in the nursery, or is beseeching the servants in the cloak-room to look for her shawls, with which someone else has whisked away an hour ago. What a man has to do in society is to assert himself. Is there a good place at table? Take it. At the Treasury or the Home Office? Ask for it. Do you want to go to a party to which you are not invited? Ask to be asked. Ask A., ask B., ask Mrs. C., ask everybody you know: you will be thought a bore; but you will have your way. What matters if you are considered obtrusive, provided that you obtrude? By pushing steadily, nine hundred and ninety-nine people in a thousand will yield to you. Only command persons, and you may be pretty sure that a good number will obey. How well your money will have been laid out, O gentle reader, who purchase this; and, taking the maxim to heart, follow it through life! You may be sure of success. If your neighbour's foot obstructs you, stamp on it; and do you suppose he won't take it away?

The proofs of the correctness of the above remarks I show in various members of the Newcome family. [95–6]

This is the passage in *The Newcomes* that corresponds to the description of the Fair in the preface to *Vanity Fair*. It is unmistakably the same world. where unscrupulous self-seeking, however disguised, is the road to success. But there are some differences of emphasis in the presentation of the

Newcome world. 'The Rev. Mr. Thumpington,' no longer called a quack, has a new eminence. The evangelical Lady Southdown is a peripheral if significant figure in *Vanity Fair*, but the Reverend Charles Honeyman, the fashionable divine, and Mrs Hobson Newcome, who conducts herself as Virtue personified, have moved into the foreground of the later novel; that is, pretension to virtue and spirituality is more standard, and the hypocrites of *The Newcomes* tend to be of that dangerous species who believe in their own deceptions. Again, *Vanity Fair* is set in the Regency, and social distinctions are still somewhat in terms of 'rank' as in the eighteenth century: birth is still the major means of gradation; and though the Osbornes are rich, they are still branded as *nouveau riche*. In *The Newcomes*, set in the more fully industrialized 30s and 40s, the definition of class in terms of money has become more standard; it is no longer so important, in the society to which they aspire, that the Newcome family is *nouveau*, for what matters is that it is *riche*. Becky, with a dubious moral reputation and an income of nothing a year, could penetrate into the houses of the great; but the aspiring Ethel needs a spotless name and a substantial fortune behind her, as well as ingenuity, to make her way in society. Becky's chief asset is a nobleman, Lord Steyne; Ethel's is a bank, Hobson Brothers & Newcome. In *The Book of Snobs* Thackeray had called birth and money 'the two humbugs which [divide] ... the social empire of this kingdom between them.' From *Vanity Fair* to *The Newcomes* the emphasis shifts from the one to the other.

The Newcomes is the 'Memoirs of a Most Respectable Family,' and their claim to respectability rests as much on their money as on their solid Quaker background and their three generations of virtuous apprentices. And Thackeray's subject is that complex union of, or confusion between, financial and moral values, good and goods, which constitutes 'respectability.'

Money, as a determinant of respectability, is a central principle that holds together at once the Newcome family and the novel, permeating language and imagery and dominating character and action. It is no accident that the Newcomes are a banking family: banking for them is not just a profession, but an existence. Through the novel people are judged by the size of their balance, relationships progress in terms of who opens and who closes how large an account, battles are fought in which the manoeuvres are transferring an account or bouncing a cheque.

As mercenary transactions dominate the action, so financial terminology pervades the language, giving a distinctive texture to the novel. Love, morality, art, and faith are all discussed in financial terms.

Colonel Newcome, bitterly disappointed, after thirty years in India, at the cold welcome accorded to him by the banking brothers, betrays his emotion to the cabman who drives him away: 'Very likely the cabman thought he was a disappointed debtor who had asked in vain to renew a bill. In fact, Thomas Newcome had overdrawn his little account. There was no such balance of affection in that bank of his brothers as the simple creature had expected to find there' [80]. The same imagery is used for Clive's frustrated love for Ethel: 'one great passion he had had and closed the account of it' [818]. The mercenary metaphor is not reserved for the mercenary marriage: even passion can be squandered like capital, where there is no steady income of affection to support a relationship:

> Many a young couple of spendthrifts get through their capital of passion in the first twelve months and have no love left for the daily demands of after-life. O me! for the day when the bank account is closed, and the cupboard is empty, and the firm of Damon and Phyllis insolvent! [491]

Love is a commodity like any other, and with no great market value either. We hear, for instance, that the only person who might be said to love the ailing Sir Brian Newcome is his valet, 'who loves him to the extent of fifty pounds a year and perquisites' [629]. Other emotions are equally reducible to pounds, shillings, and pence. Hobson Newcome's grief for his mother's death can be calculated in inverse proportion to the size of his legacy, and he speaks of it in terms of 'the weight of business which this present affliction entails' [42]. And, as Barnes Newcome hurries to the City after his grandmother's funeral, we are reminded that 'business is business, and must be attended to, though grief be ever so severe' [726].

People are evaluated by their income, as we hear in Pendennis's long lecture in which he tries to dissuade Clive from loving Ethel. Clive is not a worthy suitor for Ethel, because the best stock in the marriage market goes to the highest bidder, and Clive cannot 'count purses with Sultan Farintosh.' It is a matter of 'bargain and sale,' and, like Circassian girls who are sold by their parents to their husbands, English girls have learned to be 'proud of their bringing up, and take rank according to the prices which they fetch.' Clive is deluded if he thinks that youth, intelligence, goodness, and love, even when accompanied by a comfortable if not immense income, have much value in this trade:

'You go and buy yourself some new clothes, and a fifty-pound horse, and put a penny rose in your button-hole, and ride past her window, and think to win this prize? O you idiot! A penny rosebud! Put money in your purse. A fifty-pound hack when a butcher rides as good a one! – Put money in your purse. A brave young heart, all courage and love and honour! Put money in thy purse – t'other coin don't pass in the market.' [537]

Thrift and prudence are the virtues which have market value, not love and generosity.

The marriage market itself is of course a central image in the novel, and the repetition of the mercenary marriage and its outcome between various couples is a unifying structural principle. In the older generation Colonel Newcome, Madame de Florac, and Brian Newcome for their different reasons married people whom they did not love; and in the younger generation, Clive, Ethel, Paul de Florac, Clara Pulleyn, Barnes, and Jack Belsize are all subject to social pressures that separate them from those they love or unite them with partners they despise. According to the philosophy of Society, marriage 'is but a question of money on one side and the other' [406]. But those who hold this tenet, however substantial their actual bank balance, find through the course of the novel that there are multiple debts accruing in trust and affection.

Such selective breeding, however, has its effects: Madame de Florac reflects that 'the children of those who do not love in marriage' are themselves lacking in love [629], and so the system can proceed. The history of the progress of the main branch of the Newcome family (distinct from the colonel's branch, for he is the child of a love match) is an expanded version of the banking family of Pump and Aldgate in *The Book of Snobs*:

> Old Pump sweeps a shop, runs of messages, becomes a confidential clerk and partner. Pump the Second becomes chief of the house, spins more and more money, marries his son to an Earl's daughter. Pump Tertius goes on with the bank; but his chief business in life is to become the father of Pump Quartus, who comes out a full-blown aristocrat, and takes his seat as Baron Pumpington, and his race rules hereditarily over this nation of Snobs. [BS 299]

There is the history of the Newcomes in a nutshell. Old Thomas Newcome came from the workhouse; and his son marries an earl's daughter who, like Pump's wife, patronizes him. However, perhaps through more consistent practice of the *marriage de convenance*, the Newcomes have managed to speed up the progress through the generations, for Barnes, or Pump Tertius, bids fair to taking on himself the role of Pump Quartus as well.

'I believe in elder sons, and a house in town, and a house in the country' [596]; this is the creed of the girl bred in society. If money is made a religion, so religion is made a commodity. Religion is one of the bank's chief assets. Old Mrs Newcome, the grand old lady of Hobson Brothers & Newcome, is a Quaker, and Thomas Newcome, the founder of the family, netted this prize for a wife, along with her bank, by becoming a convert, and being careful to conciliate 'the Quaker connexion' [20]. The servants in her house, the 'serious paradise' at Clapham, are all devotees of various bizarre dissenting religions, and the visitors are a mixture of 'clerical gentlemen' and 'clerks at the bank' [21]. Her funeral is a grande fête testifying to the union of commerce and religion, which triumphantly carry the aristocracy in their wake.

> There was such a crowd you might have thought it was a Derby Day. The carriages of some of the greatest City firms, and the wealthiest Dissenting houses; several coaches full of ministers of all denominations, including the Established Church; the carriage of the Right Honourable the Earl of Kew, and that of his daughter, Lady Ann

Newcome, attended that revered lady's remains to their final resting-place. [59]

Her son and successor, Sir Brian Newcome, who has managed to shed the stigma of dissent while retaining the advantages that accrued from it, conscientiously maintains the practice of family prayers in his Park Lane residence.

> It was a Thursday morning ... The household from above and from below; the maids and footmen from the basement; the nurses, children, and governesses from the attics; all poured into the room at the sound of a certain bell ... The urns are hissing, the plate is shining; the father of the house standing up, reads from a gilt book for three or four minutes in a measured cadence ... At the very instant when the voice has ceased speaking and the gilded book is shut, the world begins again, and for the next twenty-three hours and fifty-seven minutes, all that household is given up to it. [185–6]

Even those three minutes of the day that have been set aside for spiritual matters, the reading 'from a gilt book ... in a measured cadence,' are rather an extension than an interruption of worldly pursuits.

The history of Lady Whittlesea's Chapel, Mayfair, is a study of religion as a commercial venture. Its patron saint seems to have been a society belle; its owner is a Jewish wine-merchant; its foundation is his wineshop; and its preacher is a genteel Chadband, the Reverend Charles Honeyman. Honeyman can synthesize religious fervour and convey it in calculated eloquence which he turns to good account; and his crocodile tears are current coin in certain circles of sentimental ladies. He is a kind of religious gigolo, who can excite them with his cultivated air of spirituality.

> He dashes the fair hair from his brow: he sits down to the piano, and plays one or two of [the chants], warbling a faint vocal accompaniment, and looking as if he would be lifted off the screw music stool, and flutter up to the ceiling.
>
> 'Oh, it's just seraphic!' says the widow. 'It's just the breath of incense, and the pealing of the organ.' [283]

(I suspect the sexual connotations of the vocabulary in this passage are not accidental.) For all Honeyman's unctuous piety, Fred Bayham's evaluation of him is probably accurate: 'It's my belief you'd rather lie than not'' [162]. Sherrick, who refers to Lady Whittlesea's as 'the shop overhead,' runs the chapel as a theatre. The pews are sold like boxes, and the best performers are carefully booked and billed. One of the initial illustrations shows Sherrick operating a little puppet Honeyman, pulling the string that will make it perform [577]. When Honeyman is arrested for debt by Moss the money-lender, Bayham reflects, 'One Jew has the chapel, another Hebrew has the clergyman. It's singular, ain't it?' [322].

Sherrick, a minor character in the story, has considerable thematic significance in a novel that depicts a materialistic society. For him, as for the other characters in their varying degrees, every enterprise is undertaken as a commercial venture; but he is frank about the fact where others try to drape their greed in virtue. He is quite as ready to talk about the chapel as 'a good speculaton' as he is about his theatre, his wine business, or his papers. The promoters of the *Pall Mall Gazette*, for which Pendennis writes, will talk of its literary merits, its support of the arts, and the principles it stands for; they keep quiet about their financial expectations, though Fred Bayham at least is not above prostituting his muse. But, so far as Sherrick is concerned, the paper's chief function is financial. He himself once speculated in papers, and had no scruples about principles. 'I tried a Tory one, moderate Liberal, and out-and-out uncompromising Radical. I say, what d'ye think of a religious paper, the *Catechism*, or some such name? Would Honeyman do as editor?' [329]. Religion, politics, and the arts are equally grist to Sherrick's mill, as they are in more subtle ways to the whole world of the Newcomes.

The subordination of high ideals to money is succinctly realized in the image of the silver coconut tree which adorns Colonel Newcome's table in his splendid mansion in Tyburnia. It is when the stock of the Bundelcund Banking Company is mushrooming, and when the colonel – himself now in the banking business like his heartless brothers – cannot resist a display of opulence, that he is presented with this emblem of prosperity:

There was a superb silver coco-nut-tree, whereof the leaves were

dexterously arranged for holding candles and pickles; under the coconut was an Indian prince on a camel giving his hand to a cavalry
officer on horse-back – a howitzer, a plough, a loom, a bale of cotton,
on which were the East India Company's arms, a brahmin, Britannia,
and Commerce, with a cornucopia were grouped round the principal
figures. [823–4]

Mercantilism and imperialism, war and peace, agriculture, industry, and
trade, along with religion and nationalism, are all lumped together in
silver, immortalized in 'this chaste and elegant specimen of British art,'
and set to carry pickles for the delectation of a Newcome family. The
coconut tree wanders through the latter half of the novel, performing its
own little Odyssey, until it too ends up in the hands of 'the Hebrew
gentlemen.'

For this view of *The Newcomes* as a novel about money, Barnes Newcome is the focal character. He of all the Newcomes has his heart most
firmly located in his pocket. He is the banker par excellence. His relations
with his friends and family are governed by the bank; because they have
substantial accounts, he is ready to receive into his house both Clive and
Lord Highgate – of whom one would like to carry off Barnes's sister, and
the other his wife. His chief information on such subjects as his sister's
engagement and his wife's elopement comes in the form of a wire from the
bank: 'Consol's, so-and-so. French Rentes, so much. *Highgate's and
Farintosh's accounts withdrawn*' [801]. In his feud with Colonel Newcome
he will not accept a challenge, but he strikes 'such a blow as might be
expected from that quarter' – that is, a financial one – and explodes the
Bundelcund venture by refusing to honour its bills at a critical period. He
not only buys his wife, but sells her for what he can get for her when he
finds he has made a bad bargain, exacting the last penny in damages from
the man to whom she escaped for protection from her husband. 'In the
City we have no hearts you know,' he jokes [688]. And his uncle, Colonel
Newcome, learns the truth of this through the novel, until at the end he
says bitterly to his brother, 'We understand that sort of thing. London
bankers have no hearts – for these last fifty years past that I have known
you and your brother, and my amiable nephew, the present commanding

officer, has there been anything in your conduct that has led me to suppose you had?' [840].

It is part of the intricate structure of the novel that the great world which it depicts in such painstaking detail is reflected in miniature in numerous little microcosms through the book. Each little community or institution, each gathering of people, even a single object like the coconut tree, has the quality of being complete in itself, with its own centre of gravity and its own set of revolving satellites within the major system.

The most fully realized of these microcosms in *The Newcomes* is perhaps the Ridley's lodging house in London. Appropriately, in the garret is Fred Bayham, the embodiment of literary Bohemia, who spouts flowing rhetoric while eating a mutton chop off a fork, clad in his dressing-gown at noon. On the second floor is Charles Honeyman, the representative of fashionable religion, and on the first is Bagshot, Esq., MP, who is more ready to discuss wine than politics. The landlord on the ground floor is a lord's butler, whose son becomes a great painter; another lodger, little Miss Cann, plays the piano well enough to inspire the imagination of this genius. Below stairs, of course, one finds the servants and '*servi servorum*,' Julia the cook and Slavey. Under this one roof at 23 Walpole Street is the world, with all its pretensions and aspirations, its virtues and hypocrisies. The same can be said of the colonel's party at Fitzroy Square, where the naval, military, medical, financial, and literary professions rub shoulders, or of Miss Honeyman's lodging house at Brighton, which is a miniature social hierarchy in itself. To some extent every meal and social gathering described in the novel (and there are many), with its selection and distribution of guests, becomes a significant assemblage of all the elements of middle-class society. The world is cluttered with microcosms that reflect worldliness: Baden is a congress of nations, a modern Babel in which each gambler curses his luck in his own tongue; Rosey justifiably boasts that her party is an *omnium gatherum*; and so on. The world is too much with us, we begin to feel – as does Florac's wife, the faded and lonely Princess de Montcontour (once plain Miss Higg of Manchester), who feels suffocated by her own status in her splendid Louis XVI bedchamber of mirrors.

Opposite that looking-glass, between the tall windows, at some forty feet distance, is another huge mirror, so that when the poor princess is in bed, in her prim old curl-papers, she sees a vista of elderly princesses twinkling away into the dark perspective; and is so frightened that she and Betsy, her Lancashire maid, pin up the jonquil silk curtains over the bed-mirror after the first night; though the princess never can get it out of her head that her image is still there, behind the jonquil hangings, turning as she turns, waking as she wakes, &c. [603]

It is a powerful image, suggesting, as the repeating microcosms suggest, that the world is inescapable. And in this glittering but often suffocating world there are many, like Barnes, who are in their element; some, like the colonel, are unaware of what the miror shows them; a few, like the princess, try to blot it out. But there are others too who try to face their own reflections with confidence and yet with knowledge. Learning how to live, at once with the world and with one's own consciousness, is one of the main subjects of the novel. This is the task before Ethel, who is a product of her environment and at the same time manages eventually to assert herself against it. 'You belong to your belongings, my dear,' Lady Kew tells her [426]; but Ethel has to develop in moral consciousness to the point where her belongings belong to her. In the first part of the novel she is gaining money, prestige, or suitors; but by the end she has learned how to give them away.

Ethel Newcome is Thackeray's best heroine; indeed she compares favorably with any heroine of the nineteenth-century novel. Besides being both vivid and likable, she has a dynamism which most of Thackeray's major females lack: she learns about herself, and changes as a result of her knowledge. She has a full and complex moral life and development. She has Becky's strong character, without Becky's siren's tail. She is like Beatrix in many ways – Thackeray drew her from Sally Baxter, in whom he recognized Beatrix incarnate [Letters III 149, 284] – but, where Beatrix is finally tainted by her ambition and selfishness, Ethel is redeemed, and convincingly so.

The Newcomes is slow to get going because Thackeray takes the necessary time to build up the world in which his individual dramas are to be enacted. The effect is the more powerful for being cumulative;

G

and by the time Clive, Ethel, and the rest reach their moments of decision, we have a full awareness of the complex pressures to which they are subject.

Ethel has been bred for worldly success. All along she sees the essential meanness of her family's goals: 'There never were, since the world began, people so unblushingly sordid!' she exclaims [425], and she is sarcastic about the suggestion that Clive is beneath her: 'he is only a poor painter, and we forsooth are bankers in the city' [425]. At the same time she has an appetite for the kind of success which she simultaneously despises; for, though she is too intelligent to be attracted by mere wealth and opulence, she has the instincts of a coquette, and she cannot resist the personal triumph which the adoration of rich suitors signifies in a society where they are considered the best prizes. She shows this inner conflict in her long self-examination when she talks to Madame de Florac.

> I, who pretend to revolt, I like [society] too; and I, who rail and scorn flatterers – oh, I like admiration! I am pleased when the women hate me, and the young men leave them for me. Though I despise many of these, yet I can't help drawing them towards me. One or two of them I have seen unhappy about me, and I like it; and if they are indifferent I am angry, and never tire till they come back. I love beautiful dresses; I love fine jewels; I love a great name and a fine house – oh, I despise myself, when I think of these things! When I lie in bed, and say I have been heartless and a coquette, I cry with humiliation: and then rebel and say, Why not? – and to-night – yes, to-night – after leaving you, I shall be wicked, I know I shall. [630]

In this situation of despising the very goals she aims at, she protects herself with irony; and in such actions as that of wearing the green 'sold' ticket on the front of her dress, she makes a show of rebelling while she conforms to her family's plans. It is only when she sees the disastrous end of her brother's mercenary marriage, a catastrophe that is close to her, that she learns enough to break off her own engagement to Farintosh and re-examine the values by which she has been living. The conversion is not glib, and Ethel is not let off lightly. Unlike Pen, whose almost miraculous release from the trap he prepared for himself was scarcely deserved,

Ethel has to pay in full for what happiness she gets; and the muted ending of *The Newcomes* seems a truer culmination of the whole novel than the comedy routine that ends *Pendennis*.

When Ethel rejects Farintosh, apologizing for her falsehood, he makes it clear just how bad her conduct has been:

'Yes, it *was* a falsehood!' the poor lad cried out. 'You follow a fellow, and you make a fool of him, and you make him frantic in love with you, and then you fling him over! I wonder you can look me in the face after such an infernal treason. You've done it to twenty fellows before, I know you have. Everybody said so, and warned me. You draw them on, and get them to be in love, and then you fling them away.' [799]

Ethel has learned that it is one thing to admit you are a coquette, and another and more painful experience to be told the same thing by one of your victims. It is a reproach that really touches her, and it is none the less painful for coming after her reformation, and as a direct result of it. The path of goodness is not to be an easy one for Ethel, for after she has ceased her ironic acquiescence in her family's values, she has to live with the awareness of her own responsibility for spoiled lives. Even at the end, it is not clear that she is to be united with Clive.

Clive's individual agony, which reaches tragic dimensions, is again intricately bound up with the social milieu. In many ways he is a passive victim of the world's values, for when he loses the girl he loves, to society, he loses his will too. Here again the length of the novel, with its accumulated detail of how society works and how time moves, helps to convey the protracted pain of Clive's story, for we see the slow process of his disintegration. His long suit of Ethel – dangling after her at parties, knocking on doors to which her guardian Lady Kew won't admit him, watching the favours granted to richer suitors – all this slowly demoralizes him. For he is not just the pining rejected lover: he has the additional pain of knowing that she cares for him, and not for the others. In Madame de Florac's garden he tells her: 'Look, Ethel, dear. I love you so, that if I thought another had your heart, an honest man, a loyal gentleman, like – like him of last year even, I think I could go back with a "God bless you", and take to my pictures again, and work on in my own humble way' [636]. But in losing her as he does to someone she does not love, he gives up. His is the story of how a man who is honest, generous, and industrious can be reduced not to poverty merely, but to degradation and despair, by the system of the Newcome world. Eventually, though his motives are different from Barnes's, he too sells himself, though he knows that he is bartering what he values for an empty prosperity. Social pressures, in one way or another, take from him the woman he loves, cause him to marry one he despises, and induce him to abandon his art, the only occupation in which he can preserve his self-respect; and it is the failure of a worldly endeavour he had never cared for that makes him and his family the victims of such a harridan as the Campaigner. The human situation is fully realized in the context of the society which brings it about. The last chapters showing Clive in his complex misery in Boulogne and London are the logical culmination of the progress of the world as the rest of the novel has portrayed it.

Ironically, the unworldly Colonel Newcome is the agent who forces on Clive the ways of the world. As we have seen, he is a saint whom we love and pity as a martyr; but he makes martyrs of others than himself. Good people who admire the colonel's character invest their savings and lose them in his hopelessly mismanaged financial venture. And friends are lost, and bitter enemies made, by his disproportionate sense of moral outrage against Barnes and Ethel. He is the well-meaning cause, emotionally, morally, and financially, of Clive's predicament; and as Ethel has to do penance for her worldliness, so does he for his lack of it. The Newcome world being what it is, it is a man's moral responsibility to know something of it. Innocence is baleful when it seeks to be an influence, and so the colonel, Madame de Florac, and Lady Walham, all saintly in themselves, lead their children into disaster.

It becomes a problem for the characters like Pen, Clive, and Ethel, who are all trying to find some means of living decently in an acquisitive society, to choose fit guides. Just as the saintly characters are disqualified by their innocence, so men like Honeyman, Bayham, and Florac, who all propose themselves as mentors for Clive, are tainted by their experience. The reformed prodigal like Kew is probably the only reliable moral influence, but his experience makes him like Cassandra, a figure who cannot communicate. The scene in which Ethel scorns Kew's good advice, because she has in her hands a poison pen letter describing his past misdemeanours, is a dramatic rendering of that theme of incommunicable experience.

'The letter was actually brought to me whilst his lordship was in the midst of his sermon ... I read it as he was making his speech ... He was good enough to advise me, and to make such virtuous pretty speeches, that if he had been a bishop he could not have spoke better, and as I thought the letter was a nice commentary on his lordship's sermon I gave it to him ... I don't think my Lord Kew will preach to me again for some time.' [441]

And, indeed, the incident ends their engagement. So Ethel has to gain her own experience, and achieve her own wisdom without Kew's help.

The narrative structure itself re-echoes this theme: for Pen as narrator watches Clive going through the same agonies and perplexities, with a few years' time lag, that he had himself suffered in the progress from boyhood at Greyfriars to manhood in London, with all the challenges and pains of entering society and a profession, and falling in love. Yet he can only record Clive's progress, not assist it. When Colonel Newcome asks him to act as Clive's elder brother and guardian, Pen sadly reflects on his helplessness: 'Ah! who is to guard the guardian?' [331]. Human beings remain isolated from each other, in their pain as well as their experience.

Another brief but telling scene shows how Clive and Jack Belsize, who – from the similarity of their situations as rejected lovers of women destined for wealthier suitors – might be expected to comfort one another, can only add to each other's misery. Each absorbed in his own unhappy love, they sit in the same darkened room, their cigar tips glowing separately, while Clive gazes out at the light in Ethel's window across the river.

His eyes are fixed upon a window whence comes the red light of a lamp, across which shadows float now and again. So every light in every booth yonder has a scheme of its own: every star above shines by itself; and each individual heart of ours goes on brightening with its own hopes, burning with its own desires, and quivering with its own pain. [378]

It is the same theme that Thackeray touches in *Pendennis*, when he tells his reader, 'Ah, sir – a distinct universe walks about under your hat and under mine ... You and I are but a pair of infinite isolations, with some fellow-islands a little more or less near to us' [184]. But in *The Newcomes* that loneliness, the mood of Arnold's poetry, pervades both action and tone: it is echoed by the narrator as it is lived out by the characters. There is more catastrophic action in *Vanity Fair*, more obsessive emotion in *Esmond*, but for me at least *The Newcomes* is the most moving of Thackeray's novels.

As the respectable world of the Newcomes has to justify its acquisitiveness with the suggestion that money is virtue and bankruptcy is damnation, so Thackeray uses a corresponding stylistic trick of telling a story about the dominance of the mercenary motive in terms that evoke the ideals of romance. His pattern of allusion to romance, fairy-tale, and fable[13] achieves a crossgrained texture in the novel that reproduces the contradictions of the Newcome values.

' Mr. Newcome's grandfather came to London with a satchel on his back, like Whittington. Isn't it romantic?' – so gushes Clara Pulleyn as she persuades herself that Barnes Newcome will make a good husband [420]. Such is the glamorized version of the origin of the Newcome family. Similarly, various characters see themselves in glamorous and adventurous roles, particularly from Scott's novels: Clive models his behaviour on a character from *Quentin Durward* [303], and chooses an incident from *Ivanhoe* as the subject for one of his grandiose paintings for the Academy. Florac is another admirer of 'Valtare Scott,' and enjoys playing Ravenswood to his servant's Caleb Balderstone. And Colonel Newcome, explicitly cast in the role of latter-day Don Quixote, is there to remind us of the anomalous relation between romance and actuality.

Characters and their relations are frequently painted in the bright colours of fairy-tale. Lady Kew is repeatedly described as a witch, and is

13 See Loofbourow *Thackeray and the Form of Fiction* (Princeton 1964) 67-72

Lady Kew as a witch: *The Newcomes* 681

depicted as one in Doyle's illustrations. We hear that Colonel Newcome
and Mrs Mackenzie, in planning the marriage that is to turn out so
disastrously, have a 'kind scheme ... that their young ones should marry
and be happy ever after, like the prince and princess of the fairy-tale'
[332]. Or a paragraph will begin, 'We read in the fairy stories [of] the
king and queen who lived once upon a time' [135], to introduce another
of the many incongruous analogies between fairy-tale and middle-class
Victorian England. The allusions are in ironic counterpoint to the main
theme, for the world of the Newcomes is no fairyland. Their marriages no
more allow them to 'live happily ever after' than does Clive's to Rosey;
and their rise to fortune, however like Dick Whittington's, can be called
'romantic' only by a considerable feat of self-delusion.

The 'Overture' and the epilogue of jumbled but significant beast fables,
which are also illustrated in the cover design, set the whole novel in an
ironic framework. Certain of the animals in the fables have recognizable

traits of characters in the novel – the owl talks like Mrs Hobson Newcome, the donkey in the lion's skin would be Farintosh, the lamb that beds with the wolf is Lady Clara Pulleyn, the wolf in sheep's clothing of course would be Barnes himself. The difference is that whereas all the pretentious or greedy or foolish animals in the Overture come by their deserts in the manner familiar in Aesop and La Fontaine, we see no such process in the main body of the novel. That indefinite ending for which Thackeray has been so denounced is a shock not only because in it he abandons solidity of specification, but because it wrenches us out of a world in which the operative maxim is 'if your neighbour's foot obstructs you, stamp on it; and do you suppose he won't take it away?' and substitutes one where poetic justice rules. The sentimental, Thackeray realizes, will be anxious to hear of the happy endings in store for the principal characters: and so he briefly suggests the kind of ending the sentimental require:

> My belief then is, that in fable-land somewhere, Ethel and Clive are living most comfortably together ... What about Sir Barnes Newcome ultimately? My impression is that he is married again, and it is my fervent hope that his present wife bullies him. Mrs. Mackenzie cannot have the face to keep that money which Clive paid over to her, beyond her lifetime; and will certainly leave it and her savings to little Tommy. I should not be surprised if Madame de Montcontour left a smart legacy to the Pendennis children; and Lord Kew stood god-father in case – in case Mr. and Mrs. Clive wanted such an article ... Anything you like happens in fable-land. Wicked folks die à propos (for instance, that death of Lady Kew was most artful, for if she had not died, don't you see that Ethel would have married Lord Farintosh the next week?) – annoying folks are got out of the way; the poor are rewarded – the upstarts are set down in fable-land, – the frog bursts with wicked rage, the fox is caught in his trap, the lamb is rescued from the wolf, and so forth, just in the nick of time. And the poet of fable-land rewards and punishes absolutely. [1008–9]

That phrase 'in fable-land' becomes more ironically loaded with each repetition. For the whole action of the novel has been saying that the

MR. THACKERAY'S NEW MONTHLY WORK.

THE NEWCOMES

MEMOIRS OF A MOST Respectable FAMILY

EDITED BY
ARTHUR PENDENNIS Esqre

ILLUSTRATED by RICHARD DOYLE.

LONDON: BRADBURY AND EVANS, 11, BOUVERIE STREET.
1855.

'The frog bursts with wicked rage, the fox is caught in his trap, the lamb is rescued from the wolf, and so forth': *The Newcomes* 1009. Cover design for *The Newcomes* world of the Newcomes is *not* fable-land, any more than it is fairyland. We have no dramatic depiction of the marriage of Clive and Ethel, because according to the reality of the main body of the novel it does not happen. Everyone would like to think of Barnes as hen-pecked; but we know that Warrington's prediction for him is far more likely to represent the hard facts: 'I look to see Sir Barnes Newcome prosper more and more. I make no doubt he will die an immense capitalist, and an exalted peer of this realm' [716]. Lady Kew certainly did die in time to prevent Ethel's marriage to Farintosh, but not in time to allow her to marry Clive. And the notion of Mrs Mackenzie's turning out to be a sort of posthumous fairy godmother to Clive's son is thoroughly improbable.

'Anything you like happens in fable-land' – and that is the only place it does happen. 'The poet of fable-land rewards and punishes absolutely' – but a major theme of the novel is that poetic justice does not operate in life, however it operates in romance and fairy-tale. And in his 'happy ending' Thackeray is exposing rather than capitulating to the kind of sentimentality by which readers like to delude themselves that everything comes out right in the end. In *The Newcomes* virtue is certainly not rewarded materially – Colonel Newcome dies a pauper. If 'virtue is its own reward,' its wages are meagre enough, for the saintly Madame de Florac has no more spiritual contentment than the wicked old Lady Kew: there is little to choose between Lady Kew's 'fourscore years of lonely vanity' [725] and the 'nearly fifty years dying' which is Madame de Florac's summary of her own adult life [629]. Even the promise of heavenly reward after death, the last resort of the canvasser for virtue, is treated with heavy irony. These are the glib words of her spiritual director:

'Not here, my daughter, is to be your happiness,' says the priest; 'whom Heaven loves it afflicts.' And he points out to her the agonies of suffering saints of her sex; assures her of their present beatitudes and glories; exhorts her to bear her pains with a faith like theirs; and is empowered to promise her a like reward. [608]

Vice is no more punished than virtue is rewarded. Perhaps 'crime does not pay,' but greed and hypocrisy and the selfish pursuit of one's own ends certainly do. 'To push on in the crowd, every male or female struggle must use his shoulders. If a better place than yours presents itself just beyond your neighbour, elbow him and take it' [95]. This is what *The Newcomes* is about, rather than how 'the fox is caught in his trap, the lamb is rescued from the wolf, and so forth.' In the Newcome world, your vices are your assets. A bad temper such as Lady Kew's, which makes her feared and respected, is 'one of the most precious and fortunate gifts with which a gentleman or lady can be endowed' [427]; and the man who 'abuses the men and things which he uses ... is better served than more grateful persons' [482]. The Newcome world is so far from being governed by justice that in it people like Barnes proceed from strength to strength, and from one reward to the next, while people like Clive and his father are crushed.

The animal imagery that is a connecting motif of the novel works in two ways. Much of it connects with the moral fables of the opening and closing pages; the beasts with which the human characters are compared are anthopomorphic and humorous, and evoke a moral response. Madame de Florac is a pelican; Clive and Pendennis in their moments of vanity wear 'peacock's plumage'; Honeyman's fashion-following congregation is appropriately a flock of sheep; and the social 'lions' are such as belong in the drawing-room rather than the jungle. Of Clive's preference for Ethel over Rosey we hear that 'the lad might ... be as happy as any young donkey that browses on this common of ours – but he must go and heehaw after a zebra, forsooth!' [572]. Such images present an ordered moral universe, in which behaviour can be classified as good or bad, wise or foolish.

But the animal imagery also suggests an amoral universe, and the topical view of nature as red in tooth and claw, a predatory struggle for survival. These animals – and birds and snakes predominate here – are drawn not from La Fontaine or the bestiaries but from natural history, and they are divided not into good and bad but into predators and victims. Creditors and bailiffs 'rush like vultures upon their prey' [326]; Lady Kew is an eagle, swooping on Farintosh, the lamb on whom she is to feed her eaglet, Ethel [609]; Clive and Hoby (a hobby, of which 'hoby' is an archaic varient, is a species of small falcon) are again predatory birds, hunting the mouse Rosey [743], while Rosey before her mother is 'a bird before a boa-constrictor' [935]. The struggle for survival in the Newcome world is perhaps more refined than that among the animals, but it is not ultimately any gentler. The typical product of this world is Barnes, whom Warrington shows to be even baser than 'Nature's rogues' [716]. It is the carnivores like him, rather than the herbivores like the colonel, who prosper in the main stream of evolution in English society.

And yet an exposition of *The Newcomes* suggesting that Thackeray presented English society as a savage and predatory struggle for survival needs some qualification. His faculty for seeing every side of a question prevented him from writing a *roman à thèse* in the manner of Zola and the naturalists. He is exposing the tendency of the middle classes to disguise their concern for making money as the concern for saving their souls, and to gush about romance while practising self-interest. But romance and the veneration for true goodness are not laughed out of court in the process. As Barnes Newcome represents the refined savagery of a greedily self-seeking society, so the artist J.J. Ridley stands for the truth of human ideals. He can conceive of beauty, love, and heroism in his imagination, and realize them in his art; to him 'splendours of Nature were revealed to vulgar sights invisible, and beauties manifest in forms, colours, shadows of common objects, where most of the world saw only what was dull, and gross, and familiar' [160]; and he is a greater painter than Clive, who can paint only what he sees. Ethel, who at one point justifies herself to Laura, 'If you had been bred as I have, you would be as I am' [666], has eventually to find her identity through transcending her environment; so J.J.'s imagination is awakened rather than confined by the dingy little room in Walpole Street:

> All these delights and sights, and joys and glories, these thrills of sympathy, movements of unknown longing, and visions of beauty, a young sickly lad of eighteen enjoys in a little dark room where there is a bed disguised in the shape of a wardrobe, and a little old woman is playing under a gas-lamp on the jingling keys of an old piano. [154]

Doyle's illustration for this passage was used as the frontispiece for the first edition. The ideals of romance have a certain validity as well as the

'To [J. J.] splendours of Nature were revealed to vulgar sights invisible, and beauties manifest in forms, colours, shadows of common objects, where most of the world saw only what was dull, and gross, and familiar':
The Newcomes 160

actualities of the unscrupulous struggle for success, and though the quixotic Colonel Newcome may be shown as often deluded, an existence without some measure of faith in love and honour emerges too as a barren half-life. The Colonel may be crushed, but we and characters in the novel have pity for him; and concepts like decency and justice exist and operate even in a society where the Barnes Newcomes prosper.

The Newcomes is by no means the 'loose baggy monster' of James's phrase: it is not just a sprawling narrative that contains some amusing characters and some graphic description of manners in mid-Victorian society. It is a carefully organized novel in which style and imagery, as well as character and action, contribute to a unifying theme, and in which the length is adapted to the complexity of the content. The action takes place, and the characters find their moral being, in a minutely realized milieu in which 'respectability' is the dominant operative standard. In relating his story in language that elevates 'fumbling in a greasy till' to heroism and reduces love and faith to mere commodities, Thackeray conveys society's confusion of values by stylistic means. And that counterpoint between style and matter does more than illuminate a contemporary vice: it reflects some of the contradictions of human existence. As the animal imagery suggests both the ordered moral universe of fable and the savage jungle of popular Darwinianism, so the pattern of contrasts between illusion and reality, fantasy and hard fact, aspiration and achievement, conveys how far human practice falls short of human ideals.

5

Ambivalent Relationships

THACKERAY IS, AFTER ALL, AN ACKNOWLEDGED MASTER OF THE
novel of manners, but his novels are also subtle and intense studies of
human psychology. So far, I have considered his characters as animals in a
social jungle, and as human beings for whom this society is a context for
moral choice; but of course they exist at a level that is deeper than either of
these, with motives that cannot be fully explained by social or moral
aspirations, though they may be influenced by them.

It is curious to what an extent the active and often furious or agonized
psychic life of Thackeray's characters has been overlooked. Amelia has
been analysed this way and that; Rachel Esmond has been given the full
treatment, by Tilford and others; and Dorothy Van Ghent has marvellously illuminated the panic, the disease, and the madness inside even a
Jos Sedley's tight unwrinkled skin, and suggested not only the cruelty of
Vanity Fair but also its crazy perversity. But to a great extent the critics have
concerned themselves with the surfaces of things. There is a usual assumption, which is indeed part of the truth, that Thackeray depicts a superficial
society, typified by superficial characters, tenth-rate people always trying
to prove they are ninth-rate, uninterested in each other except as they are
higher or lower in the pecking order, and operating according to a consistent
if unpleasant rationale. Such seems to be Leavis's conviction in dismissing
Thackeray's novels as having '(apart from some social history)' nothing to
offer in the way of 'the essential substance of interest.'[1] For Lubbock,
Vanity Fair is less a study of people in their intimate relations to each
other than 'the impression of a world, a society, a time ... a chapter in the
notorious career of well-to-do London.'[2] And, according to Edmund

1 *The Great Tradition* (London 1948) 21
2 *The Craft of Fiction* (London 1921) 95

Wilson, Thackeray 'is unable to interest himself in personalities or relations for their own sake.'[3]

Extended analysis of a character or a relationship, of course, Thackeray does not give us. He does not enter the mind and describe its workings in detail in the manner of George Eliot, or chronicle the minute fluctuations of a relationship like James. What we know of his characters we must gather for the most part from speech and gesture, external manifestations. From these and from occasional supplementary comments the reader must do the work of the psychiatrist himself. But there is plenty of material to work on; for in the packed incident and among the crowds of characters there is always more going on than meets the eye. In an image or an apparently insignificant scene, in a word, a kiss, a blush, the reader has glimpses of depths of motive and ambivalence of emotion of which the characters themselves are often unaware.

The conflict of conscious and unconscious motivation is a strong force in all of Thackeray's work. This is why his characters so often escape close examination, for they themselves often rationalize in social terms the motives that have a deeper origin. Generations of readers have believed, as she would have them believe, that Rachel Esmond denounced Harry only for bringing the smallpox into the house, when it was jealousy for the blacksmith's daughter that was the underlying cause of her passionate rebuke. Mrs Baynes turns against Philip as a suitor for her daughter ostensibly because he has insufficient money and social standing, but also because her tenderness for him has been thwarted. Barry Lyndon sets about catching a rich wife in order to achieve an easy berth in life, and then takes a savage pleasure in subjecting her to his tyrannical will and perversely squandering her fortune. Helen Pendennis is a conscientious mother who earnestly wishes the best for her son: but there is a sexual element in her passionate fondness for him that makes her neurotically resist all his attachments to other women.

It is particularly the ambiguity in the relations between the generations that interests Thackeray. The love of two young people of marriageable age, which he is so ready to dismiss as just another instance of the same old

3 'An Old Friend of the Family: Thackeray' in *Classics and Commercials* (New York 1950) 357

inevitable attraction, becomes tense and absorbing when seen in relation
to the love and demands of the parents' generation. Mothers and sons,
daughters and fathers! – Thackeray, whose marriage and love life were
arid if not disastrous, informs his fictional relationships with the energy of
his own compensatory relations with his mother and his daughters.
Freudian psychology has given us a terminology for the relationships
Thackeray depicts, but it would otherwise have had surprisingly little to
teach him. 'I have no doubt,' he says, speaking of Helen's jealous super-
vision of Pen's loves, 'there is a sexual jealousy on the mother's part, and a
secret pang' [P 298]. That is strong language for a Victorian, and it shows
his high degree of consciousness in the depiction of the Oedipal relation.
In one sense he goes beyond Freud, for his vision does not limit significant
experience to infancy, and hence he is as perceptive about the parent as the
child: as interested, in fact, in the Jocasta and the Agamemnon as in the
Oedipus and the Electra.

These concerns were close to home for Thackeray, an integral part of
his own experience, as his letters show. He made no secret of the fact that
Helen Pendennis was a portrait of his mother, and in 1852 he wrote of her:

> It gives the keenest tortures of jealousy and disappointed yearning to
> my dearest old mother (who's as beautiful now as ever) that she can't
> be all in all to me, mother sister wife everything but it mayn't be –
> There's hardly a subject on wh. we don't differ. And she lives away at
> Paris with her husband a noble simple old gentleman who loves
> nothing but her in the world, and a jealousy after me tears & rends
> her. Eh! who is happy? When I was a boy at Larkbeare, I thought her
> an Angel & worshipped her. I see but a woman now, O so tender so
> loving so cruel. My daughter Anny says O how like Granny is to Mrs.
> Pendennis Papa – and Granny is mighty angry that I should think no
> better of her than that. [Letters III 12–13]

This gives some indication of the extent of Thackeray's awareness of the
implications of the ambivalent relationships he depicts.

The same pattern of jealousy between parent and child emerges, though
not so persistently, in the relationship of father to daughter, where the
daughter may devote herself to the father to the exclusion of a lover, or

become, like Beatrix, a rival of her mother. General Lambert admits jocularly, 'We men don't wish to part with [our daughters]. I am sure, for my part, I should not like yonder young fellow half as well if I thought he intended to carry one of my darlings away with him' [v 219]. But this is more than a joke, for his daughter Hetty, out of devotion to him, does remain a childless old maid.

The central emotional relationships in the novels repeatedly take the form of a triangle of which parent and child, either as lovers or as sexual rivals, are two of the corners. In a Victorian novel such a situation must necessarily be suggested rather than analysed in detail, but it was perennially interesting to Thackeray.

Before we consider the tensions of these triangle relationships in the different novels, it is worth studying separately one particular form which depends on the ambivalence of the mother-daughter relationship: that of the mother, daughter, and daughter's lover. It is in many ways the one seen most clearly from the outside, for Thackeray's definitely male point of view gave him the most objective vision of the other two corners of the triangle in which two women are in love with the same man. And it explains, too, the psychological evolution of that recurring and appalling figure in Thackeray's novels, the mother-in-law.[4]

This is the typical pattern. The bond between mother and daughter is seen as being so close that they seem like twins, and their looks, their reactions, and apparently their interests, are identical. But this very identity of interest must turn to enmity when a suitor enters the picture; for in the nature of things he can take only one half of the composite being that is mother and daughter, though he may want with some part of himself to take both, and may vacillate between them: Henry Esmond's vacillation lasts for ten years, during which he tries to make Rachel his mother-in-law before he finally makes her his wife instead. Generally, however, the suitor takes the daughter; and, though for a while the mother can live through her daughter and so carry on a vicarious love

4 Some of this material has already been published in my article, 'Thackeray's Mothers-in-Law,' in *Literature and Psychology* xv (1965) 171–9, and in *Thackeray: A Collection of Critical Essays* ed. Alexander Welsh (Englewood Cliffs, NJ, 1968) 55–64.

Mother and daughter as sirens: *The Newcomes* 658

affair, eventually she finds that her daughter is no longer an extension of herself, but her rival instead, and usually the successful rival at that. The mother is excluded from the tender relationship; and her reaction is to swing to the opposite extreme of hostility – to become, in fact, one of the savage mothers-in-law that Thackeray so often depicted.

Mother and daughter are often presented as a single composite image, entwined and wrapped up in one another. '*Matre pulchra filia pulchrior*,' someone says of Beatrix and Rachel in *Esmond*; their shoes are made from the same last, and Rachel says of her daughter, 'We are like sisters, and she the eldest sister, somehow' [301]. The singing Mrs and Miss Sherrick, who perform the chants at Lady Whittlesea's, dressed alike in nunlike habits, are represented, in one of Doyle's delightful little designs for chapter initials, as a brace of latter-day sirens, equally appealing to the wandering male. Mrs and Miss Bolton similarly work as a team with their charming visitor Pendennis:

> Fanny clapped her hands with pleasure: her face beamed with it. She looked and nodded, and laughed at her mamma, who nodded and laughed in her turn. Mrs. Bolton was not superannuated for pleasure yet, or by any means too old for admiration, she thought. And very likely Mr. Pendennis, in his conversation with her, had insinuated

some compliments, or shaped his talk so as to please her ... When two women get together to like a man, they help each other on – each pushes the other forward – and the second, out of sheer sympathy, becomes as eager as the principal. [P 612–13]

Mothers and daughters are characteristically entwined in mutual embraces, like Mrs Mackenzie and Rosey: 'More caresses follow. Mamma is in a rapture. How pretty they look – the mother and daughter – two lilies twining together' [N 287]. The floral imagery is recurrent: it is when Pen sees Laura giving her foster-mother Helen a rose that 'the image of the two women remained for ever after in his mind' [P 299]. Similarly, Charlotte Baynes is said to be 'blooming like a rose ... the very image of her mother'; though here the narrator comments drily, 'In this case poor Charlotte must have looked like a yellow rose, for Mrs. Baynes was of a bilious temperament and complexion' [AP 290].

An early instance of this identification of mother and daughter occurs in 'The Ravenswing,' where Mrs Crump and her daughter meet the dashing Mr Walker at the hairdresser's:

> [Mr Walker] looked round at the ladies with such a fascinating grace, that both ... blushed and giggled, and were quite pleased. Mamma looked at 'Gina, and 'Gina looked at mamma; and then mamma gave 'Gina a little blow in the region of her little waist, and then both burst out laughing ... and both fixed their large shining black eyes repeatedly on Mr. Walker ...
>
> 'He can't stay,' said Mrs. Crump, all of a sudden, blushing as red as a peony.
>
> 'I shall have on my peignoir, mamma,' said miss, looking at the gentleman, and then dropping down her eyes and blushing too. [IV 335]

Here mother and daughter (peonies this time), with the same black eyes, and the same gestures and reactions, both blush for the same man, whom they both find attractive. Mrs Crump is good-humoured, even if Mr Walker pays more attention to Morgiana, for when Morgiana lets down her beautiful black hair, her main sexual attraction, and he is rapt in admiration, she is able to make 'her daughter's triumph her own':

'Heigho! when I acted at the Wells in 1820, before that dear girl was born, *I* had such a head of hair as that, to a shade, sir, to a shade. They called me Ravenswing on account of it [the name that her daughter afterwards inherits]. I lost my head of hair when that dear child was born, and I often say to her, 'Morgiana, you came into the world to rob your mother of her 'air.'' [IV 356]

The sexual symbolism of such a passage suggests the deep rivalry that is implicit in the identification of mother and daughter. Later Thackeray was to recall it in *Esmond*, where Rachel loses her hair and her beauty during the smallpox, after which her daughter begins to monopolize the love of both her husband and Harry.

While the identification of mother and daughter lasts the mother can live through her daughter, and this is why mothers are such ardent match-makers; they themselves are in some sense carrying on a vicarious love-affair with their daughters' suitors. General Lambert may well ask in bewilderment, 'What is this burning desire all you women have for selling and marrying your daughters?' [V 219]. The answer is in the same novel:

No woman was ever averse to the idea of her daughter getting a husband, however fathers revolt against the invasion of the son-in-law. As for mothers and grandmothers, those good folks are married over again in the marriage of their young ones; and their souls attire themselves in the laces and muslins of twenty – forty years ago. [V 339]

No wonder Mrs Mackenzie can say cheerfully, 'I live for my darling girls now' [N 286], as she spreads her net to catch Clive as a husband for Rosey.

The sexual motive in the development of Thackeray's termagant mothers-in-law is often suggested and even asserted in the novels. Nor is it a one-way attraction: the son-in-law is shown as finding some attraction in both the mother and the daughter, the two of whom he so often sees as closely identified. We tend to think of Mrs Mackenzie as the dreadful

Campaigner of the last part of *The Newcomes*, but we should also remember that she was not always such a dragon. When Clive is considering
Rosey as a wife, we hear that he 'laughed and joked and waltzed alternately with Rosey and her mamma. The latter was the briskest partner of
the two' [N 284]. And once he even admits half-jocularly of Mrs Mackenzie
'I thought her delightful for three days, I declare I was in love with
her' [315]. George Warrington in *The Virginians* describes a stage in his
relations with the Lambert family when Mrs Lambert, during her promotion of his match with her daughter Theo, preens herself on her attractions, dislikes being reminded of her age, and pays George all sorts of
sentimental attentions which he enjoys and reciprocates. He later recollects
this with surprise: 'Strange infatuation of passion – singular perversity of
reason! At some time before his marriage, it not unfrequently happens
that a man actually is fond of his mother-in-law!' [V 705–6]. Even Philip
in his relation with Mrs Baynes – who, being old and of bilious complexion,
is the least physically attractive of these mothers-in-law – was not always
as hostile as he becomes in later life, when 'he fumes, shouts, and rages
against them, as if all were like his' [AP 618]. There was a time when he
espoused her cause against his friend Pendennis, and when he listened
respectfully to her endless anecdotes about military life in India [236–9].
Similarly, we remember there was also a time when she considered him
her family's great deliverer, and was eager to promote his match with
Charlotte. Her initial motivation is exposed in a revealing dialogue
between her and her sister, Mrs MacWhirter, who becomes Philip's
defender after Mrs Baynes has turned against him:

'Of course, as a feeling mother, I feel that poor Charlotte is unhappy,
my dear.'
'But what makes her so, my dear?' cries Mrs. MacWhirter, who
presently showed that she was mistress of the whole controversy.
'No wonder Charlotte is unhappy, dear love! Can a girl be engaged
to a young man, a most interesting young man, a clever, accomplished,
highly educated young man – '
'*What?*' cries Mrs. Baynes.
'Haven't I your letters? I have them all in my desk. They are in

that hall now. Didn't you tell me so over and over again; and rave about him, till I thought you were in love with him yourself almost?' cries Mrs. Mac.

'A most indecent observation!' cries out Eliza Baynes, in her deep, awful voice. [AP 399]

Inevitably there comes a time when the mother ceases to be able to live a vicarious love affair through her daughter, a time when she finds that her daughter has the young man's whole allegiance and that he has forgotten his sentimental attachment to her and may even actively dislike her. Her reaction, when she finds herself thus excluded, is a violent change from tenderness to hostility. So there is in fact a carefully conceived psychological basis for the metamorphosis of the charming Mrs Mackenzie into the terrible Campaigner of *The Newcomes* and for that of Mrs Baynes from match-maker to match-breaker in *Philip*. In Mrs Mackenzie the two stages of identification and rivalry actually overlap, and express themselves alternately in her private and public roles: upstairs she mercilessly scolds and pinches Rosey, but when they descend to the company she is all effusion and caresses.

Thackeray usually offers a social motive as well for this change in the mother. Mrs Baynes says she wants a better financial match for Charlotte than the out-at-elbow Philip, and Mrs Mackenzie is at her worst when Colonel Newcome has lost her money. But the sexual motive of thwarted tenderness is undoubtedly present too, and is perhaps the more genuine. Freud describes this process when he is discussing the impulse towards incest and its suppression:

A mother, as she grows older, saves herself from this [the uneventfulness of her emotional life] by putting herself in her children's place, by identifying herself with them; and this she does by making their emotional experiences her own ... A mother's sympathetic identification with her daughter can easily go so far that she herself falls in love with the man her daughter loves; and in glaring instances this may lead to severe forms of neurotic illness as a result of her violent mental struggles against this emotional situation. In any case, it very frequently happens that a mother-in-law is subject to an *impulse* to fall in love in this way, and this impulse itself or an opposing trend are added to the tumult of conflicting forces in her mind. And very often the unkind, sadistic components of her love are directed on to her son-in-law in order that the forbidden, affectionate ones may be the more severely suppressed.[5]

It is clear that Thackeray does have such a situation in mind, and that he regards a woman like Mrs Baynes as a neurotic. 'Ah fond mother of fair daughters!' Mr Batchelor moralizes in *Lovel The Widower*, 'how strange thy passion is to add to thy titles that of mother-in-law! I am told, when you have got the title, it is often but a bitterness and a disappointment' [LW 90].

In his *Electra*, Sophocles portrays three roles of the daughter in the children of Agamemnon and Clytemnestra. Iphigenia is the father's victim, and has the mother's allegiance; Chrysothemis is ready to forget her father and to become an extension of her mother's will; and Electra is so devoted to her father that she becomes her mother's mortal enemy. But Electra is also her father's victim, for she wastes her life in devotion to him.

Thackeray shows the daughter in all three of these roles. Mr Osborne, the tyrannical father who marries one of his daughters to a rich stuffed shirt and keeps the other at home to minister to him until she becomes an embittered spinster, has good reason to decorate his drawing-room with a clock 'surmounted by a cheerful brass group of the sacrifice of Iphigenia' [VF 149]. General Lambert, for all his loving kindness, extorts the same sacrifice from Hetty, and General Baynes almost does the same with Charlotte. The mothers live through their daughters while they can; then when they are excluded they turn vindictive. But the element of rivalry between mother and daughter is potentially present from the first: Mrs Crump loses her beautiful hair when her daughter is born; and in Thackeray's last work, the unfinished *Denis Duval*, the mad Countess de Saverne, like a Clytemnestra turning the tables on Electra, tries to drown her baby daughter. It is a symmetrical reversal of the incident in

5 *Totem and Taboo* in *The Standard Edition of the Complete Psychological Works of Sigmund Freud* ed. James Strachey (London 1955–) XIII 15

Esmond where Francis Castlewood almost allows his baby son to perish by fire.

The rivalry between mother and daughter is not only for the lover but for the husband and father as well. Mrs Baynes is at last a pathetic figure: 'That sad, humiliated, deserted mother goes out from her daughter's presence, hanging her head' [AP 415]. And she is cast off not only by Charlotte and Philip, but by General Baynes too, who changes his allegiance from his wife to his daughter. In a powerful passage, a long remorseful self-examination by General Baynes while he lies sleepless in bed beside his wife, we are shown how he at last realizes that at her instigation he has made an Iphigenia of his daughter: 'You stab her to the heart, and break your plighted honour to your child. "And it is yonder cruel, shrivelled, bilious, plain old woman who makes me do all this, and trample on my darling, and torture her!" he thinks' [AP 410]. After this realization, he turns from his wife to cleave to his daughter.

This intricate set of interlocking triangles – father between wife and daughter, mother between husband and son-in-law, and daughter between father and lover – is the emotional core of *Philip* which, among all Thackeray's novels, has the balance of interest weighted most heavily on the psychological relationships between the characters rather than on the hero's progress through society.

The mother-daughter-lover triangle is only one of the various possibilities of allegiances and rivalries between the generations that Thackeray explores. Such ambivalent relationships are not only the focus of emotional interest in the novels, but their recurrence and variation constitute a structural pattern which often has as much force as the formal plot. To demonstrate this we must examine these patterns as they occur in the separate novels.

BARRY LYNDON

Barry Lyndon is to a great extent a picaresque novel in which Barry goes through many adventures, and travels in various capacities to several countries. But at the beginning and at the end the focus of interest is on a particular set of relationships rather than on what the protagonist does or sees in the world.

We are told in detail initially of Barry's first love and finally of his marriage; and both involve him in a triangle situation. Like nearly all Thackeray's young men, he first falls in love with a woman older than himself – eight years is the usual age difference: 'She is eight years older than you (that follows, of course)' [20], says Barry. She is his cousin Nora; and what follows just as automatically is that his mother is at once jealous of her. She abuses Nora as being fat, freckled, and red-haired [22]. Then when Barry is ill, and will take nothing but from Nora's hand, she becomes the pathetic figure of the rejected beloved:

> [I] would look rudely and sulkily upon the good mother, who loved me better than anything else in the world, and gave up even her favourite habits, and proper and becoming jealousies, to make me happy ... She must have been very sad, that poor mother of mine – Heaven be good to her! – at that period of my life; and has often told me since what a pang of the heart it was to her to see all her care and affection of years forgotten by me in a minute, and for the sake of a little, heartless jilt. [28–9]

Nora herself drives Barry wild with jealousy by treating him 'sometimes ... as a child, sometimes as a man' [23]. The situation is one that Thackeray portrays more than once, and with sympathy: where the hero is off with the older mother and on with the new mother-surrogate.

At the other end of the novel is Barry's marriage with the widow, Lady Lyndon. Barry has by now developed from the almost sympathetic young scapegrace to the dyed-in-the-wool villain. But at the same time there is a startling psychological realism about his relation with the woman he marries, and a convincing exploration, in the study of her feelings for him, of emotional ambivalence.

He woos her as peremptorily as Gloucester woos Lady Anne, and he knows that the more she is afraid of him, the more likely he is to win her. 'Terror, be sure of that, is not a bad ingredient of love' [218], he says, and he knows he is prospering in his suit when 'the widow was growing dreadfully afraid of me, calling me her *bête noire*, her dark spirit, her murderous adorer' [219].

> 'Can this monster,' she wrote, 'indeed do as he boasts, and bend even Fate to his will? – can he make me marry him though I cordially detest him, and bring me a slave to his feet? The horrid look of his black serpent-like eyes fascinates and frightens me; it seems to follow me everywhere, and even when I close my own eyes, the dreadful gaze penetrates the lids, and is still upon me.' [220]

'When a woman begins to talk of a man in this way,' Barry comments drily, 'he is an ass who does not win her'; and of course he does win her, and proceeds to play Bluebeard to her Fatima. It is interesting that in Thackeray's version of the Bluebeard myth, which he handled more than once, women are particularly attracted to Bluebeard, even when they know of his nefarious deeds; in 'Barbazure' Fatima's cousin 'would give her eyes' to become his tenth wife, and actually stands by at the proposed execution of her predecessor so as to be first in line for the succession [VIII 132–7]. *Barry Lyndon* is a more realistic and extended version of the story, but the same perversity is in operation. Lady Lyndon is fat and unromantic, and to some extent a figure of fun – though it is macabre fun at best. But she is more interesting as a psychological study in masochism: for there is a subtle insight in the depiction of her adoration of Barry in spite of, or because of, his brutal treatment:

> My Lady Lyndon's relation with me was a singular one. Her life was passed in a crack-brained sort of alternation between love and hatred for me. If I was in a good humour with her (as occurred sometimes), there was nothing she would not do to propitiate me further, and she would be as absurd and violent in her expressions of fondness as, at other moments, she would be in her demonstrations of hatred ... I had got my lady into such a terror about me that when I smiled it was quite an era of happiness to her; and, if I beckoned to her, she would come fawning up to me like a dog ... I brought my high-born

wife to kiss my hand, to pull off my boots, to fetch and carry for me like a servant. [299]

So in this early novel Thackeray is already exploring the combination of love and hatred, and of attraction and fear, and its result in a definite masochism.

Lady Lyndon has a young son, Lord Bullingdon, who from the first is Barry's enemy. At the wedding, 'when called upon by the Countess to embrace his papa, he shook his fist in my face, and said, "*He* my father!"' [233]. He might well have added, 'A little more than kin, and less than kind,' for there is a strong parallel here with the Hamlet situation. Step-father and step-son are immediate rivals and hate each other. Barry would like to disinherit Bullingdon, who is his father's heir: 'The insubordination of that boy was dreadful. He used to quote passages of *Hamlet* to his mother, which made her very angry. Once when I took a horsewhip to chastise him, he drew a knife, and would have stabbed me' [240]. Barry reveals his feelings in one of his characteristic attempts at self-justification:

For the first three years I never struck my wife but when I was in liquor. When I flung the carving-knife at Bullingdon I was drunk, as everybody can testify; but as for having any systematic scheme against the poor lad, I can solemnly declare that, beyond merely hating him (and one's inclinations are not in one's power), I am guilty of no evil towards him. [252]

The *Hamlet* parallel is maintained, though not explicitly, in Bullingdon's scholarly habits, and in the love the common people bear him. Thackeray seems to have been aware of the Oedipal situation which, as Freud and Jones have pointed out, is implicit in the play.[6] There is a scene in which Bullingdon knocks over the drunken and wife-beating Barry, and 'catching his fainting mother in his arms, took her into his own room, where he, upon her entreaty, swore he would never leave the house as long as she continued united with me' [268]. Like Claudius, Barry plots to send his

6 See Ernest Jones' *Hamlet and Oedipus* (New York 1949) for a full elaboration of Freud's analogy

step-son abroad on a fatal mission, but Bullingdon manages to frustrate the attempt, and finally returns to castigate the already dethroned step-father.

Lady Lyndon is certainly no Gertrude; but her curious mixture of feelings for Barry and her divided allegiance between her second husband and her son make her part of the novel that which holds our interest. And Barry's career takes the shape of a development from the son who is adored by his mother to the father figure who is the deadly enemy of the son.

VANITY FAIR

Dorothy Van Ghent, in a perceptive passage of her study of the novel, has pointed out the importance of the theme of the fathers in *Vanity Fair*. The tyrannical Osborne and his household of frightened females, the mild and ineffective Sedley, old Sir Pitt Crawley, and the cynical Lord Steyne are the father figures. The fatherless heroine, Becky, is twice involved in a triangle between her husband and an older man, at the beginning and at the end of her career. The first time she is actually wooed by father and son, Sir Pitt and Rawdon Crawley. When she is obliged to refuse the old man's proposal because she is already married to his son, she weeps 'some of the most genuine tears that ever fell from her eyes' [178]. 'I might have been somebody's mamma, instead of – ' she writes to Rawdon, suggesting all the psychological complexity of the situation [187]. Sir Pitt is disappointed but good-humoured and even amused when he hears she must reject his proposal because she is married already: "'Vamous,'" said Sir Pitt. "Who'd ha' thought it! what a sly little devil! what a little fox it waws!" he muttered to himself, chuckling with pleasure' [VF 182]. But when he knows the identity of his rival he is enraged.

> When Sir Pitt Crawley heard that Rebecca was married to his son, he broke out into a fury of language, which it would do no good to repeat in this place ... We will shut the door upon the figure of the frenzied old man, wild with hatred and insane with baffled desire. [199]

In *Vanity Fair*, with the siren Becky at its centre, we see more of undisguised male rivalry than in the other novels. Esmond and the Duke of Hamilton have their moments of hauteur and perceptible hostility in one another's presence, but they always preserve the rules of decorum. Becky's various suitors, on the other hand, snarl and growl at one another, and physical violence erupts more than once. There is something of the primal situation of the leader of the pack challenged by the younger male, for the difference in generation always seems to contribute to the violence of the jealousy. A memorable scene is that where Becky flirts with the dashing young George Osborne in her box at the opera, while her old beau General Tufto furiously looks on. He 'stared at the newcomer with a sulky scowl, as much as to say, who the devil are you?' While he pretends to examine the audience with his opera-glass, 'Rebecca saw that his disengaged eye was working round in her direction, and shooting out bloodshot glances at her and George.' And when, delighted with her mischief, Becky leaves on George's arm, Tufto stays behind in the box, muttering curses in an access of 'lust and fury, rage and hatred' [350–1].

At the beginning of her career Becky betrays the father (at least in his own eyes) for the son; and at the end she betrays the son, her husband, for another old and powerful lover, Lord Steyne, who is the 'wolf' as Sir Pitt had been the 'hyena':

> He had her hand in his, and was bowing over it to kiss it, when Becky started up with a faint scream as she caught sight of Rawdon's white face. At the next instant she tried a smile, a horrid smile, as if to welcome her husband: and Steyne rose up, grinding his teeth, pale, and with fury in his looks.
>
> He, too, attempted a laugh – and came forward holding out his hand. 'What, come back! How d'ye do, Crawley?' he said, the nerves of his mouth twitching as he tried to grin at the intruder. [675]

There are obvious similarities between the old aspirants to Becky's affections, including even their appearance – they are all bald, toothy, and stocky in build – which emphasize the repetition of this father-woman-son triangle.

Becky is not the only woman in *Vanity Fair* who is 'a match ... for father and son too' [130]. In *Pendennis* and *Esmond*, where the focus is on the man between the girl and the mother, there are repeated relationships of young men with older women. But in *Vanity Fair* the woman is characteristically seen between the young man and the father figure. Maria Osborne, engaged to young Frederick Augustus Bullock, would as soon marry 'gouty, old, bald-headed, bottle-nosed Bullock Senior' [138]. When George Osborne shows himself reluctant to espouse Miss Swartz, the West Indian heiress, his father is quite ready to do the job himself: '"Gad, if Miss S. will have me, I'm her man. *I* ain't particular about a shade or so of tawny." And the old gentleman gave his knowing grin and coarse laugh' [279]. And he does in fact propose to her [535]. Society sanctions the marriage of young girls to decrepit rich old men. We hear how Miss Trotter, arrayed in orange blossom and bridal gown, 'trip[ped] into the travelling carriage at St. George's, Hanover Square, and Lord Methuselah hobbled in after. With what an engaging modesty she pulled down the blinds of the chariot – the dear innocent! There were half the carriages of Vanity Fair at the wedding' [138].

The theme of the mothers in *Vanity Fair* is almost as pervasive as that of the fathers. This is connected mainly with Amelia's part of the story, while the fathers have most to do with Becky's. Amelia's mother, Mrs Sedley, follows the pattern of Thackeray's other mothers in being eager to marry off her daughter but indignant at the thought of her son's marriage. 'Nothing is more keen, nor more common, nor more justifiable, than maternal jealousy' [37], the narrator tells us; he is referring to Mrs Sedley's anger at the idea of Jos marrying Becky, which emerges in a little colloquy between Jos's parents:

'Here is Emmy's little friend making love to him as hard as she can; that's quite clear; and if she does not catch him some other will. That man is destined to be a prey to woman ...'

'She shall go off to-morrow, the little artful creature,' said Mrs. Sedley, with great energy.

'Why not she as well as another, Mrs. Sedley? The girl's a white face at any rate. *I* don't care who marries him. Let Joe please himself.' [36]

The parents' positions are reversed when it comes to Amelia's marriage. In helping Amelia to buy her trousseau 'Mrs. Sedley was herself again almost, and sincerely happy for the first time since their misfortunes' [322]. But Mr Sedley's reaction, when he hears that George will after all condescend to marry a bankrupt's daughter, is savage: 'I won't have his name mentioned in my house. I curse the day that ever I let him into it; and I'd rather see my daughter dead at my feet than married to him' [243].

During the time of Amelia's early widowhood, when she is living with her parents in reduced circumstances, her allegiance is always to her father, and she is estranged from her mother. We hear of Mrs Sedley that 'the bitterness of poverty has poisoned the life of the once cheerful and kindly woman' [621]: but it is not only poverty that embitters Mrs Sedley, as it is not only poverty that turns the 'once cheerful' Mrs Mackenzie into a cruel tyrant in *The Newcomes*. The primal rivalry between mother and daughter is at work as well.

It is only for her father's sake that Amelia can make up her mind to part with Georgy to his grandfather Osborne, to save her family from their increasing hardship. The decision becomes necessary when old Sedley confesses that he has muddled away Jos's annuity, their last source of income.

> 'Ah!' said he, with quivering lips and turning away, 'you despise your old father now.'
>
> 'Oh, papa! it is not that,' Amelia cried out, falling on his neck, and kissing him many times. 'You are always good and kind. You did it for the best. It is not for the money – it is – O my God! my God! have mercy upon me, and give me strength to bear this trial;' and she kissed him again wildly, and went away. [624]

Amelia as a mother devotes herself to Georgy as she had devoted herself to George. She in fact almost makes a husband of Georgy, and constantly sees him as the image of his father.[7] Now, after she has deserted the father for the husband, she finds she must sacrifice the son for the father. The roles of father, husband, and son are strangely interchangeable, each

7 See Myron Taube: 'Georgy becomes an unknowing lover for Amelia, an object of her worship': 'The Character of Amelia in the Meaning of *Vanity Fair*' *Victorian Newsletter* 18 (1960) 6

substituting for the other in Amelia's love.

The time span of *Vanity Fair* allows history to repeat itself in the generations; and the father-daughter, mother-son pattern of the Sedley family is lived again in the quadrangle of the Dobbin ménage. The final image of the novel shows the structure of the Dobbin family as they retreat from Becky's baleful presence:

> Emmy scurrying off on the arm of George (now grown a dashing young gentleman), and the colonel seizing up his little Janey, of whom he is fonder than of anything in the world – fonder even than of his *History of the Punjaub.*
>
> 'Fonder than he is of me,' Emmy thinks, with a sigh. [877]

So there is a cyclical pattern for Amelia as for Becky, and the repeating patterns of sexual and family relationships is part of the structure of the novel.

PENDENNIS

The parent and child relationship, which is an underlying theme in *Vanity Fair*, is in the foreground of *Pendennis*. Pen's story is to a large extent the history of his loves; and each relation he has with a woman turns into a three-cornered one in which his mother plays the most significant part.

We hear only in summary of Helen Pendennis's youth and Arthur's childhood. She had fallen in love with a young man who was already engaged to another woman. The brief love of the two was broken off, and he fulfilled his engagement; but Helen later becomes the guardian of her early lover's daughter, and so in a sense the mother of his child. After this unhappy love she consents to marry the elderly apothecary-turned-gentleman, John Pendennis. She comes to worship this fatherly figure, but she also adores her boy Arthur. The mother and son are in the habit of taking sunset walks together which 'generally ended in a profusion of filial and maternal embraces' [P 13]. We hear that John Pendennis takes care to be otherwise occupied during 'the sunset business': 'It is probable that he did not much care for the view in front of his lawn windows, or take any share in the poetry and caresses which were taking place there'

H

[14]. It is an apparently casual touch, and we are to hear little more of John Pendennis except for the news of his death; but the situation of the son's love for his mother and rivalry with his father has been set up deliberately. And when the father dies, we are prepared for what is, in a Victorian novel in which the hero, with all his faults, is meant to retain our sympathy, a most un-pious filial reaction:

> As for Arthur Pendennis, after that awful shock which the sight of his dead father *must have* produced on him, and the pity and feeling which such an event *no doubt* occasioned [the italics are mine, but the irony, I suggest, is Thackeray's], I am not sure that in the very moment of the grief, and as he embraced his mother and tenderly consoled her, and promised to love her forever, there was not springing up in his breast a sort of secret triumph and exultation. He was the chief now and lord. [25]

So we are prepared for Pen's series of loves where his mother's attitude is always to have some effect on his own. His first love, Emily, is an obvious mother figure: she is placid and serene, and of course eight years older than he is. Pen's emotions are fully and ardently engaged, but his mother's feelings about the match are from the first of primary importance to the principals.

> 'Does your mother know of this, *Arthur*?' said Miss Fotheringay slowly. He seized her hand madly and kissed it a thousand times. She did not withdraw it ... 'Calm yourself, dear Arthur,' she said, in her low rich voice, and smiled sweetly and gravely upon him. Then with her disengaged hand, she put the hair lightly off his throbbing forehead. He was in such a rapture and whirl of happiness that he could hardly speak. At last he gasped out, 'My mother has seen you and admires you beyond measure. She will learn to love you soon: who can do otherwise? She will love you because I do.' [78]

It seems strange that Helen is not as jealous of this first ardent love as she is of the later and comparatively mild ones. One reason is perhaps that she does not feel deeply threatened by Emily Costigan, who gives little indication of requiting Pen's passion. His marriage to this woman, then, would not absorb his love exclusively, and there would still be room for a deep relationship with his mother. But it is also possible that Helen realizes to some extent that this passionate attachment to an older woman is an outlet for his unconscious feelings for her. There is a passage in which she goes to him in his bed, when he is sleeplessly composing poems for Emily:

> All the love-songs he had ever read, were working and seething in this young gentleman's mind, and he was at the very height and paroxysm of the imaginative frenzy, when his mother found him.
>
> 'Arthur,' said the mother's soft silver voice [not 'Helen' or even 'his mother,' but '*the* mother'] : and he started up and turned round. He clutched some of the papers and pushed them under the pillow.
>
> 'Why don't you go to sleep, my dear?' she said, with a sweet tender smile, and sat down on the bed and took one of his hot hands.
>
> Pen looked at her wildly for an instant. 'I couldn't sleep,' he said – 'I – I was – I was writing.' – And hereupon he flung his arms round her neck and said, ' Oh, mother, I love her, I love her!' [88]

Thackeray's illustration for this passage shows Pen and his mother embracing in bed. To a determined Freudian, the crescent moon beyond the window bars and the overturned chair, symbols of the mother and father, might suggest Pen's Oedipal impulse, for Thackeray frequently includes allegories in his illustrations. There is no need to labour the point: but the Oedipus pattern is undoubtedly present in the rest of the book.

The pattern is developed in another parallel with *Hamlet*. Here the parallel emphasizes Hamlet's relation to his mother rather than to his father, as in *Barry Lyndon*; and it is fully explicit, and elaborated in various incidents. Emily Costigan plays the part of Ophelia in the play at Chatteris, and during the play within the play, 'as Hamlet lay at Ophelia's knee, Pen felt that he would have liked to strangle [the actor] Mr. Hornbull' [75]. And when Pen defends his love to his mother, he speaks to her 'with a soothing, protecting air, like Hamlet with Gertrude in the play' [80]. There is also a parody of the graveyard scene in which one of a group of factory youths gathered in the churchyard 'began repeating Hamlet's verses over Ophelia, with a hideous leer at Pen'; and Pen is sufficiently provoked that he 'knocked the bewildered young

'Oh, Mother, I love her, I love her!' Arthur and Helen Pendennis: *Pendennis* 88

ruffian into the grave which was just waiting for a different lodger' [173].
Much later in the book, too, and in reference to his political position, Pen
disclaims Hamlet's responsibility: 'If the time is out of joint, have I any
calling or strength to set it right?' [795]. Again Jones's interpretation of
Hamlet seems relevant to an interpretation of Thackeray's novel.

While Pen is attached to the mature Emily, Helen has attracted the
love of the young curate, Pen's tutor. 'Poor dear Mrs. Pendennis might
be his mother almost,' we read in a passage which Thackeray cut in later
editions [988]. Smirke is a comic figure, destined to spend his time
languishing in love and falling off his horse, and he is not taken seriously
as a possible step-father for Pen. But he does bear a significant relation to
Pen's story. For a short while, when the affair with Emily has been broken
off and Pen is nursing a broken heart, there is a very tender relationship
between the two young men, Helen's son and her lover. In another
subsequently excised passage there is even a suggeston of a brief homo-
sexual attachment on Pen's part: he plies Smirke with presents, and his
'affection gushed out in a multitude of sonnets to the friend of his heart'
[986]. The relationship remains tender only until Pen learns of Smirke's
pretensions to his mother. Over several bottles of claret the curate at last
works up the resolution to confess his passion:

> 'For two years my heart has been filled by one image, and has
> known no other idol. Haven't I loved you as a son, Arthur? – say,
> hasn't Charles Smirke loved you as a son?'
>
> 'Yes, old boy, you've been very good to me,' Pen said, whose liking,
> however, for his tutor was not by any means of the filial kind …
>
> 'Arthur, Arthur!' exclaimed the other wildly. 'You say I am your
> dearest friend – let me be more. Oh, can't you see that the angelic
> being I love – the purest, the best of women – is no other than your
> dear, dear angel of a – mother?'
>
> 'My mother!' cried out Arthur, jumping up and sober in a minute.
> 'Pooh! damn it, Smirke, you must be mad – she's seven or eight years
> older than you are.'
>
> 'Did *you* find that any objection?' cried Smirke piteously, and allud-
> ing, of course, to the elderly subject of Pen's own passion.

> The lad felt the hint, and blushed quite red. 'The cases are not similar, Smirke,' he said. [192–3]

Pen goes on to adduce social reasons why Smirke should not become his step-father, but his floundering objections are only a part of the story. Smirke is dismissed without ever having the chance to declare his love to Helen (who, as Arthur is aware, would find him no substitute for her son). The incident, however, serves to reconcile Pen to the loss of Emily. It is as though Pen's loss of a mother-surrogate has been compensated by his dismissal of a step-father, and the intimacy between him and his mother is re-established.

> Pen ... described the dismal but ludicrous scene which had occurred. Helen heard of it with many blushes, which became her pale face very well, and a perplexity which Arthur roguishly enjoyed ... Pen and his mother had a long talk that night, full of love, confidence, and laughter, and the boy somehow slept more soundly and woke up more easily than he had done for many months before. [194–5]

Helen's sexual jealousy is fully aroused by Pen's other two flirtations, with Blanche Amory and Fanny Bolton. Both of these are siren figures, though in different ways, and in both cases Pen falls under their influence to some extent because of his relationship with his mother. His flirtation with Blanche represents a direct revolt from the maternal influence, for she is the major's and the world's candidate for his hand. He falls under Fanny's spell because she sees him as his mother has made him think of himself, as the 'prince of Fairoaks.' His attraction to her is sensual, but it is also a kind of auto-eroticism.

It is in the case of Fanny Bolton that Helen's jealousy, and the vindictiveness that goes with it, fully manifests itself. (The Blanche affair is more important to the social and artistic themes of the book, but Pen's love for the porter's daughter is more interesting from a psychological point of view.) The mother readily believes the rumours of Pen's licentiousness, and she savagely turns on Laura to blame her for her earlier refusal of Pen when she might have prevented this new guilt. 'I will never forgive you, never,' she tells Laura, who is quite blameless in the affair [639]. Her reaction is in fact neurotic, as is shown by her hysteria:

'And now – if this woman loves him – and you know they must – if he has taken her from her home, or she tempted him, which is most likely – why still, she must be his wife and my daughter. And he must leave the dreadful world and come back to me – to his mother, Doctor Portman. Let us go away and bring him back – yes – bring him back – and there shall be joy for the – the sinner that repenteth. Let us go now, directly, dear friend – this very – '
Helen could say no more. She fell back and fainted. [640]

There is an evident discrepancy between her stated intention of accepting Fanny as a daughter-in-law and her actual behaviour, for she dismisses her from Pen's sickbed, suppresses her letters to him and never mentions the matter to him during his convalescence.

And it is over this issue that Pen finally asserts himself and breaks his mother's hold on him. His indignation at the 'persecution which his woman-kind inflicted upon him' [729] over Fanny finally causes his outburst, which as he intends is overheard by his mother:

'They have kept her letters from me; they have treated me like a child, and her like a dog, poor thing! My mother has done this.'
'If she has, you must remember it is your mother,' Warrington interposed.
'It only makes the crime the greater because it is she who has done it,' Pen answered. 'She ought to have been the poor girl's defender, not her enemy.' [726]

In the classical Freudian view he has achieved maturity and asserted his identity by mastering the Oedipus complex. Pen accomplishes this task by virtually killing his mother: he is told that if he speaks out about his anger Helen will die, and in spite of all the grief and anguish over her death scene the fact remains that he does speak and she does die. Oedipus has changed into Orestes.

However, the picture is complicated by the figure of Laura, whom Helen is so anxious to match with her son. It is not difficult to see that

Helen and Laura here fill the roles of mother and daughter – Laura does in fact call Helen 'mother' and Pen 'brother' – and that the two are to some degree symbolically identified, like Thackeray's other mothers and daughters. Thus Helen, in promoting the marriage of her daughter Laura like any other mother, is to some extent wooing Pen for herself. There certainly seems to be some sexual gratification for her in her avid match-making here:

'O you profound dissembler,' he said, kissing his mother. 'O you artful creature! Can nobody escape from your wicked tricks? and will you make your only son your victim?' Helen too laughed, she blushed, she fluttered, and was agitated. She was as happy as she could be – a good, tender, match-making woman, the dearest project of whose heart was about to be accomplished. [341]

There is even a suggestion that Helen would be disappointed and so turn vicious, after the manner of Thackeray's other mothers, when she found herself excluded. For Laura is shrewd enough to realize that once Pen showed himself as loving her rather than Helen, Helen's love would change to hostility: 'If Pen had loved me as you wished, I should have gained him, but I should have lost you, mamma, I know I should' [716], she says.

It is no accident that the only woman Helen would like her son to marry is her own foster-daughter. And this raises the question whether Pen does free himself from the Oedipus syndrome at all, for he does marry his 'sister' Laura, who in many ways was brought up as an extension of Helen's personality. However, Laura does assert her own independent existence; and Pen does not marry her until *he* wants to, and that is after his mother's death.

Pen has no actual father through most of the book; but it is noticeable that the same old man turns up as his rival in two of his amours. Old Bows, with his hopeless but touching adoration first for Emily Costigan and later for Fanny, is a sympathetic figure. Symbolically, however, there is something sinister about him. Though he cannot possess the women himself, he has a certain power over them and, through them, over their suitor: it is he who teaches Emily the doll to act and Fanny the siren to sing. When Pen is running through the crowded streets with Fanny's image in his mind, he unexpectedly meets this shadowy supervisory figure:

> As he was talking thus, and running, the passers-by turning to look at him, he ran against a little old man, and perceived it was Mr. Bows.
> 'Your very 'umble servant, sir,' said Mr. Bows, making a sarcastic bow, and lifting his old hat from his forehead.
> 'I wish you a good-day,' Arthur answered sulkily. [629]

The encounter is a chilling one, and is reminiscent of that in Keats's 'Lamia' between Lycius and the sage Apollonius, who seems 'the ghost of folly haunting my sweet dreams.' Rapaccini, in Hawthorne's tale 'Rapaccini's Daughter,' is another embodiment of this demonic but powerfully rational father figure who is the hero's antagonist. There is, as I have said, something archetypal about the sequence of Pen's loves.

Reinforcing the central theme of the relationship of mother and son and son's loves, there is the repeating pattern of young men falling in love with old women, and usually living to regret it. So Francis Bell, Laura's father, has to marry old Miss Coacher; Pen loves Emily Costigan; Smirke loves Helen Pendennis; Madame Fribsby waxes sentimental over Mirobolant, who regards her as a mother; Mrs Bonner the maid marries Lightfoot the footman, who is twenty-five years younger than she, and whom she regards 'with a fondness at once parental and conjugal' [845]. The same kind of unlucky attachments are prevalent in Society; and 'misery, undeviating misery,' is their inevitable result, as we are told in Major Pendennis's characteristic manner:

> 'Look at Lord Clodworthy come into a room with his wife – why, good Ged, she looks like Clodworthy's mother. What's the case between Lord and Lady Willowbank, whose love match was notorious? He has already cut her down twice when she has hanged herself out of jealousy for Mademoiselle de Sainte-Cunegonde, the dancer; and mark my words, good Ged, one day he'll *not* cut the old woman down.' [93]

Again a pattern of relationships gives thematic cohesion and works as a unifying structural principle in the novel.

I

HENRY ESMOND

The same theme of sexual love and rivalry between the generations is developed in *Esmond*. Rachel was only fifteen when she married Francis, Lord Castlewood, who was several years her senior, and at first she worships him as an idol. Then, with their daughter and son growing, the familiar pattern of allegiances establishes itself: little Beatrix knows how to pain the mother and placate the father: 'From her mother's sad looks she fled to her father's chair and boozy laughter. She already set the one against the other: and the little rogue delighted in the mischief which she knew how to make so early' [118]. And Lord Castlewood is already calling his wife a jilt for being more concerned with little Frank than with him [119]. But of course there is another 'son' in the family, who is the real cause of the growing dissension between husband and wife. By the time Harry is sixteen and Rachel twenty-four (Beatrix incidentally would be eight, for the symmetry of the eight-year age difference is maintained), she has noticed her idol's feet of clay, and is in love with Harry. At the same time, Harry remains in a sense a son to her, and he continues throughout to think of her as his mother.

Rachel's sense of guilt in this situation is a major source of emotional tension in the novel; for she is more aware than most of Thackeray's characters of the conflicting state of her own emotions. And Harry, of course, only adds to her torment by acting as her husband's advocate for her love. As we have seen, when Francis is killed in the duel with Mohun, she is conscious of her own secret gladness, and horrified by it. Her behaviour indicates a classic case of emotional ambivalence. Her outward reaction is one of wild grief, and a furious accusation of Harry, who had in fact tried to prevent the fatal duel. Her long speech in the prison scene reveals the turmoil of contradictory emotions, to only some of which can she give expression. She demands of Harry, 'Why did you stand by at midnight and see him murdered?' and she blames him, though again she is not clear on how he is responsible, for spoiling her marriage since he first came as 'an orphan child.' 'I worshipped him: you know I worshipped him,' she asserts hysterically. 'And I lost him through you – I lost him – the husband of my youth, I say ... my kind, kind, generous lord.' And the whole is not only Harry's fault, but also 'a just judgement on my wicked heart' [167].

Rachel proceeds from the wife who is torn between her fatherly husband and her filial lover to the widow who must agonizingly watch her lover woo her daughter. And again Harry, either with boundless tactlessness or with consummate cruelty, increases her suffering by making her a spectator and his confidante. A focal scene is that where Harry, kneeling to put on Beatrix's dainty red slipper, kisses her foot while Rachel looks on.

> Mamma's feet began to pat on the floor during this operation, and Beatrix, whose bright eyes nothing escaped, saw that little mark of impatience. She ran up and embraced her mother, with her usual cry of, 'Oh, you silly little mamma: your feet are quite as pretty as mine,' says she: 'they are, cousin, though she hides 'em; but the shoemaker will tell you that he makes for both off the same last.'
>
> 'You are taller than I am, dearest,' says her mother, blushing over her whole sweet face – 'and – and it is your hand, my dear, and not your foot he wants you to give him,' and she said it with a hysteric laugh, that had more of tears than laughter in it; laying her head on her daughter's fair shoulder, and hiding it there. They made a very pretty picture together, and looked like a pair of sisters. [336–7]

Once more, Thackeray dwells on the symbolic identification of mother and daughter, and the deep rivalry that is inherent in it. This rivalry extends itself even to Rachel's second daughter, the child of her old age when she is married to Harry. We hear in the preface from the young Rachel that her father had to conceal his love for her to avoid arousing his wife's jealousy [9].

The question of incest has been raised in criticism of *Esmond* (as it might be raised about *Pendennis* or any of his novels: but here it is to the fore). Does the hero, in marrying the woman whom he has for years felt for and spoken of as a 'mother,' commit 'psychological incest'? Tilford has considered this question, and he feels that this obstacle to Rachel's marriage with Harry must definitely be present, to her mind at least, for after her husband's death there is no other reason for her to consider her love for Harry sinful. Tilford suggests that Thackeray has avoided this issue in an over-hurried resolution, and that the final union of Harry and Rachel, in spite of the careful preparation for it all through the book, is facile.[8] There is certainly no dramatic scene which shows Rachel at last overcoming her scruples and Harry at last discovering the true conjugal nature of his love for her. There is, however, an indication of what incidents and reactions would have constituted such a scene. In the last two pages of the novel Esmond tells us that he and his 'dear mistress' would have remained tenderly attached but unmarried, but for 'circumstances.' These circumstances are that Beatrix has defected from the parental care (this process we have seen at large), and that Frank has shown himself to be entirely occupied with his wife and her family. ''Twas after a scene of ignoble quarrel on the part of Frank's wife and mother ... that I found my mistress one day in tears, and then besought her to confide herself to the care and devotion of one who, by God's help, would never forsake her' [463]. In other words, Rachel marries Harry when her daughter is out of the way and her son has rejected her. It is evident that at least part of Harry's function is to take the place of Frank.

After Harry's reunion with Rachel at Walcote, and at the beginning of his love for Beatrix, he at one point pauses to examine his feelings.

> As for his mistress, 'twas difficult to say with what a feeling he regarded her. 'Twas happiness to have seen her: 'twas no great pang to part; a filial tenderness, a love that was at once respect and protection, filled his mind as he thought of her; and near her or far from her, and from that day until now, and from now till death is past, and beyond it, he prays that sacred flame may ever burn. [232]

'Come now, Esmond, *what* flame?' Dodds asks, with justifiable exasperation. 'Your "filial tenderness," long before this writing, must have been sublimated at the marriage altar.'[9] However, it seems to me that, on the contrary, the maternal and filial element is present at the consummation of their relationship, just as the sexual element was present at its incep-

---

8 See 'The "Unsavoury Plot" of *Henry Esmond' Nineteenth-Century Fiction* VI (1951) 121–30, and 'The Love Theme of *Henry Esmond' PMLA* LXVII (1952) 684–701

9 *Thackeray: A Critical Portrait* (London 1941) 170

tion. If Pendennis masters his Oedipal impulse, Esmond succumbs to his. He too has been a Hamlet in his jealousy of his 'mother's' affections: when he hears a rumour that Tom Tusher aspires to her hand he determines in such a case 'to take a private revenge upon the ears of the bridegroom.' His violent reaction is of course quite at variance with his declared social principles:

'Tis true Mr. Esmond often boasted of republican principles, and could remember many fine speeches he had made at college and elsewhere, with *worth* and not *birth* for a text: but Tom Tusher to take the place of the noble Castlewood – faugh! 'twas as monstrous as King Hamlet's widow taking off her weeds for Claudius. [207]

And this is a Hamlet who lives to marry Gertrude.

THE NEWCOMES

In *The Newcomes*, as in *Pendennis*, Thackeray uses a recurring set of relationships to form a thematic pattern, but this time, as we have seen, the mercenary marriages have more relation to the social theme than to his preoccupation with the love and rivalry between the generations.

But the pivotal situation, the emotional centre for which the rest of the novel seems an eleborate preparation, is the domestic life of Mr and Mrs Clive Newcome, with father-in-law and mother-in-law in attendance; and here the familiar antagonisms and allegiances between parents and children are again in operation. This part of the novel is extraordinarily painful. Thackeray has been particularly skilful in evoking, in all its detail, the impossibility and at the same time the inevitability of this social and psychological situation.

In Clive and Colonel Newcome we have an instance of what Thackeray showed more often with mothers and daughters: the identification and simultaneous rivalry of parent and child. The father is a match-maker for his son, first in his pursuit of Ethel, in whom he sees the reincarnation of his own lost love, Léonore; and then, when that fails, in his championship of Rosey. But the identity of interests of father and son ends with the loss of Ethel. In marrying Rosey Clive is merely passive, yielding equally to

Ethel and Colonel Newcome: *The Newcomes* 201

his father's pressures and the world's. The colonel naturally consults his own inclination when he thinks he is consulting Clive's. We would expect him to turn into the wicked father-in-law after the marriage when he finds himself excluded; but in fact Rosey's allegiance remains with him, and it is rather Clive who is excluded. So, in an ironic version of the courtly love situation, the old colonel is the gallant courtly lover, while the young husband finds himself *de trop* in his own household.

We hear of the colonel's devotion to his daughter-in-law, and how during the time of his prosperity he gives her jewels, a carriage, and the best of everything. At their opulent evening parties, he attends her with constant fidelity:

That solemn happiness of the colonel, who shall depict it: – that look of affection with which he greeted his daughter as she entered, flounced to the waist, twinkling with innumerable jewels, holding a dainty pocket-handkerchief, with smiling eyes, dimpled cheeks, and golden ringlets! He would take her hand, or follow her about from group to group, exchanging precious observations about the weather, the Park, the Exhibition, nay, the Opera ...

Very likely this was the happiest period of Thomas Newcome's life. No woman (save one perhaps fifty years ago) had ever seemed so fond of him as that little girl. What pride he had in her, and what care he took of her! [N 816–17]

'All this while,' Pendennis continues, significantly, 'we have said little about Clive, who in truth was somehow in the background in this flourishing Newcome group.' Laura too realizes the situation, and sees it as a reason for Clive's evident unhappiness. 'I think ... that Colonel Newcome performs all the courtship part of the marriage' [843], she observes. And Clive sums up his situation, 'I am not quite the father of my own child, nor the husband of my own wife, nor even the master of my own easel' [885]. Silly little Rosey, who is so comfortable with her gallant father-in-law, cannot communicate with her husband, though she dutifully goes to his studio to

practice artless smiles upon him, gentle little bouderies, tears, per-haps, followed by caresses and reconciliation. At the end of which he would return to his cigar; and she, with a sigh and a heavy heart, to the good old man who had bidden her to go and talk with him. He used to feel that his father had sent her; the thought came across him in their conversations, and straightway his heart would shut up and his face grow gloomy. [828]

Rosey constantly acts in a way to antagonize father and son. She seems, and no doubt is, quite ingenuous; but Thackeray can indicate the com-plexity that underlies ingenuousness, and we can no more dismiss Rosey as a silly little harmless thing than we can so dismiss Amelia. Some part of her knows and delights in the mischief she is causing. 'The colonel and I are walking on a mine,' says Clive, 'and that poor little wife of mine is perpetually flinging little shells to fire it' [854]. There is constant tension between father and son.

'We don't understand each other, but we feel each other as it were by instinct. Each thinks in his own way, but knows what the other is thinking. We fight mute battles, don't you see, and our thoughts, though we don't express them, are perceptible to one another, and come out from our eyes, or pass out from us somehow, and meet, and fight, and strike, and wound.' [855]

The situation becomes yet more intolerable when Colonel Newcome goes bankrupt, and the dreadful Campaigner moves in as a permanent appendage to the family. We know that Mrs Mackenzie, besides having been through the usual temporarily tender relationship with her son-in-law elect, had once set her cap unsuccessfully at the colonel [332]. So she has been doubly thwarted, and she is doubly vicious towards father and son. On her daughter she maintains something like a strangle-hold. Jung describes just this kind of mother-complex of the daughter: 'The mother lives out for her beforehand all that the girl might have lived for herself ... The daughter leads a shadow existence, often visibly sucked dry by her mother, and she prolongs her mother's life by a sort of continuous blood transfusion.'[10] The image recalls Mrs Shum of *The Yellowplush Papers*, another blood-sucking mother-in-law figure, 'who stuck to [her daughter's] side as close as a wampire, and made her retchider and retchider' [I 182]. It is exactly the relationship of Mrs Mackenzie and Rosey, which Thackeray depicts with such appalling clarity. When Pendennis visits the family in Boulogne, it is perceptible that the mother, for all her seeming love for her daughter, has become a vampire, and Rosey is sickening.

> The young woman being in the habit of letting mamma judge for her, continued it in this instance; and whether her husband stayed or went, seemed to be equally content or apathetic. 'And is it not most kind and generous of dear Mr. and Mrs. Pendennis to propose to receive Mr. Newcome and the colonel?' This opportunity for gratitude being pointed out to Rosey, she acquiesced in it straightway – it was very kind of me, Rosey was sure. 'And don't you ask after dear Mrs. Pendennis and the dear children – you poor, dear, suffering, darling child?' Rosey, who had neglected this inquiry, immediately hoped

10 'Psychological Aspects of the Mother Archetype' *The Collected Works of C.G. Jung* ed. Sir Herbert Read (London 1954–) IX pt ii

Mrs. Pendennis and the children were well. The overpowering mother had taken utter possession of this poor little thing. Rosey's eyes followed the Campaigner about, and appealed to her at all moments. She sat under Mrs. Mackenzie as a bird before a boa-constrictor, doomed – fluttering – fascinated. [935]

The boa-constrictor inevitably devours the bird, and Rosey dies a victim to her mother. This image of cannibalism, of the parent devouring the child and love become rapacity, is not isolated in Thackeray's works.

THE VIRGINIANS

The Virginians suffers from a lapse in tension. A sense of literary fatigue is perceptible not merely in the wandering of the story, but in Thackeray's inability to evoke a sense of urgency or uniqueness about the characters' relations with one another. He is dealing with the same subject matter, but partly because it *is* the same and partly because he felt he had written himself dry, it all seems obvious and so, in comparison with the other novels at least, boring to him. He settles for telling more and showing less: there is less dramatic depiction in relation to commentary in this novel than in any of the previous ones. The ironic tension of love and hostility between parent and child, which gives the domestic situation of *Esmond* its telling impact, somehow relaxes: *of course* young men always fall in love with older women, Thackeray seems to be wearily telling us; of course fathers are jealous of their daughters, and mothers of their sons. The same emotional situations which in *Esmond* had the quality of being universal, often seem in *The Virginians* to be merely commonplace.

This is an over-all judgment. But there are still individual scenes and relationships which come alive in the old way: Harry's love for Maria is not just a tired reworking of Pen's for the Fotheringay, but has its own quality. And the evocation of the feelings of the Baroness Bernstein for Harry and George – the grandsons of the only man she could have loved – this is a subtle picture. Even in George's ruminative loquacities there is an atmosphere of strong feeling recollected in tranquillity that has its own force.

'A Stepfather in Prospect.' George and Harry Warrington furious to discover that they have a rival in their mother's affections: *The Virginians* 95

The 'plot' of *The Virginians* was to have hinged on the conflict of the two brothers who find themselves on different sides of the American War of Independence. However, Thackeray evidently lost interest in this, and again he binds his novel together by a system of relationships rather than with the development of action. This time he creates a symmetrical structure from the relations of a mother with her two sons and a father with his two daughters.

To demonstrate Thackeray's continuing concern with the sexual element in the parent-child relationship in this novel, one has only to summarize the story. Rachel Warrington, or 'Madam Esmond,' appropriately the daughter of Henry and Rachel Esmond, has twin sons, one dark and saturnine and the other fair and lively. When she has hopes of marrying a young man both the sons are furiously jealous, and George, the elder, challenges the rival to a duel. At the same time, both are anxious to escape from the maternal apron-string. Harry, in England, falls in love with his cousin, a woman older than his mother who treats him with 'a maternal tenderness.' When each finally finds the woman he wants to marry, their mother does all she can to prevent both marriages.

General Lambert, a sympathetic character who is presented as in many ways an ideal husband and father, is Thackeray's major study in the relation of father to daughters. He cheerfully admits to being in no hurry to find husbands for his girls, and to being antagonistic to anyone who comes courting them. His daughter Hetty falls in love with Harry, but she is impatient with the emotion: 'I am not going to set my cap at Mr. Harry. No; our papa is ten times as good as he is. I will stay by our papa, and if he asked me to go to Virginia with him to-morrow, I wouldn't' [v 345]. When her resolution is finally put to the test she stands by it, for she does at last refuse Harry, and all her other suitors, to devote herself to her father: 'She loved best to stay with her father, Hetty said. As long as he was not tired of her she cared for no husband' [913]. George woos General Lambert's other daughter, Theo, and this time the daughter is ready to part with the father; but the father is not so willing to part with his daughter. He finds a reason for his determined effort to part Theo and George, but it is clear, as George points out, that this is a trumped-up

Harry Warrington, smitten by a Cupid who is not only blind but headless, woos a motherly Maria: *The Virginians* 181

excuse. The father stands in the way of the daughter's marriage as the mother of the son's. When George knows of his mother's unjust bid to dismiss Theo, he asks, 'Who had a right to stab such a soft bosom?' [797]. And to her father he says, 'You may part us: and she will die as surely as if she were Jephthah's daughter. Have you made any vow to Heaven to compass her murder?' [817]. This is strong language. But the demands of loving parents for the exclusive fidelity of their children come to seem more and more like tyranny and rapacity in Thackeray's novels.

The history of the Esmond family and its descendants, as we have it in *Henry Esmond* and *The Virginians*, is a prolonged account of the mating of different generations. 'It runs in the family,' as Eugene Esmond says, with a resignation born of experience [v 205]. Rachel Esmond first marries a man who is considerably older than herself, then one who is considerably younger and who has been the suitor to her daughter. Her son Frank breaks from the maternal tie only to marry a mother-surrogate. Her second husband, Harry, first loves a girl to whom his relaton is 'almost paternal' then the girl's mother whom he had for years called his own mother. When Rachel and Henry are married they have a daughter of whom the mother is jealous, and who is proud 'to supply the place which she was quitting' by Henry's side when her mother dies. This daughter marries a Mr Warrington, whom she despises in comparison with her father; and after his death she so devotes herself to her sons that she does all she can to prevent their marrying. The sons, for their part, are jealous of her affections, and one tries to kill the young man she wants to marry; the other himself almost marries an old woman. And finally we gather from George's armchair narrative that he is exasperated at the place his son Miles holds in his mother's affections, and much disturbed at the thought that his daughters may some day leave him to get married. And so it continues from generation to generation.

PHILIP

Philip is usually considered inferior in quality to Thackeray's other novels. And so it is, as a social document at least. We have come to expect so much of Thackeray in the way of delineation of social types and the depiction of the incongruities of the social scene, that when we are presented with such obvious re-working of old materials as Talbot Twysden and Sir John Ringwood we feel that the book is a failure.

But if *Philip* is far inferior to *Vanity Fair* as an entertaining social panorama, it still shows a resurgence of vigour in Thackeray's ability to imagine and convey certain anomalous characters and relationships. Tufton Hunt, the reprobate priest, Caroline Brandon, and Mrs Baynes are psychologically bold conceptions. And there is a certain intensity, even violence, about the imagery which is reminiscent of Dickens. Images of death, of stabbing and sacrificing, and of devouring are recurrent; and it is particularly the parent-child relationship that is visualized in these terms. Philip and Dr Firmin are a powerful incarnation of the antagonism of father and son, and this relationship dominates *Philip* as the attachment of mother and son dominates *Pendennis*.

Philip's somewhat feeble mother had died when he was a boy. But he finds a substitute mother in the nurse, Caroline Brandon, the 'Little Sister.' She is a woman of the lower classes whom his father had seduced years previously by means of a bogus marriage, and then deserted, and who had borne the doctor's stillborn child. This Little Sister is a complex character. For instance, she shows herself all through the book to have no illusions about the 'gentleman' who had betrayed her; but when she hears of his death she puts on widow's weeds and acts as though she had been his legal wife for thirty years. She stands in relation to Philip midway between mother and beloved. There is a scene in which Philip knocks down a man who is in many ways identified with his father (and to whom she herself afterwards acts as Judith to Holofernes); and she shows her satisfaction.

> She took him into her little room. She was pleased with the gallantry of the boy. She liked to see him just now, standing over her enemy, courageous, victorious, her champion. 'La! how savage he did look; and how brave and strong you are! But the little wretch ain't fit to stand before such as you!' And she passed her little hand down his arm, of which the muscles were all in a quiver from the recent skirmish. [AP 146]

We are not surprised, when Philip is married, to notice that the Little

Sister and Charlotte are bitterly jealous of each other.

Philip's allegiance to this woman is the greater for the fact that his father betrayed her. The son has a bitter grievance against his father, for like Esmond he can feel 'no love towards the man who had ... stained his mother's honour and his own' [HE 69]. 'He clings to the woman and shrinks from the man,' we are told. 'Is it instinctive love and antipathy?' [AP 121].

Dr Firmin, of all Thackeray's fathers, gives most reason for the son to shrink from him. 'Talk of the ***,' say a group at the club, as the doctor enters.

> The personage designated by asterisks was Phil's father, who was also a member of our Club, and who entered the dining-room, tall, stately, and pale, with his stereotyped smile, and wave of his pretty hand. By the way, that smile of Firmin's was a very queer contortion of the handsome features. As you came up to him, he would draw his lips over his teeth, causing his jaws to wrinkle (or dimple if you will) on either side. Meanwhile his eyes looked out from his face, quite melancholy and independent of the little transaction in which the mouth was engaged. Lips said, 'I am a gentleman of fine manners and fascinating address, and I am supposed to be happy to see you. How do you do?' Dreary, sad, as into a great blank desert, looked the dark eyes. [24]

Here are all the characteristics of the devil incarnate, and the doctor is reminiscent of Dickens' Rigaud in *Little Dorrit*. He does not quite maintain this diabolic stature, for he is reduced to human proportions, and mean ones too, in the later part of the novel. But the images which refer specifically to his role as a father are just as vivid. He is a parasite on his son, and one illustration depicts him as the Old Man of the Sea, maintaining a stranglehold on his preserver [553]. As old Osborne's room is decorated with the sculptured group of the sacrifice of Iphigenia, so is Dr Firmin's with a picture of the sacrifice of Isaac:

> 'You remember that picture of Abraham and Isaac in the doctor's study in Old Parr Street?' [Philip] would say. 'My patriarch has tied

me up, and had the knife in me repeatedly. He does not sacrifice me at one operation; but there will be a final one some day, and I shall bleed no more.' [555]

Charlotte is similarly the victim of her parents, particularly of her mother. The way the hero's father and his wife's mother both cheat their children financially in an image for a deeper psychological deprivation. Of all Thackeray's novels, *Philip* shows the parents most clearly as the villains. The central image is the parable of the Good Samaritan; and in the last part of the novel Philip is forced to the reflection: '"Ah," thought poor Philip, groaning in his despair, "I wonder whether the thieves who attacked the man in the parable were robbers of his own family?"' [616].

In the dramatic opening of the novel, a scene in the youth of Pendennis before his marriage or the death of his mother, Dr Goodenough comments of Helen Pendennis and her son, 'If that child were hungry, you would chop off your head to make him broth.'

> 'Potage à la bonne femme,' says Mr. Pendennis. 'Mother, we have it at the club. You would be done with milk, eggs, and a quantity of vegetables. You would be put to simmer for many hours in an earthen pan, and –'
>
> 'Don't be horrible, Arthur!' cries a young lady, who was my mother's companion of those happy days. [AP 2]

This is no accidental joke. In a passage in *Pendennis* we are told that

> the noble family of which, as we know, Helen Pendennis was a member bears for a crest, a nest full of little pelicans pecking at the ensanguined bosom of a big maternal bird, which plentifully supplies the little wretches with the nutriment on which, according to the heraldic legend, they are supposed to be brought up. Very likely female pelicans like so to bleed under the selfish little beaks of their young ones: it is certain that women do. [P 997]

This tells us a good deal about the ambivalent feelings of the mother: but in a book of heraldry compiled by Thackeray we could be sure that all the pelican chicks would be male; just as we can be sure that the only person offered *potage à la bonne femme* on his menu, other than the son of the

Thackeray's and Walker's chapter initials for *The Virginians* [222] and *Philip*
[553], showing the young man's strangling obligation to a parent figure

bonne femme, would be her father. (Such imagery is not unusual with
Thackeray, who frequently sees human relations in terms of cannibalism.
The Roundabout Paper on 'Ogres' is an example of the elaboration of
this image.)

The bulk of *Philip,* and of *The Virginians* too, is concerned with the
sacrificing rather than the self-sacrificing side of parenthood. So Theo
Lambert is Jephthah's daughter; Charlotte Baynes is Iphigenia; and
Philip Firmin is Isaac to Dr Firmin's Abraham. The image of the Old Man
of the Sea, burdening and almost strangling the young Sindbad, is used
alike for Harry Warrington's obligations to the motherly Maria and for
Philip's responsibilities to his parasitic father. In calling Mrs Baynes Lady
Macbeth Thackeray no doubt had in mind her lines about her readiness to
pluck her baby from her breast and dash its brains out; and when in
Esmond he compares the deserted Rachel with Medea forsaken by Jason,
he could not have forgotten one of the first images of the novel: 'Queen
Medea slew her children to a slow music' [HE 13]. There is evidence that
Thackeray was to develop this theme even more fully in his last novel, for
in his notes for *Denis Duval* he refers to the story of the heroine, who was

to be sacrificed to an evil older man, as that of 'Henriette Iphigenia' [XVII 338]. Parents become progressively more guilty, or at least more patently so, through the novels. But it is always worth remembering, even when Thackeray is dwelling on the self-sacrificing side of parenthood, that it is part of the pelican legend that the mother needs to revive her young with her heart's blood because she has herself killed them' Thackeray is constantly exploring this deep irony of the parent-child relationship.

All through his works we see his ability to convey a sense of the un-realized possibilities of human relationships, and of the realized improb-abilities. 'I might have been somebody's mamma, instead of – ' Becky writes to her husband. 'The maternal passion is a sacred mystery to me, says the narrator of *Pendennis*, who proceeds to explore what is maternal and what is passionate in a mother's love for her son. 'Is it mamma your honour wants, and that I should have the happiness of calling you papa?' Beatrix asks her ardent suitor Henry. 'Should you like a stepmother, Mr. Clive, or should you prefer a wife?' a gossip inquires, as he and his father separately contemplate the attractions of Mrs Mackenzie. 'Can this monster ... make me marry him though I cordially detest him, and bring me a slave to his feet?' wonders Lady Lyndon of the man she is going to marry. Such questions, and the sense of multiple possibilities which they evoke, reverberate through the novels.

The question of how far Thackeray's depiction of these ambivalent rela-tionships has autobiographical significance does not primarily concern me here, since the novels themselves are my subject rather than their relation to Thackeray's life. Criticism of Thackeray has been much occupied with the close relation between his life and his work – witness Gordon Ray's *The Buried Life*[11] and his standard critical biography, and also Lambert Ennis's study of certain anomalous relationships which Thackeray has reproduced from his life in his fiction.[12] Thackeray's letters are of course the main source of information about the parallels between his fictional characters and his friends and family. Not only is Helen Pendennis his

11 (London 1952)
12 *Thackeray: the Sentimental Cynic* (Evanston 1950)

mother, whose 'jealousy after me tears and rends her,' but the Campaigner was avowedly his 'she-devil of a mother-in-law' [Letters III 465n],
as was Mrs Baynes. But he had not always considered her a she-devil, for
there was a time when he wrote tenderly to his fiancée, 'give a kiss to your
dear Mother ... for me' [I 305]. It is also no accident that between
Pendennis, of 1848–50, and *The Virginians*, of 1857–9, during which time
his daughters had grown from children to young women, the emphasis
shifts from the son's relation with the mother to the father's relation with
his daughters. On the whole, Thackeray is fair. General Lambert is
certainly a more sympathetic character than Helen Pendennis; but it is
characteristic of Thackeray's readiness to find fault with himself as well
as with the rest of the world that he speaks of his still unmarried daughters
as 'beginning to bewail their Virginity in the mountains,' and so identifies
himself with Jephthah.[13]

In applying Freudian psychology to an interpretation of Thackeray's
novels, there is a danger of being too solemn and so forgetting the air
of amused ironic detachment that often plays about his depiction of these
primal situations. And to reduce all his characters to Oedipuses and Electras
is to rob them of both their humour and their individuality. Of course the
novels are far from being just a set of textbook variations on *Totem and
Taboo*. But, again, it is a question of emphasis. I assert only that Thackeray
concerned himself, consciously and repeatedly, with that aspect of
human relationships that Freud had best analysed, and this is one reason
that his novels have subtlety and intensity. And not only subtlety and
intensity, but humour too. There is irresistible comedy in the prostration
of Pen before the Fotheringay, or Harry before his 'elderly Calypso,'
mother-surrogates or no; and Mrs Sedley's jealousy of Jos's affections and
Mr Osborne's awful solemnity in his rule over his daughters are matter
for laughter as well as psychiatry. Thackeray is ready to parody his own
preoccupations with considerable zest. So, in *Our Street*, an amateur pro-
duction of a play shows the hero madly in love with a woman who turns
out to be his grandmother. And in *The Rose and the Ring*, where so many
of Thackeray's themes and character types turn up in a fairy-tale setting,
the hero, Giglio, like another Pendennis or Harry Warrington, gets him-

13 See *Letters* IV 272 and Judges 11: 38.

'The dear old woodman fell down on his knee ... and in token of his fealty, he rubbed his venerable nose three times on the ground, and put the Princess's foot on his head.' A faithful subject vows allegiance to Rosalba: *The Rose and the Ring* 393. The sexual symbolism of the knife and bowl is probably not accidental for Thackeray frequently made his backgrounds allegorically significant.

self engaged and almost married to the hideous old hag Gruffanuff, while the heroine is constantly wooed by alternately tender and savage father figures.

'If Fun is good, Truth is still better, and Love is best of all' [BS 493]: it is Thackeray's familiar maxim. But a study of the triangle relationships between the generations involves yet another qualification to his moral of 'the vanity of success and of all but Love and Goodness'; for the more carefully we read the novels the more we can see that love is no more the *summum bonum* than is goodness. We are shown love that 'beareth all things, believeth all things, hopeth all things, endureth all things.' But we are also shown love that demands all things, grasps all things, and devours all things.

Indeed, in his best work Thackeray has in effect revised that scale of values he outlined in *The Book of Snobs*. Fun he never abandoned, though his fun is tinged with the sadness that made him think a 'jaundiced livery' best suited his part numbers, for all the jester's antics they contained. But love, and goodness too, he had examined so intently in all their operations in this fallen world of Vanity Fair that his reservations about them matched his veneration. It is truth, finally, that he values highest. 'Look you,' he reminds us in the great passage where he speaks at once as artist, moralist, fool, quack, and our own confidential associate, 'one is bound to speak the truth as far as one knows it, whether one mounts a cap and bells or a shovel-hat; and a deal of disagreeable matter must come out in the course of such an undertaking' [VF 95]. He will not shirk the disagreeable matter that he finds so intricately involved with the agreeable. For his vision is one that recognizes primarily the contradictions of existence. Whether we examine his personal standpoints, his social, moral, or psychological pre-occupations, we find him showing how the quest for social eminence be-comes snobbery, how the aspiration to sainthood becomes moral tyranny, how tenderness fosters aggression and an embrace turns into a strangle-hold, and how truth itself includes a measure of illusion.

He will not let his reader shirk the business of assessment, either. We are to know the Beckys of this world for what they are; but his ironic stances, tempting us to align ourselves with the sentimental or the worldly-wise, undercut any glib judgments, for they make us know too the precarious moral bases from which we judge. We understand that it is too easy to cast Becky into outer darkness if we are among the safely respectable classes, or to despise Amelia if we do not possess her peculiar virtues.

His very technique of maintaining a confidential relation with his reader is determined by his desire to be honest, to look his audience straight in the eye, and so avoid as far as possible the posturing which he finds comes so easily to himself and to all who take it upon themselves to address a listening public. In the preface to *Pendennis* he refers to his novel as 'a sort of confidential talk between writer and reader,' and contends 'this kind of composition ... at least has the advantage of a certain truth and honesty, which a work more elaborate might lose ... I ask you to believe that this person writing strives to tell the truth. If there is not that, there is nothing.'

In his major work at least, I believe Thackeray satisfies us, not only that he can tell the truth, but that the breadth of his vision, the truth he has to tell, is worth our listening to. His alternate poses as sentimental novel-reader, pillar of respectability, and detached cynic add up not to successive retreats but to a brave attempt to know all round a character or situation, from various viewpoints. The shifts of sympathy in which he involves us are not an evasion of judgment, but an inducement to us to judge responsibly. And his probing into the sensitive spot in the most hardened snob, and explorations of the ulterior motives and secret agonies that underlie the humdrum lives of ordinary individuals, are part of a deeply perceptive vision of humanity. His irony is a means of knowing.

Index

References to characters or works by writers other than Thackeray are indexed under the name of the author. Material within the quotations is not indexed. Major references under given entries are italicized.

This book
was designed by
WILLIAM RUETER
under the direction of
ALLAN FLEMING
and was printed by
R & R Clark, Ltd, Edinburgh
for
University of
Toronto
Press